100 THINGS
MAVERICKS FANS
SHOULD KNOW & DO
BEFORE THEY DIE

Library of Congress Cataloging-in-Publication Data

Names: Cato, Tim, author.
Title: 100 things Mavericks fans should know & do before they die / Tim Cato.
Other titles: One hundred things Mavericks fans should know and do before they die | A hundred things Mavericks fans should know and do before they die
Description: Chicago, Illinois : Triumph Books LLC, [2017]
Identifiers: LCCN 2017020476 | ISBN 9781629374222
Subjects: LCSH: Dallas Mavericks (Basketball team)—History. | Dallas Mavericks (Basketball team)—Miscellanea. | Basketball—Texas—Dallas—History. | Basketball—Texas—Dallas—Miscellanea.
Classification: LCC GV885.72.T4 C37 2017 | DDC 796.323/64097642812—dc23 LC record available at https://lccn.loc.gov/2017020476

This book is available in quantity at special discounts for your group or organization. For further information, contact:
Triumph Books LLC
814 North Franklin Street
Chicago, Illinois 60610
(312) 337-0747
www.triumphbooks.com

Printed in U.S.A.
ISBN: 978-1-62937-422-2
Design by Patricia Frey
All photos courtesy of AP Images

*To Mom and Dad, who always took me
to the library and didn't get mad when I
stayed up reading under the covers*

Contents

Foreword

If you're a Mavs Fan For Life like me, it means we share some crazy, amazing memories.

The most unforgettable one is the championship. In 2011 I refused to let myself think we would win until there were about 90 seconds left in Game 6. Too many times, I had seen something that seemed like a sure thing go away in a moment. I remember the yellow tape going up around the court and hugging Rick Carlisle when the buzzer finally sounded after what felt like an eternity. We were finally champions. Let me tell you, it felt tremendous. Still does. If you're an MFFL, you know exactly what that feeling is, too.

But you don't have to win a championship to experience something you'll never forget. If you're an MFFL, you probably know exactly who hit the shot in Game 5 to beat the Utah Jazz in 2001—Calvin Booth, coming off the bench out of nowhere to save our asses. You can fondly recall why the team all grew beards in 2013 and how Dirk looked like one of those GEICO Cavemen with his grown all the way out. We didn't make the playoffs that year, but we did make it to .500, which was important for every player on that team. There's Jason Terry, and everyone can picture him running down the court after hitting a huge three-pointer with his arms stretched out. JET truly was someone special.

My Mavericks memories started a long time before I bought the team in 2000, though. I still remember the amazing 1988 team that took the seemingly invincible Los Angeles Lakers to a Game 7. I still remember the sickening feeling when Roy Tarpley went down with a knee injury, and his career never recovered. I remember trying to go to Moody Madness except I couldn't get a ticket. It was all sold out!

I remember how awful the 1990s were because the team just couldn't figure it out, even after Jason Kidd and the Three J's seemed so promising. But then a tall dude from Germany came along, and that changed everything.

Dirk and I both joined the Mavericks around the same time. No one knew what to expect from us, and now we're still here, almost 18 years later. This dude made things so easy for me and everyone else by being the best damn player on the court and coolest person off of it that I've ever seen. If you're not a MFFL, you'll never fully understand what he means to the Mavericks and all of us.

If you're a longtime MFFL and you remember all these moments, or if you're a new fan who wants to know more about the wonderful moments that made the Mavericks who we are today, then *100 Things Mavericks Fans Should Know & Do Before They Die* is the perfect book for you. All of those unforgettable moments from 1980 to 2017 are in here.

And with exciting young players and our bright future, so many moments like these are ahead for MFFLs, too. There has never been a better time to be rooting for the Mavericks. For Life.

—*Mark Cuban*

1 Dirk Nowitzki Means Everything

Dirk Nowitzki pulls his jersey over his eyes as television cameras broadcast his short trip back to Miami's visiting locker room. There was a reason he had run off the court as soon as the final buzzer sounded, a reason he had hurdled the scorer's table and fled the court even as the Mavericks achieved the everlasting validation of a championship.

It's June 12, 2011, and he isn't going to let anyone see him cry.

He does it in the locker room instead, where the television cameras couldn't follow, while his teammates are still celebrating on the court. Only when his eyes dry minutes later is a team official able to coax him back onto the floor to accept his NBA Finals MVP and to cradle the Larry O'Brien trophy, moments he had wondered if he would ever experience. "I still really can't believe it," Nowitzki says when a microphone is put in front of him. "We worked so hard and so long for it. The team has been unbelievable, riding through ups and downs and always staying together and working. I still can't even believe it."

Left unsaid—both in this answer and in many more of his words that followed that evening—was his own role in making this unbelievable accomplishment a reality. But Nowitzki has never been one to talk about himself, so we'll have to do it for him. He brought Dallas a championship. Narrowing his impact to just that, though, is superficial and trite. The truth is Dirk Nowitzki means so much more than that.

* * *

It's June 24, 1998, and the Mavericks are calling Dirk Nowitzki to welcome him to the team. They don't know that the decision will make this the most important day in the team's history. Nowitzki changed the Mavericks as a franchise—and Dallas as a city. With him, he brought so many moments worth remembering. They came in the form of trophies and awards ceremonies and by way of unforgettable shots and cherished games. They triggered celebration, induced pride, produced tears, and brought joy. Sometimes, they came quickly—many memories blending together hours, days, and weeks at a time—and sometimes, they slowed down, giving enough time to hold on and cherish them.

But none could have happened before that day in June. In the year 2022 or 2023, or maybe even 2024 or 2025, Nowitzki will be elected to the Naismith Memorial Basketball Hall of Fame. It'll happen unanimously, and on the first eligible ballot, because Nowitzki's championship, MVP, 13 All-Star appearances, and 12 selections to an All-NBA team speak for themselves. It'll be entirely deserved because he's only the sixth player to ever score 30,000 points in his career and the greatest European basketball player ever. It'll be celebrated in the Dallas streets because Nowitzki leads the Mavericks franchise in games played, points, rebounds, and wins and is unquestionably the greatest player in the team's history.

Nowitzki's statistics are prodigious, and his accomplishments could stretch on for an entire book. An ever truer testament to the player he is, however, is his influence. Nowitzki wasn't the first big man to shoot three-pointers or dribble the ball on fast breaks, but he quickly became the best. He played like a guard in a seven-footer's body, and that itself changed basketball.

You see Dirk Nowitzki everywhere you look in the NBA today. Centers shoot threes, and power forwards run fast breaks, and some seven-footers never even need to step into the paint. There are direct tributes, when big men and guards alike shoot Nowitzki's patented fadeaway off of one leg. Nowitzki isn't the only reason for the league growing in this direction, but him joining the league at the turn of the century legitimized a trend and sped it along even faster.

Nowitzki deserves credit for the rising popularity of basketball internationally, too. It wasn't just him, of course. Other foreign-born superstars like Hakeem Olajuwon and Pau Gasol had equally strong influences. Commissioner David Stern also played an enormous role in the globalization of his league in the 1990s and 2000s. But basketball continues to morph into a world phenomenon, and the league proudly announced that a record 113 international players from 41 countries and territories were on Opening Night rosters to begin the 2016–17 season. Nowitzki helped inspire that.

Still, the German's swooping global influence doesn't resonate as personally as his impact on Dallas itself. The Mavericks have now played more seasons with Nowitzki (20) than without him (18), and he has radically transformed the city's entire sporting history. The Mavericks were the league's laughingstock in the 1990s. From 1991 to 1999, the team won an average of 22 games per season, even going 11–71 in 1993. Nowitzki joined a failing franchise and turned it into a perennial playoff contender, one that won 50 games in 11 straight seasons and made the playoffs 15 times in 16 years.

That's how good Nowitzki really was. He took basketball—a sideshow to the Dallas Cowboys in the country's fourth largest metropolitan area—and turned it into the city's most consistently successful sport. With Nowitzki came heartbreak in the 2006 NBA Finals and elation when they finally won it all in 2011. The Mavericks remain the only major sports team in Dallas to win a league championship since the turn of the century.

Like most sports figures this successful, Nowitzki is beloved. He has made thousands of shots and produced hundreds of storybook memories. Dallas adores him, and we shouldn't limit that love to the city limits. Nowitzki has created Mavericks fans everywhere—children who grew up in the area and moved away, German citizens who felt pride at one of their own becoming so successful, and even basketball aficionados who marveled when they saw a seven-footer with a gorgeous jump shot and who still can't look away after so many years. All these people, separated by borders and oceans, languages and culture differences, all share a singular feeling: an undying love for a seven-foot man who is spectacular at putting a ball through a hoop.

This all describes Dirk Nowitzki the basketball player. Dirk Nowitzki, the global icon. Dirk Nowitzki, the hometown hero. Even Michael Jordan, notoriously critical of modern basketball, named Nowitzki one of the four current superstars who could play in his era.

It doesn't say anything about Dirk Nowitzki the person.

* * *

It's May 4, 2014, and Dirk Nowitzki is miserable.

He's always miserable when a season ends in a loss. This year it was expected—the Mavericks were the lowest seed in the 2014 playoffs, and the San Antonio Spurs had won 62 games. But Nowitzki and the Mavericks pushed the Spurs to Game 7, and then anything could happen.

No miracle occurred, and the Spurs clobbered Dallas for an excruciating 48 minutes to move on. In the locker room, Nowitzki dresses slowly. The Mavericks' PR staff comes to fetch him for a postgame press conference—the lone player representing Dallas on the podium—but he stops at the door. Sometime during the four road games in San Antonio, Nowitzki had befriended the two teen-aged locker room attendants. He wishes them both a good summer, briefly calling across the room to each one by name. Only then does he disappear through the door to a press conference, answering depressing questions about another season ending short of his goal.

Nowitzki would still be beloved by his fans if he didn't care so much. He could still be a future Hall of Famer if he didn't sign every autograph and accept every photo request. Many of the greatest athletes are narcissistic and disagreeable, to put it mildly, and they're still seen for their skills on the court. If Nowitzki was like that, it would be easy to look past all that while focusing on the triumphs instead.

But Nowitzki isn't. He visits Children's Medical Center at Dallas every year, distributing gifts as Uncle Dirk, and his annual charity events raise money in support of the well-being, health, and education of underprivileged children. He was presented with the Magic Johnson Award in 2014 for his constant and tireless cooperation with the media, partly encompassed by his self-deprecating, dry humor that can draw laughs in any situation.

Just ask those around him. "I've been around this for three decades, and this is the most special individual I've ever come across in NBA basketball," said Rick Carlisle after Nowitzki passed 29,000 points in 2016. "And I've met some very special people. I'm honored just to come to work with him every day."

"He [is] one of the most professional people I've ever met," Wesley Matthews said. "Not even in sports, not even as an athlete, just as a professional. Dirk, I've never seen him say no to a picture. I've never seen him say no to an autograph, greets everybody, says hi to everybody, complains a lot, but he works his ass off. I think after 39 years, you can complain a little bit. He's awesome."

Those around him adore him unequivocally, stars and role players alike. "He's like a brother. Inspiration. A teacher, learned so much from him, just watching him," Tyson Chandler told me. "Not only what he means to me, but what he means to the game, what he means to the city of Dallas. I was just telling my teammates: I've never seen that level of basketball in my life in that 2011 run. I've never seen a player play at that level, just seeing how locked in and focused he was as an athlete and a competitor. I'll be forever indebted to him and I love him forever because he helped me reach my ultimate goal as an athlete and winning a championship. He can call me anytime for anything, and the only thing I can even describe it like is brothers."

"He was such a humble guy," Ian Mahinmi told me, "such a great teammate. He goes from one to 15 guys in the locker room, he likes to joke with everybody, likes to make everybody feel like they're a part of something."

Nowitzki himself would protest any depiction that makes him seem perfect. He's human, of course. He curses out referees, picks up technicals, and takes out his frustrations on inanimate objects after games. Occasionally, he can't resist subtle cracks at competitors or former teammates—usually because he feels they aren't approaching basketball the right way.

It doesn't make anyone love him any less. *Did you ever in your wildest dreams think you'd accomplish what you did?* That's the question Mavericks legend Derek Harper often asks Nowitzki, and this superstar always answers honestly: no.

2 2011 Was Different

It's May 17, 2011, and Tyson Chandler is walking into the American Airlines Center. He's arriving earlier than most for the team's shootaround before Game 1 of the Western Conference Finals, but he's not the earliest. As Chandler laces his shoes on the sideline, Dirk Nowitzki is already taking jump shots on the floor. DeShawn Stevenson sidles up next to Chandler, and they both marvel at the sight. Stevenson leans over to Chandler. "All we've got to do is get that man there," Stevenson said. "And we'll have a ring."

Chandler knew he was right. Nobody in the world could stop him, he thinks. The rest of the team just had to do their part.

* * *

The second most important day in the history of the Dallas Mavericks is June 12, 2011. It's the day the Mavericks became champions. It was supposed to happen years before. In 2003 the Mavericks made the conference finals only for Dirk Nowitzki to be shut down with a knee injury in Game 3. When Dallas lost in the 2006 NBA Finals in heartbreaking fashion, the one thing the team held onto was that they were in position to do it again. The next year, they became the ninth team (at the time) to win 67 games in the regular season…only to face in the first round the only team they hadn't beat all year. Instead, Dallas succumbed in one of the greatest playoff upsets of all time.

After a decade of missed chances, the Mavericks' playoff disappointment earned them a label. They were relying on a superstar who was incredible but couldn't lead a team by himself, people said. They shot too many jump shots, and teams would never win that way, they said. In 2011 the Miami Heat had just formed a LeBron James-led superteam, the Los Angeles Lakers were looking for a third straight championship, and the San Antonio Spurs were looming as large as ever.

But it happened.

What will always stand out about the 2011 series is how magical it felt. It had the touch of a film writer who relied on a few too many cliches, who scripted an underdog story with a lovable but flawed protagonist and an extraordinary leading man who outmatched his role. Maybe the author could have eased up on perfect comeback endings and sappy moments from people achieving lifelong dreams, but man, this movie always made you tear up at the end.

When I sat down to interview Rick Carlisle for this book, he used the word *magic* to describe it. "It was a magical thing going on and it was a team and a group of guys that truly did understand that this was their time and their moment," he told me. "It was really an amazing group."

For Nowitzki, the championship was validation. It meant he would never leave Dallas to chase a ring during his final few seasons and it made sure he would never end up on those hideous lists, ranking the best players who never won one. Because Nowitzki doesn't draw much attention to himself, sometimes we forget how competitive he is. But it meant everything to him.

For Jason Kidd it was the same thing. Kidd will be a first-ballot Hall of Famer one day soon, and his ring makes sure his career doesn't end with any regrets. For Carlisle, the championship meant longevity. Without it, who knows if he would be approaching his second decade in Dallas.

For the other veterans, this was their final chance to be champions. Shawn Marion is a borderline Hall of Fame candidate, and the others—Jason Terry, Tyson Chandler, and Peja Stojakovic—won't make it, but they were all wonderfully talented NBA players for years. They had all fatefully ended up in Dallas together, and 2011 gave them the ultimate award.

It's magical how all those storylines converged on one team. As the postseason progressed, it seemed like every player had their moment to shine. If we carry on the Hollywood film analogy, it was an episodic progression with every actor getting a chance to shine. Of course, Nowitzki earned the most screen time, but there was the Corey Brewer moment and Stojakovic's chance for payback. When Brendan Haywood was injured, it opened the door for Brian Cardinal and Ian Mahinmi.

Of course the opponent was the Miami Heat, too, offering a chance for vindication. Naturally, it ended in Game 6, just like it had five years before. After years of criticism for being too soft or not clutch enough, Nowitzki repeatedly succeeded when asked to deliver for Dallas late in games. It was all a supernaturally scripted run. "Very seldom in life, when somebody steals your bicycle or your girlfriend, do you literally have a chance to go back to the scene of a crime and right a wrong," Mavericks president Donnie Nelson told me. "That just never happens in life and at that level. To go back to the core, it was very gratifying. And I think, just like him, you don't allow your emotions, just because you're trying to dispatch the enemy, you are literally trying, and that's the ramifications of this franchise and the history that the fans went through. If we would have not grabbed that trophy, it would have been a whole different landscape."

3 Mark Cuban

Donnie Nelson has never forgotten his initial reaction upon hearing someone named Mark Cuban had bought the Mavericks franchise. "The name 'Cuban,'" Nelson told me. "The first thing that goes through my mind is, *This guy's from Cuba. I'm going to have to learn how to speak Spanish to communicate with this guy.* I didn't know!"

It was January 4, 2000, and owner Ross Perot Jr. had sold the team to Cuban, a self-made billionaire from the dot-com boom. What Nelson and the Mavericks didn't know is that this would become the third most important day in the franchise's history. Since Cuban's arrival the Mavericks have been one of the most successful teams in all of professional sports.

It was Cuban who changed the trajectory of the Mavericks and Cuban who became one of the first celebrity owners. Traditionally, owners sat in luxury boxes and watched their teams from afar. Cuban has always sat courtside in team apparel, even jerseys, while celebrating big shots and screaming at referees in the meantime.

When Cuban bought the Mavericks days into the new year and the new millennium, they were still fresh off the terrible 1990s and were only just starting to show flickers of success. Neither Dirk Nowitzki, Steve Nash, nor the coaches had proven themselves yet. In fact, Donnie Nelson went for drinks with the coaching staff that night, expecting they would be cleaned out by Cuban so the owner could install his own people. "That was when Steve Nash was getting booed in his own building," Nelson said. "Dirk was getting thrown around like a rag doll. Mark had every right to come in, and I think it was a popular sentiment at the time…like a lot of owners, you come in, you wanna get your own guys, you wanna clean house. That's what we felt. And Mark embraced us at our darkest hours."

Cuban's loyalty stood out, as did his hands-on enthusiasm. He became a personality directly involved with the team instead of someone who just signs checks and watches from afar. Of course, this was displayed most with Cuban's spats with officiating. In his first two years alone, Cuban racked up more than $1 million worth of fines. Once, he had the still shot of a missed call put up on the Jumbotron as he berated an official and another time he said he wouldn't let the NBA's head of officiating "manage a Dairy Queen." When Dairy Queen protested, Cuban actually spent a day managing one, showing up at 6:00 AM to begin training and serving ice cream to more than a thousand customers who showed up to the carnival-like atmosphere. Though Cuban reined in his temper somewhat over the years, his fines are over $2 million and counting.

Another quirk of the personable owner is his frequent media sessions, occurring before nearly every home game and often on the road, too. Cuban usually works out before games, chatting with beat writers on a StairMaster behind the Mavericks locker room for as long as and about whatever they want. Given that some

Brash, outspoken, and one of the best owners in sports, Mark Cuban celebrates the Mavericks' championship in 2011.

team owners don't even talk openly to reporters once a year, it's an unprecedented gesture.

Sometimes, Cuban was even more transparent, blogging directly to fans on his website, blogmaverick.com, about why the Mavericks made certain moves. In 2015 during the DeAndre Jordan debacle, Cuban posted several updates to CyberDust, a messaging app that he had invested in. Famously, Cuban will read at least the first sentence of every email he receives. Not every fan likes Cuban's style of ownership, wishing he would stop drawing headlines and distracting attention from the team, but you can't deny how accessible he is.

The Mavericks' only losing seasons since Cuban bought the team was the first one and in 2016–17, and he only purchased the franchise halfway through that first year. Of course, Cuban lucked out by having a first-ballot Hall of Famer already on the roster, but it was the combination of Cuban's zeal and Nowitzki's greatness that has propelled Dallas into this historical run of success since 2000.

4 How the Mavericks Came to Dallas

The Dallas Mavericks came into existence on a napkin in a diner booth. The restaurant, Coco's, has long since been replaced by a gas station and pawn shop. A sparkling new In-N-Out Burger now sits across the street. The people in the booth were Don Carter, Norm Sonju, and an attorney. Carter and Sonju had been trying to bring a team to Dallas for more than two years. At first they tried separately before meeting and linking up their plans. In fact, Carter had already agreed in principle to buy an NBA team twice with plans to move it to Dallas. Both times the league refused to approve his purchase.

Carter and Sonju realized the only way a team was coming to Dallas would be through expansion. Carter wrote the $100,000 check, giving him exclusive rights to expand to Dallas, but actually agreeing to expansion terms proved much more difficult. At the 1980 All-Star Game, two years after Carter and Sonju had started their quest, seven teams voted against Dallas receiving an expansion team. It was enough to block the move.

The franchises against the move wanted more demanding terms of entry. The league raised the price three separate times and lowered the expansion team's traditional first pick to the 11th overall selection. Twenty-four investors had been interested in helping fund the purchase, but that number had fallen to fewer than five. Sonju, originally a Chicagoan, had spent nearly two years in Dallas, trying to make this purchase happen. Confronted with the rising demands, he was about ready to give up when he met Carter in that diner. Carter wasn't. Ultimately, he agreed to fund an 87 percent ownership stake of the $12 million expansion price requested by the NBA, which set a record for the most ever paid for an expansion team at the time. The figures were scribbled on that napkin in Coco's, and at the time, Carter and Sonju might have been the only two who expected good things for this franchise, especially when so many current teams in the league were losing money. But the duo pushed forward anyway, and the Dallas Mavericks officially became the NBA's 23rd team on May 1, 1980.

* * *

Don Carter wasn't exactly a basketball fan. In fact, he had never even attended an NBA game before beginning his fight for a franchise. But the multimillionaire's wife, Linda, grew up playing the sport, and she convinced him that Dallas deserved professional

The Chaparrals

The honor of the first professional basketball team in Dallas actually belongs to the Dallas Chaparrals, which spent six seasons in the Dallas-Fort Worth area as a part of the American Basketball Association. Founded in 1967, the Chaparrals went to the playoffs in five straight seasons before missing in their sixth and final year.

For one season the team rebranded themselves as the Texas Chaparrals, splitting games between Dallas, Fort Worth, and Lubbock. The experiment was a failure, and the team returned solely to Dallas in 1971 until their departure. The Chaparrals moved to San Antonio in 1973 and became the Spurs. Unlike in Dallas, where the team had struggled to draw decent crowds, San Antonio loved them. When the ABA merged with the NBA in 1977, the Spurs were one of the four ABA franchises to be directly assimilated into the league. But despite the Chaparrals' short time in Dallas, they deserve credit for setting the stage for the Mavericks just a few years later.

basketball. Norm Sonju had spent a season as the general manager of the Buffalo Braves, a couple seasons before they moved to California to become the Clippers. Sonju saw how little Buffalo cared about the sport, and his idea was to move the Braves to Dallas. He thought it was going to happen, too, but it fell through at the last minute.

Bringing a team to Dallas became Sonju's new passion, even though he had no connection to the city. First, Sonju realized that Dallas had higher television ratings for the NBA than any other city without a franchise (and even some cities that did have teams). There was also a new stadium being built, Reunion Arena, that made North Texas a perfect fit.

The NBA wasn't a lucrative market in 1979. Only a few teams were in the black, and even the NBA Finals that year—and the season after—were shown on tape delay after the evening news, which often spoiled the results. Dallas was and is a football town, but Carter and Sonju were convinced they could develop a passion for basketball. Their critics collectively thought, *I told you so*, after the Mavericks had 18th best attendance (out of 23 teams) their first season. But it was Carter and Sonju who were laughing when Dallas ranked fifth best in the NBA just three years later.

Mark Cuban says Carter, whom he calls Mr. C, is the person the franchise owes the most thanks. "He is Mr. Maverick," Cuban told the *Fort Worth Star-Telegram* in 2015. "There are no Mavericks without Mr. C and Mrs. C. There's nobody more important to this organization, and I would put him ahead of Dirk. Without him, we are not here."

After a reckless youth—Carter's mother, Mary Crowley, once wrote in her autobiography that she prayed, "Lord, I know Don is going to do something great; please let it be legal"— Carter became a devout Christian. He cared deeply about the franchise he had brought to Dallas but also the players who came through.

One Carter story is that when he had to cut Ollie Mack shortly before Christmas, he felt so bad about it that he presented him with a $3,000 going-away present. In another anecdote, Carter took Mark Aguirre off the trading block when his mother unexpectedly died. With Aguirre already coping with one traumatic event, Carter didn't want to put him through another dramatic life change. Carter owned the team until 1996, with Sonju serving as the team's general manager and president the entire time. The Mavericks weren't the first professional basketball team in Dallas, but they were the ones that stuck. For that, you can thank Carter and Sonju.

5 The 1980s

Nothing stands out about the Mavericks' first season except for the obvious: they were horrendous.

It wasn't a surprise. Don Carter and Norm Sonju had found their coach, the veteran Dick Motta, who already had 12 years head coaching experience, an NBA Coach of the Year award, and an NBA championship. Besides him, though, the team was starting from scratch. The Mavericks' first pick in the 1980 NBA Draft—picking 11th overall instead of first—was Kiki VanDeWeghe, who refused to play until he was traded in December. The team's second selection, Roosevelt Bouie, never played a season in the NBA, while their third-round pick, Dave Britton, only played one. It wasn't with Dallas.

A scraggly group of journeymen went 15–67 in that opening 1980–81 season, but Motta wasn't phased. The experienced coach wanted to be in Dallas. He had sought out Carter and Sonju, leaving the Washington Bullets to avoid a rebuilding process, even though he had won a championship with them just three seasons prior. Leading a brand new franchise appealed to him.

In some respects it's amazing the Mavericks even won 15 games the first year. The team was made up of "basically four types of people," Motta has said. "People with bad contracts, people with a bad injury, people with a bad attitude, or a bad player. Some of them qualified for three of the four categories."

A terrible season meant the Mavericks earned the first overall selection in the following draft, and that's when the team's fortunes began to change. Dallas picked Mark Aguirre with their top pick that year and selected Rolando Blackman with another top 10 pick. They nabbed power forward Jay Vincent, who ended up leading the team in scoring that season, in the second round, and the team improved its record that season by 13 wins.

By the 1982–83 season, the Mavericks began looking like a team that could really make the playoffs. At that year's All-Star break, Dallas was 25–24 and had won 12 of their last 15 games. Unfortunately, they faded in the second half, finishing 38–44 and missing the postseason. But they used the offseason to draft Derek Harper, adding the point guard to a steadily improving young roster.

The next season the Mavericks finally broke through, making the playoffs for the first time in the team's history. It was the team's first winning season (43–39) and it featured the Mavs' first All-Star in Aguirre, who averaged 29.5 points per game—second most in the league—that season. The Mavericks exploded for a quick start, winning 13 of their first 17 games, including eight in a row, and carried it all the way to the season's end, where they finished strong with four wins in their last six games.

Dallas was matched up against the Seattle SuperSonics in the first round, an experienced playoff team who had won the NBA Finals five seasons prior. After the Mavericks fell behind two games to one, they recovered to win Game 4 in Seattle and carried their success to a series win in Game 5, which is colloquially called "Moody Madness." That's still one of the most iconic games in the franchise's history.

Though Dallas quickly lost in the next round against the Los Angeles Lakers, it was still a sparkling achievement to not only make the playoffs, but also advance in a series during the team's fourth year in existence. That playoff appearance was the first of five straight. The Mavericks fell in the first round the next year, made another run to the semifinals during the 1985–86 season before falling to the Lakers again, and got ousted yet again in the first round the next year. In 1988 the Mavericks suffered their biggest playoff disappointment: facing the Lakers in the Western

Conference Finals—only to fall short of the team's first trip to the NBA Finals because of a heartbreaking Game 7 defeat.

The Mavericks' roster morphed and changed over those five seasons. In 1984, using a high draft pick pilfered from the terrible Cleveland Cavaliers, they selected big man Sam Perkins, who locked down the position for six years. The next year they nabbed Detlef Schrempf, a German-born shooter, though his best seasons came once he left Dallas. James Donaldson rolled through town, joining Perkins in the frontcourt and representing the Mavericks in the All-Star Game in 1988. He's still the only Mavericks center to make the team.

Harper played the second half of the 1985–86 season as the team's starting point guard before taking over the position full time a year later. It moved starter Brad Davis to the bench, a role he filled for Dallas until his retirement in 1992. The last crucial move Dallas made came with the selection of Roy Tarpley in the 1986 NBA Draft. Tarpley was one of the most talented players in the team's history, but his career is also one of the saddest. Off-court issues and addictions derailed his career until he was permanently banned from the NBA in 1995 for substance abuse.

That team's failure to knock off the Lakers in 1988 marked the beginning of the end. Donaldson went down with a season-ending injury the following season, causing Dallas to miss the playoffs. They traded Aguirre midway through the year. Dallas made the playoffs once more, the next year in 1990, the only postseason appearance in the coming decade.

Moody Madness

No Mavericks game has stood the test of time quite like one played in 1984. The franchise, only four years old, made the 1984 playoffs with a 43–39 record and was matched against a much more experienced Seattle SuperSonics in the first round of the playoffs. Despite falling down two games to one, the Mavericks shockingly won Game 4 to push the series to a fifth and conclusive game.

Dallas was hosting Game 5, but Reunion Arena was booked by the World Championship Tennis Finals in late April. When the series started, the location of Game 5 read "TBD." No one really believed that the Mavericks would make the playoffs and certainly no one believed they would win two games against a Sonics team that had been crowned NBA champions a few years before.

The solution was Southern Methodist University's Moody Coliseum, about five miles north of downtown. The Coliseum held only 9,007 fans compared to Reunion's 17,007, and the technology was out of date. In the hours leading up to tipoff, it looked like the only television broadcast of the game—to an old pay-per-view channel, no less—might be without sound. The Mavericks' equipment crew even had to measure and paint the NBA three-point line onto the court.

As many fans that could fit packed into Moody anyway. It was win or go home, and nobody cared that the Mavericks were huge underdogs who had never been to the playoffs before.

In a back-and-forth game, Seattle led 93–86 with 2:08 left in the game. Mavericks legend Derek Harper was a rookie coming off the bench that season and he remembers thinking that there was no way Dallas could win that game. But despite that the Mavericks surged back anyway. Rolando Blackman stole the ball for a dunk that made it a two-point game. On the game's final possession, he knocked down a game-tying jumper to force overtime. "I watch that game over and over," Blackman told the *Dallas Observer* in 2009. "It's probably the highest I ever jumped in my career."

It had been a wild game played under ludicrous circumstances, but it wasn't Moody Madness until that five minutes of overtime. Up six halfway through the period, the Mavericks' lead shrunk to just one point. On the final possession with a single second left on the clock, the Sonics' Tom Chambers attempted a half-court shot that missed. The referees whistled the game over, and the jubilant Mavericks paraded into the locker room. "Pandemonium, man, is what comes to mind for me," Harper told me. "Any time you're a part of a game you think you're going to lose, you don't see any way you can come back and win the game, when you find a way to do that, I get goose bumps right now just thinking back on it. I'm not kidding, I'm really getting goose bumps because it was incredible, man. It was one of those never-say-die moments by a team that looked like they were dead in the water."

But wait. The referees realized the clock hadn't started on Chambers' last-second shot, and they spent 14 minutes discussing the final play. They ultimately ruled that the Sonics would replay one final possession with a second remaining. Seattle had one last chance, and the Mavericks literally had to put their uniforms back on and return to the court after thinking they had won. "Coming back out, all kinds of things go through your mind, like what kind of things could go wrong that we don't win this game," Harper said. "It was an emotional roller coaster."

The do-over made no difference, as an alley-oop attempt was broken up instead—this time with the clock running out successfully. Moody Coliseum worked itself into a frenzy, one that witnesses say was unmatched by anything they've seen then or since.

The Mavericks moved on to the Western Conference Semifinals, where they lost to the Los Angeles Lakers in five games, but Moody Madness lives on. It's a hallmark moment in the franchise's history—its first playoff series win, its first unforgettable game, and the first time Dallas realized this Mavericks team might truly be special. "It was," said Harper, who went on to play more than 1,200 games in the NBA, "the most exciting thing I've ever experienced inside a basketball court."

The 1990s

To describe how quickly the Mavericks went from a model franchise in the 1980s to a 1990s disaster, we need to borrow from Charles Dickens. *It was the best of times, it was the worst of times.* As incredible as it was for the Mavericks to climb from an expansion franchise to an annual playoff team, it all came crashing down once the decade turned. After losing in the first round of the 1990 postseason, Dallas embarked on a 10-year postseason drought.

It started in the 1990 offseason, when center Sam Perkins left for the Los Angeles Lakers in free agency. The Mavericks acquired Lafayette "Fat" Lever, but he underwent season-ending surgery four games into the year. The next game Roy Tarpley was also lost for the season due to injury. (His substance abuse problems had alrcady cost him timc thc previous two years.) Dallas had also signed Alex English that offseason, a former scoring champion who had spent his past 11 seasons with the Nuggets, averaging around 26 points. But English was 37, his production fell off drastically, and he retired the next year.

With all those bad turns, the result was a 28-win season. The next year, the Mavericks fell even further, winning just 22. Tarpley, a 1986 lottery selection, was arrested for his second DWI offense the previous season and suspended by the league. Even Brad Davis, the most steady and reliable player on the roster who had been with the team since its inception, suffered a back injury. In January the 36-year-old had no choice but to retire.

The rebuilding process began in earnest after that year in the 1992 offseason, when the team traded Rolando Blackman. Now the Mavericks' all-time leading scorer (having passed Mark Aguirre), Blackman had hung around with the team—even through those previous two miserable seasons. Though he was 32, the New York Knicks were willing to send a first-round pick, an offer the Mavericks had to accept, for him. Blackman played the two worst seasons of his career in New York before hanging it up.

The other major acquisition from the 1990 offseason, Lever, only played 35 games through his first three years in Dallas. After his first season-ending knee surgery, Lever suffered another one in January the next year and required a third surgery that caused him to miss the entire 1992–93 season. The 33-year-old guard, twice an All-Star and once an All-NBA team selection with the Denver Nuggets, managed to play 81 games in his final season. The injuries, however, had totally robbed him of his old skill, and Lever retired after the season in 1994.

After two bad seasons, the Mavericks kept sinking. An 11-win season was followed by a 13-win campaign—both by far the worst in the league. Four days after Christmas in 1992, the Mavericks suffered the worst loss in franchise history: a 139–81 demolition by the Sacramento Kings. Since that date in 1992, only one team has ever lost by more than 58 points like Dallas did on that evening. But hey, huge margins of defeat were a common theme; the Mavericks lost games by an average of more than 15 points that season.

The Mavericks have never had coaching inconsistency like they did in the 1990s. From 1989 to 1997, seven head coaches cycled in and out of Dallas—including briefly Dick Motta, the team's first coach who had left in 1987. His return lasted only two seasons.

Of course, the Mavericks' futility meant they routinely received high draft picks. Thanks to the NBA's lottery system, Dallas never drafted higher than second (1994) in that decade. But in three straight years, they selected Jim Jackson, Jamal Mashburn, and Jason Kidd—coined as the Three J's. Dallas was sure this trio was their path back to the glory days. It was a hope that was never realized.

Three J's

Nothing from the Mavericks' history promised more and delivered less than the Three J's. It's a stark reminder that everything in the NBA must be earned—even when there's a flashy nickname already in place.

With the fourth overall picks in the 1992 and 1993 NBA Draft, the Mavericks selected Jim Jackson and Jamal Mashburn, respectively. A year later with the second overall pick, Dallas drafted Jason Kidd. This trio of youngsters immediately made impacts on the floor. Jackson and Mashburn both averaged more than 24 points per game during that 1994–95 season. Meanwhile, Kidd was awarded Co-Rookie of the Year honors for his excellent debut season, when he immediately showed an ability to score, rebound, defend, and run an offense. With two top six scorers in Jackson and Mashburn on his team, it felt like a perfect fit.

The Mavericks were on the rise that season, too, with the Three J's leading Dallas to a 36–46 record. But by the next season, it was already falling apart. The Mavericks regressed, only managing a 26–56 record during their 1995–96 campaign. Much of it had to do with the personalities of the Three J's. "We've matured enough to understand that we had a great thing in Dallas," said Jackson looking back in 2003. "It may be the timing wasn't right."

Dick Motta, the first ever Mavericks coach who had returned for a second stint, unexpectedly resigned in 1996. In his place came Jim Cleamons, who found that his three stars— particularly Kidd and Jackson, who had previously been close friends—were barely on speaking terms. "As soon as I got to Dallas, it was a matter of putting out fires," Cleamons said in hindsight.

Blame can be passed around. Cleamons was the Mavericks' fifth coach since Jackson was drafted, causing instability. In what was supposed to be a breakout year for Dallas during the 1995–96 season, Mashburn only played 18 games after suffering a severe ankle injury. The team lacked a veteran presence. Journeyman (and future NBA head coach) guard Scotty Brooks was the only player who was at least 30 years old who played the whole season with Dallas. "I thought those Three J's were going to make it that first year," Motta said after the fact. "Halfway through the second year, shoot, I wouldn't give you 15 cents for the three of them together."

The most persistent rumor was that R&B star Toni Braxton was involved in the breakup of the Three J's. The details of the story are still vague. It supposedly happened in Atlanta, or maybe New York, and involved a limo intended to pick up Kidd that Jackson knowingly took instead. The players and their teammates at the time have denied anything like that actually happened. But Braxton, when reached for an interview, only fueled a firestorm of rumors about the trio's bad terms. "As far as dating, whether it's true or not, I can never kiss and tell," she said coyly.

The teammates were broken up by the next season. Kidd requested a trade and was the first player shipped out. The Mavericks dealt him in December for Michael Finley and Sam Cassell of the Phoenix Suns. The Mavericks hired Don Nelson as the team's general manager in February, and within weeks he lined up separate trades for Jackson and Mashburn that completely

Thought to be saviors of the franchise, the Three J's—Jamal Mashburn, Jason Kidd, and Jimmy Jackson—instead let chemistry issues get in the way of their immense individual talent.

revamped the team's roster. Finley turned into a crucial building block for the future, while the 7'6" Shawn Bradley also arrived in one of the deals and spent the next eight seasons of his career in Dallas.

The Three J's had all the promise in the world, and they appeared to be the Mavericks' ticket out of the mediocrity that plagued them the entire decade. Instead, they only sucked Dallas further into the mire—one they wouldn't start to break out of until Dirk Nowitzki was drafted in 1998. All three players admitted wondering what could have been when they looked back on the team years later. "We were young," Mashburn said. "And everybody wanted the limelight just a little bit too early."

9 Just a Kid from Germany

Dirk Nowitzki's journey to the NBA began on a court in Germany. Not a basketball court, though. A tennis court.

Nowitzki's mother played basketball for the German national team, and his older sister, Silke, had followed suit. Because of that Dirk Nowitzki decided early on that basketball was a women's sport. Instead, he played tennis and followed his dad into handball, a sport in which his father had played professionally in Germany.

Attending a cousin's basketball practice when he was 13 helped change Nowitzki's mind, and soon he was playing basketball constantly. Nowitzki kept growing taller, too, so basketball made sense for him. It wasn't long before he quit the other sports to focus on basketball, and by the time he was 15, he joined a professional basketball club called DJK Wurzburg X-Rays, a second-division team in Germany. At the time it bothered his father, who thought he could be a great handball player, but Nowitzki clearly had made the right choice.

With his height and athleticism, Nowitzki was destined to become a great German basketball player. But his path reached a higher trajectory when Holger Geschwindner, a former star on the German national basketball team, spotted the gangly 15-year-old in a chance encounter at a local gym. Right away, he saw the potential for a star who could transcend Germany and reach the NBA. Even better, Geschwindner knew Nowitzki's mother from their time on the national teams and quickly earned the Nowitzkis' approval to start coaching their son individually several times a week. "Holger's just the best thing that happened to Dirk from a basketball perspective," Mavericks president Donnie Nelson said.

Geschwindner's training styles were unorthodox. He even used algebra to calculate the optimum release point for Nowitzki's jump shot, but it all worked. Nowitzki went from a scrawny teenager to a sensation with his club team, joining the starting lineup at DJK Wurzburg in his second year and spending four seasons overall dominating the German leagues. Still, Nowitzki was tearing up a virtually unknown second-tier league in Germany in a time before the Internet allowed teams to scout players with just a few clicks on a computer. Two American events helped push him onto a national scale.

In 1997 Nike's "Hoop Heroes Tour" had NBA stars tour internationally, playing against international professionals. Nowitzki participated in a game facing Michael Jordan, Charles Barkley, and Scottie Pippen, and Barkley swears to this day he dropped 50 points despite Pippen's best efforts to guard him.

The performance helped earn him an invite to the Nike Hoops Summit in March 1998, which served as a national scouting spectacle for the NBA. One squad was the USA Basketball Junior National Select Team, while the other was made up of selected international players from around the world. Obviously, the U.S.

team—with more knowledge of each other and home country advantage—was favored. With Nowitzki on the international team's side, it didn't matter.

Playing against top prospects like Al Harrington, Rashard Lewis, and Quentin Richardson, it was Nowitzki who recorded a game-high 33 points to go along with 14 rebounds and three steals while leading the World Team to a 104–99 victory. It was a head-turning performance for everyone in the building, especially since many had never even heard of Nowitzki before.

Still, most teams didn't take Nowitzki seriously yet. Publicly, Nowitzki had talked about needing to spend another year in Germany's required military service, and there was an impression that he wasn't ready to make the leap to the United States. The Mavericks were interested anyway and hopeful they could persuade him to come over right away but willing to wait a year if not. "I didn't think I was ready," Nowitzki said, looking back. "It was a big jump coming over right away from Europe to the best league. I didn't know if I should make it or not."

The week he was drafted, Geschwindner even told *The Dallas Morning News* that Nowitzki wouldn't head to the U.S. before 2000, meaning the Mavericks would have had to wait two seasons. Instead, after a last-second lockout resolution saved the 1998–99 season, Don Nelson—now the team's head coach as well as general manager—and other Mavericks executives convinced the 20-year-old to give it a shot. "I told his parents I would try to be his father away from Wurzburg and I'm trying to do that as best I can," Mavericks coach Don Nelson said in a 1998 television interview.

Like a proud father, Nelson couldn't help but brag about his new "son" and unfairly inflated expectations for Nowitzki when he publicly predicted the scrawny German would win Rookie of the Year. Instead, Nowitzki was frequently benched, often bullied by bigger players, and never fully comfortable. Challenges came on the court, but Nowitzki needed just as much help off it, too.

Nash still pokes fun at Nowitzki, saying that early in his career all he ever said was "sure." As the youngest child in his household (where he also lived with two cousins), Nowitzki had always been on the quiet side. It was a difficult transition to be living by himself for the first time in a foreign country, speaking a language he still wasn't totally comfortable with—while his family and then-girlfriend were an ocean away. "When I came to Dallas, I was 20," Nowitzki said. "I barely said a word."

It took help from everyone around him in those early years. Steve Nash showed Nowitzki how to pay his cable bill and how the postal service worked; journeyman forward Chris Antsey helped show him how to cook and clean. Maybe the most important person to Nowitzki's acclimation was Lisa Tyner. The motherly Mavericks senior accountant and payroll manager, who has now worked with the Mavericks for more than 35 years, helped walk Nowitzki through his basic finances and developed a friendship with the floundering youngster. "He needed help with a lot of things but not really much more than a lot of kids who show up here," Tyner told *The Oklahoman* in 2016. "We try to look out for our guys, not just throw them out there for the wolves."

Tyner and Nowitzki remain friends to this day. Between his teammates, Tyner, and visits from his family and Holger Geschwindner, Nowitzki's off-the-court life slowly grew more comfortable. By the final two months of the abbreviated lockout rookie season, Nowitzki was playing more minutes, averaging more points, and shooting much better from the field. You could see him slowly becoming the player the Mavericks had believed he could be when they drafted him.

10 Steve Nash

Steve Nash's opening press conference is an unforgettable snapshot in Mavericks history. On the left is Dirk Nowitzki, the gangly, newly drafted seven-foot German sporting a terrible bowl cut. In the middle is head coach Don Nelson, whose arms are around both of them. Nash stands on the right with unfortunate spiky, bleached blond hair, holding up his new Dallas jersey emblazoned with No. 13. In that moment Nash and Nowitzki looked more like the frontmen of an early 2000s boy band. Who would have guessed they were two future Hall of Famers?

When Nash enters the Hall of Fame in 2019, he'll be recognized first as a member of the Phoenix Suns. But his six seasons with the Dallas Mavericks are unforgettable, and Nash was an instrumental part of helping morph Dallas from a laughingstock to a perennial playoff power, and the point guard had fun while doing it.

Nowitzki and Nash, still close, were best friends during their shared years in Dallas. A few drunken photographs exist from their late nights spent in Uptown, or you can refer to grainy videos of them both playing the guitar and singing original songs in the Mavericks locker room. Those moments are as memorable as their hundreds of pick-and-rolls over six seasons in Dallas, which roasted opponents with perfect precision.

Nash grew up in Canada and spent four years at Santa Clara University, turning enough heads in a small conference to be drafted by the Phoenix Suns in the first round. Although the youngster showed promise in his initial two seasons, he was stuck in an impossible situation behind two of the NBA's best guards at the time, Jason Kidd and Kevin Johnson. At first the Suns wanted to keep Nash and declined to trade him at the 1998 deadline despite numerous requests. But during the 1998 draft, Phoenix finally relented and shipped him to the Mavericks for several players and a future first-round pick. (That pick became Shawn Marion, so you could say the deal worked out for both sides.)

Though the Mavericks saw Nash and Nowitzki as the future of their franchise, the early returns weren't good. Both struggled in their first years in Dallas, and Nash shot only 36 percent in his first season there. Though Nash improved in Year Two, he missed nearly a third of the season with an ankle injury. It wasn't until his third year that Nash made the leap Dallas expected, and the Mavericks rose along with him.

Nash averaged nearly 18 points and eight assists over the next four seasons, emerging as a deadeye shooter from any spot on the floor and a clever passer who thrived with Nowitzki as a pick-and-roll partner. When Nash's contract expired in the summer of 2004, everyone expected him to return. After all, he and Nowitzki seemed like a perfect pairing, and the team had been a couple wins away from the NBA Finals in 2003.

Then, a day into free agency, Nash signed with the Phoenix Suns. "That was shocking," Ben Rogers, longtime Dallas sports radio host, recalled. "That didn't make sense...This guy, who is Dirk's best friend, and you're going to let another team outbid you?"

Though Phoenix insisted that Nash make his decision quickly, Mark Cuban had a chance to match the five-year deal worth more than $65 million. In the years since, Cuban has said his belief that Nash wouldn't stay healthy factored into the decision. He's also said it was his biggest mistake and a learning moment for him.

Still, Nash's sudden departure shocked Mavericks fans and those with the team alike. "The thing I remember the most about that, the next day at Moody Coliseum…all the Mavericks employees were there," said Jeff Wade, Rogers' co-host and Mavericks television announcer. "They were in shock. It was like someone came up to you and said, 'Oh my God, our best friend died.' It was like, they were in total shock. I remember in particular [Mavericks director of communications] Sarah Melton was like catatonic because he was so loved."

What would have happened if the Mavericks had kept Nash—and whether they should have—is still one of the most contentious questions in Dallas sports history. It's amplified by Nash's career after the Mavericks, which included two MVP awards but no championships. Either way, though, his departure doesn't take away from Nash's impact on the franchise in those formative years.

11 The Early 2000s

The basketball renaissance in Dallas that began with Dirk Nowitzki and Steve Nash didn't happen instantaneously. Both players struggled their first season, a frenzied lockout-shortened one played in three and a half months. The Mavericks finished with 19 wins, albeit with a winning home record that showed promise.

The next year, in the 1999–00 season, the team began to click. Michael Finley had been acquired from the Phoenix Suns when the Mavericks held a fire-sale on the Three J's and he led the team in scoring for a third straight season that year. Nowitzki broke out, averaging nearly 18 points per game in his sophomore campaign. Although Nash lagged behind slightly due to an injury-plagued season, the team's potential was clear.

On January 14, 2000, Ross Perot Jr. and his ownership group sold the franchise to Mark Cuban. He immediately brought an enthusiasm and excitement to a team with a bright future, and his unorthodox, hands-on style with the team attracted attention to Dallas from around the league.

The Three J's had collapsed right after their "breakout" season, but any fears that the same thing would happen to Dallas' new Big Three were unfounded. The team kept rising, winning 53 games in the 2000–01 season, serving as just the third time in team history they had a 50-win season. Nash's breakout year and Nowitzki's steady improvement had quickly accelerated the team's development—along with a savvy trade for veteran forward Juwan Howard.

In 2001 Dallas won their first playoff series—against the Utah Jazz—since 1988. After falling behind 2–0 in the best-of-five series, the Mavericks won the next two games and took Game 5. Calvin Booth, the team's backup center, hit the game-winning layup and forever etched his name in Mavericks lore.

The Mavericks kept rising in 2003 with 60 wins and the deepest playoff push yet. Unfortunately, Dirk Nowitzki went down with a knee injury in Game 3 of the Western Conference Finals against the San Antonio Spurs. Without him, the Mavericks lost in six games.

That injury proved to be contentious. Nowitzki wanted to play through it, and Mark Cuban thought he should, but Don Nelson insisted that Nowitzki sit unless he was 100 percent. "It was certainly Dirk's health first and foremost," Mavericks general manager Donnie Nelson told me. "We always had to protect him from himself. If he had his druthers, he would be out there 40 minutes every night."

The Mavericks made another trade that offseason, acquiring Antoine Walker and Antawn Jamison, but lost in the first round. In the summer of 2004, Cuban failed to match Phoenix's contract to Steve Nash, losing a player everyone expected to spend years more in Dallas. Nash's departure may have been the final straw for Nelson, who resigned as head coach halfway through the 2004–05 season. He appointed Avery Johnson in his stead, and the Mavericks fell out of the postseason in the second round of a transition year for them. For the first few seasons, the Mavericks were just happy to be winning again. By the time 2006 arrived, though, real championship expectations had arrived.

12. Watch *The Finish Line* and Wonder What Dirk and Nash Could've Been

My favorite thing ever created by Grantland—the beloved sports and pop culture website shut down way too soon—was a mini-documentary series called *The Finish Line* filmed during Steve Nash's final season before his 2014 retirement. The last episode is titled "Dinner With Dirk," and it's exactly what it sounds like. "What do you think would have happened," Nash asks Nowitzki, sitting next to him on camera, "if I would have re-signed with the Mavs in 2004?"

"I'm not sure what ever would have happened," Nowitzki replies. "Obviously, people ask me that sometimes, and you think about it a little bit, but some people say it was good for our careers to be apart, to grow without each other. I'm not sure. It would have been a hell of a time, though, I know that."

The 10-minute production offers an unprecedented look at one of the biggest questions in Mavericks history—directly from the mouths of the two players involved. Sure, it's not their uncensored thoughts. They still know they're on camera, of course, even in this unconventional setting. But it might be as close as we ever get and it's definitely a reason to check out the video online at Grantland.com.

In 2014 Mark Cuban said letting Steve Nash sign with the Phoenix Suns was the worst mistake he ever made. Many Mavericks fans have agreed with him for a decade. "I learned an expensive lesson," Cuban told *Rolling Stone*. "It's easy to look back and see my mistakes today. I wish I would have been smart enough to know

Close buds Dirk Nowitzki and Steve Nash hang out at a 2003 Texas Rangers game. Mavericks fans are left to wonder what could have been—if the team had retained the duo.

better back then. I loved taking risks to win. Unfortunately, some of them were not as educated as they should have been."

It's clear that Nash never would have become the version of himself that won two MVPs without going to Phoenix under Mike D'Antoni's mentorship, where his possessions increased and the tempo accelerated. Dallas was coached by Don Nelson then, and his mismatch-heavy offenses often took the ball out of Nash's hands. Cuban said in 2012 that the fear that Nash's body would break down again—like it did his first two years in Dallas—impacted the team's decision to let him go. At the time it was a valid concern.

There's also the question of whether two average-at-best defenders could have started on a championship-caliber defense. Perhaps, if the Mavericks filled out the other three spots with strong defenders, it could have worked. But who can say for sure?

Because the basketball gods have a sense of humor, the Mavericks and the Suns faced each other in the playoffs in the two years after Nash's departure. Phoenix won the first series, ousting Dallas in the semifinals before the Mavericks topped them in next year's Western Conference Finals to make their 2006 Finals appearance. Nash admitted he couldn't really root for Nowitzki that year despite their close friendship because the Mavericks had beaten him. That's why he was so glad Nowitzki went back in 2011, when he could root on his longtime friend as he finally won his first ring.

Still, the two will always wonder from time to time what would have happened if they hadn't separated. "On the one hand, I feel like we would have gone on and won a championship because you did it without me," Nash said. "A part of me is like, 'Yeah, we both grew in different ways and better ways because we were apart.' But a part of me thinks we would have won for sure."

At this point, we can only speculate, imagine, and run video game simulations. Maybe, like Nash asks rhetorically in the video, they could have won multiple championships. Maybe they wouldn't have won one at all. "It's weird to think about," Nash said.

2006 Western Conference Finals

The Dallas Mavericks won 60 games headed into the 2006 postseason, but their path to the NBA Finals required them to go through San Antonio. What resulted was one of the greatest playoff series ever witnessed. Seven times in that playoff series, the two Texas teams battled, and each ending became more dramatic than the last. When regulation ended in Game 7, the score was tied.

Of course it was.

In 2013 ESPN ranked the series third best of all time. Six of the seven games went to overtime or were decided by five or fewer points with ejections, clutch performances, and ridiculous moments sprinkled throughout. Michael Finley, beloved Maverick, had switched sides that offseason, while Avery Johnson's 10 seasons with the Spurs had led him to the head coaching gig in Dallas. All of it added to the drama. "It was the best series I've ever played in," Tim Duncan said after it ended.

* * *

In 2003 Dallas lost to the San Antonio Spurs in the Western Conference Finals after an ill-fated Dirk Nowitzki knee injury. "The Spurs were always the big brother, beating up on the little brother," said Nowitzki, describing the two teams' relationship.

The Spurs and the Mavericks were the two best teams in their conference in 2006, both delivering 60-win seasons, but a quirk in the seeding placed the two opponents against each other in the West semifinals. San Antonio was defending champions, while Dallas had disappointed in back-to-back postseason appearances. Thus, it was no surprise that the Spurs were heavily favored.

San Antonio took Game 1. Bruce Bowen's three-pointer with about two minutes left put his team up by three, and Dallas scored only one more point the rest of the way. Still, despite a 87–85 score, Jerry Stackhouse lost his mind on the game's final possession. After collecting a deflected pass from Nowitzki, Stackhouse appeared to have an open path to the basket. Instead, down by two, he dribbled back to the three-point line and took a contested shot that never had a prayer of going in.

The Mavericks moved Devin Harris into the starting lineup and responded purposefully in Game 2, winning big in the series' only blowout. Game 3, though, quickly brought the series back to its roots. In the final six minutes, there were 12 lead changes and nine ties, and each team answered each other back and forth on virtually every shot. Nowitzki shot 9-of-10 from the line in the fourth quarter, including the game-winning pair with eight seconds left.

Game 4 went to overtime. After Finley hit an enormous three putting San Antonio up two, Nowitzki tied the game with free throws. Two midrange jumpers from Jason Terry and two more layups from Harris in the extra period helped Dallas escape with a 123–118 win and a 3–1 series lead. But the Spurs came back to tie the series anyway, winning 98–97 in Game 5 and 91–86 in Game 6. Terry was suspended one game for a below-the-belt punch on Michael Finley in Game 5, crippling the Mavericks' chances of closing the series out at home. Instead, the incredible series moved on to a finale that surpassed everything that had come before it.

* * *

Why did Jason Terry stop guarding Manu Ginobili at the three-point line? No one knows. Ginobili, realizing how far off Terry was playing, calmly pulled up for three and drained it.

"I saw everything slipping away, the great season we had," Dirk Nowitzki admitted.

Ginobili's shot came with 33 seconds left in Game 7 and put San Antonio up 104–101. It was the first time the Spurs had led the entire game. Dallas had built a 20-point lead in the first half, starting the game shooting a preposterous 15-of-17 from the field in a collective team effort. They led by double figures at halftime but were clinging to a four-point lead with two minutes left.

Ninety seconds later, Ginobili nailed his three.

Nowitzki answered. He caught the ball in the post with Bruce Bowen guarding him, spun past him toward the rim, and laid the ball in while being fouled by Ginobili. He hit the and-one free throw. Besides the 2011 Finals, that layup in the waning seconds of Game 7 is the most iconic moment of Nowitzki's career.

In overtime, the Mavericks put San Antonio in a chokehold and never looked back. The 119–111 final score was the second largest of the series, and the margin was the most misleading. After all, of all the Game 7s that have ever been played, this one has to rank near the top. Dallas moved by the Phoenix Suns in the next round, setting up the franchise's first NBA Finals appearance.

14 2006 NBA Finals

It has been more than a decade now since the heartbreaking 2006 NBA Finals. It's the series where the Mavericks went up 2–0, where the plans to their championship parade leaked, where their star missed a free throw that could have sent a game into overtime, where they allowed Dwyane Wade (and the referees) to dominate them for four straight games.

That the Mavericks earned vindication against the Miami Heat in the 2011 championship helps, but it doesn't ever completely take away the disappointment. It's more of a historical lesson now, sometimes a bit uncomfortable but featuring a series of events that can't be changed. That won't stop fans from always wondering how that series could have been different.

For those first two games, Dallas cooked the Heat. The Mavericks won by 24 points combined, featuring a 32-point outing from Jason Terry in Game 1, and Dirk Nowitzki notching 26 points and 16 rebounds in Game 2. They were confident enough in Dallas that the route for the championship parade was drafted and subsequently leaked to the media, which was nothing more than the city working ahead but turned out to be all the motivation Miami needed.

If Dallas had won Game 3, the series was practically over. No team has ever come back from down 3–0. After Nowitzki drew a foul with the Mavericks down two points and seconds remaining, he hit the first free throw...and missed the second. Dallas really never recovered from that moment and subsequent loss.

Game 4 was a blowout in the Heat's favor—a humiliating one at that with Dallas scoring only 74 points. What if the Finals format hadn't still relied on an antiquated 2–3–2 format, rather than the typical 2–2–1–1? Not only did Miami have the momentum after two straight wins, but they got to play Game 5 at home yet again.

No self-respecting Mavericks fan will ever get over Game 5. Dirk Nowitzki nearly won it in regulation, tying the game at 91 with a jumper and assisting an Erick Dampier layup that put Dallas up by two. Wade, in a deified performance, tied it with a floater to force overtime. With nine seconds remaining, Nowitzki once again nailed a jumper, giving Dallas a 100–99 lead.

Nine seconds remained. Just nine. That's it.

The Mavericks pressured Wade on the ensuing inbounds. At one point or another, four players tried to slow him down. He barreled past Terry and away from Josh Howard, splitting through Nowitzki and Devin Harris while attempting a wild layup. It missed, but the farthest official from the play, Bennett Salvatore, whistled a foul. Maybe it was. The Mavericks still insist it never happened. Even impartial fans have referred to it as the "phantom call."

Wade hit them both, and Dallas botched their final timeout, ruining any chance of a last-second game-winning inbounds. Game 6 was a three-point Heat win to take the series, but Dallas had already been broken. Though Nowitzki dropped 29 more points—the narrative of being unclutch that he received after this series really only came from that single Game 3 missed free throw—he couldn't quite match Wade's 36 in a win. "We actually partied harder when we lost the Finals [than when we won], maybe even to forget about it," Nowitzki admitted in an interview for this book. That will never happen, nor will the dissatisfaction that came with it. But after a decade, it's easier to make peace with it.

15 Jason Terry

Jason Terry tattooed the Larry O'Brien trophy onto his bicep right before the season the Mavericks won the championship. Let me repeat that: 12 seasons into his career—with experts projecting Dallas to be nothing more than a solid playoff team—Terry put an image of basketball's greatest achievement, which is won by only one team each year, onto a visible place on his body *in permanent ink*. That says everything you should know about the man they call "JET."

Terry was the best teammate with whom Dirk Nowitzki played. He may not have been the most talented, and his career won't be remembered like certain Hall of Famers paired with him.

But Terry stuck with Nowitzki through his toughest moments and deserves as much credit as anyone else for helping him reach that pinnacle in 2011.

If there's one essential attribute that made Terry, it was his confidence. The 6'2" shooting guard never saw a pull-up jumper or a fast-break three he didn't like, whether he had made or missed 10

DeShawn Stevenson

DeShawn Stevenson was only expected to be a throw-in piece when the Mavericks traded for Caron Butler and Brendan Haywood in 2010. He turned out to have the biggest impact of the three. During the championship season, Stevenson settled in as the team's starting two-guard. Jason Terry usually closed games as a sixth man, but Stevenson was a reliable defensive presence who routinely knocked down three-pointers. After struggling with his shot and falling out of the rotation, Stevenson reemerged late in the year and hit 13 threes in the NBA Finals, more than anyone else on the team.

Stevenson, though, was more than an incredibly effective role player. He was pure entertainment. He rarely censored himself talking to the media, notably beefing with LeBron James earlier in his career when he played for the Washington Wizards. When Stevenson compared himself to Soulja Boy, James said he was Jay-Z. It escalated to the point where Jay-Z wrote a diss track about Stevenson.

There's also Stevenson's neck tattoo of Abraham Lincoln. When too many people failed to recognize who the tattoo was of, Stevenson went back to the tattoo artist and had him turn it into a $5 bill, just so no one would be confused.

The best DeShawn Stevenson story came from the NBA Finals that year. Though Rick Carlisle has never confirmed it, two people around the team swear this exchange happened in the locker room leading up to that series. "Nobody talk shit to LeBron," Rick Carlisle was telling his team.

"Coach, I'm gonna talk shit," Stevenson responded.

Carlisle didn't even miss a beat when he changed his message to the team: "Nobody but DeShawn talk shit to LeBron."

straight. Sometimes, that made him an incredibly frustrating player to watch, but it also made sure Nowitzki never felt like he had to win every game and take every clutch shot himself. Terry hit dozens of momentum-swinging jumpers or dagger threes over the course of his career. None are more memorable than the final minute of Game 5 of the 2011 Finals, when the shot clock ran down, and Terry pulled up from nearly 30 feet to shoot it over LeBron James' outstretched hands. That sealed the game.

His nickname comes from his full name, Jason Eugene Terry. From there, the JET persona naturally evolved, spreading his arms like a plane taking off after big shots and inspiring catchphrases from announcers across the league as they described "the JET is on the runway" if he was heating up.

Terry's first five seasons came in Atlanta, where he flourished as a scoring combo guard, but the Hawks didn't re-sign him in the summer of 2004. So, the Mavericks brought in Terry to replace Steve Nash, providing unfair comparisons, especially since Terry wasn't a natural point guard.

But no Maverick played better in the 2006 Finals than Terry, who opened the series with a 32-point explosion and put up 35 points (and 50 minutes) in the team's Game 5 overtime loss. Dallas lost, but Terry averaged 22 points on 48 percent shooting to solidify him as an important cog on the team moving forward.

Although Nowitzki could probably run an effective two-man game with a traffic cone, the pairing of him and Terry proved particularly lethal. If the defense focused too much on the Nowitzki screen, Terry had a deadly pull-up jump shot that he could get off on a whim. If they stopped him, Nowitzki could slip into an empty space at a moment's notice and bury you with midrange missiles.

After the 2007 collapse to the Golden State Warriors, Terry moved to the bench. He had always been more of an off-the-ball player and better at spotting up and running weak-side pick-and-rolls than initiating an offense every possession. To his credit he took on the role with aplomb. It worked well, and Terry won the NBA's Sixth Man of the Year during the 2008–09 season. He was the third Mavericks player to earn that reward, following Roy Tarpley in 1988 and Antawn Jamison in 2004.

Terry inked his bicep tattoo in 2010 and nine months later justified it. In the last two games of the NBA Finals, Terry scored a combined 48 points on 19-of-28 shooting as Dallas staved off the Miami Heat for its first championship. That three-pointer over James in Game 5 will live on forever as his defining shot.

After a final season in Dallas, the two sides parted, and Terry bounced around the league as a journeyman. He nearly rejoined the team in 2015, only backing out after the DeAndre Jordan reversal. Still, fans would have welcomed any reunion with the beloved guard, who is called "Mavericks Royalty" and a part of their family for life. Mark Cuban has publicly offered Terry a role with the organization whenever he's ready to accept it. The exact role hasn't been determined yet. Maybe he'll be an assistant coach, running around with a Mavericks warmup jacket on, or perhaps he'll join the front office, wearing a crisp white-collared shirt. But either way, rest assured: that trophy tattoo will always be hiding out underneath his sleeve, a perpetual reminder of the time he promised a championship and then helped deliver it.

16 A Bittersweet 2007 MVP

Dirk Nowitzki's short, spiky hair was thick with gel and just as artificial as his forced smile.

The mood filling the 2007 Most Valuable Player Award press conference was unfamiliar. The NBA had done dozens of these, and the vibe was always similar: light in places, emotional in others, but always cheerful and celebratory. They were never somber. Yet this one was, as Nowitzki stood up on the podium answering questions and making sure he grinned occasionally. It was a facade that even he knew wasn't fooling anyone. "At this stage for me, it's still a little hard to be happy," Nowitzki confessed.

Two weeks before the Mavericks—with a league-best 67 wins, then only the ninth time a team had ever reached that figure—played the Golden State Warriors in the first round, a team that snuck into the playoffs on the final day of the regular season. In one of the greatest playoff upsets in league history, the Warriors beat them.

It was a moment without precedent. So yeah, it was a little hard for Nowitzki to be happy.

Dallas was only a year removed from the humiliating 2006 NBA Finals, where its championship parade plans leaked before the team lost four straight games to the Miami Heat. The Mavericks came into the 2007 season frustrated, and it didn't help when they lost the season's first four games. But it quickly turned around, and Dallas won 52 times in their next 57 matchups.

Nowitzki was sensational that season, averaging 24 points, nine rebounds, and three assists. He joined the 50-40-90 club that year by shooting 50 percent on field goals, 42 percent on threes, and 90 percent on free throws, becoming one of only seven players in league history to do that. Just as important was how much better the Mavericks played with him on the floor. His shooting and his size opened up a world of opportunities. Josh Howard's career-best season earned him an All-Star nod, averaging 19 points on 46 percent shooting. Jason Terry thrived in his role as shooting guard, while Devin Harris locked down the starting point guard spot even if he wasn't really a pure passer. (He averaged fewer than four assists that year.)

The team had the top overall spot in the playoffs wrapped up by late March. If they had wanted, the Mavericks could have pushed for a 70-win season. They also could have done more to influence who they faced in the first round. Dallas clearly preferred to face the Los Angeles Clippers instead of the Golden State Warriors.

You could argue Dallas should have. The Warriors were the only team that the Mavericks hadn't beaten in the regular season, and a midseason trade for Al Harrington and Stephen Jackson helped Golden State finish the year by winning 16 of its final 21 games. But in the two teams' third and final matchup, the Mavericks rested their starters rather than attempting to beat the Warriors.

The Mavericks were the league's best team, so it's hard to blame them. More baffling is why they didn't keep acting like it. Against any other first-round opponent, the Mavericks would have had an easier time. Against the Warriors, led by former Mavericks coach Don Nelson, the team collectively lost their heads.

In Game 1 Avery Johnson decided to match the Warriors' successful brand of small ball and bench Erick Dampier, who had started all season for Dallas. That's exactly what Golden State wanted, and the Warriors easily won the series opener.

The Mavericks rebounded in Game 2, reinserting Dampier back into the lineup and giving more minutes to backup center DeSagana Diop. Golden State answered with a big win at home in Game 3, and a 33-point Baron Davis performance carried them to a four-point win in Game 4. Dallas won a narrow Game 5 thanks to Nowitzki, who scored 12 points in the final minutes in a six-point victory, but the Mavericks were embarrassingly blown out in Game 6 to end their previously wonderful year.

It was a magical series for Golden State, whose fans rallied around the slogan "WE BELIEVE." The Warriors were inspired, and Davis, Jackson, and Jason Richardson all took turns hitting wild shots—none more absurd than Davis' half-court buzzer beater

The Hole in the Wall

You can imagine how Dirk Nowitzki felt as he left the court of Oracle Arena after losing Game 6 and the series. He was humiliated, yes, and perhaps had never been more frustrated. As he passed an innocent trash can on his shameful walk back to the locker room, Nowitzki snapped. The trash can, once flightless, clanged off the wall and left a small hole in the sheetrock 12 or 13 feet up in the tunnel before returning to the ground.

The hole is still there, now framed with a "We Believe" T-shirt next to it. Years later, Golden State asked if Nowitzki could autograph it, and, of course, he agreed. The Warriors even have plans to cut out that part of the wall and take it with them when they move stadiums. "In a dumb way, it's part of my career," Nowitzki admitted.

in Game 4. Still, the Warriors deserved the win. Nelson smoked Johnson in the coaching department, while Nowitzki shot just 38 percent across those six games.

If Nowitzki had his wish, he would have immediately skipped town, but that wouldn't work, the Mavericks told him, because he was needed in two weeks at the MVP ceremony. (He ended up going to Australia for five weeks later that summer.) It was his award, but never had the ultimate individual basketball achievement felt so shallow.

Nowitzki's original plan was to make a few jokes and keep the atmosphere light, but an emotional Cuban took it in a completely different direction. "He's the guy you don't have to encourage to get in the gym; he's the guy you have to lock out of the gym," Cuban said. "He's not the guy who you wonder if he cares. He's the guy who hurts so much when things don't go the way he wants. And that's what makes him an MVP of this league."

It wasn't really what Nowitzki wanted to hear at the time, but Cuban was right, of course. Though the award and Nowitzki's biggest playoff failure are intrinsically linked together, even today, nobody remembers Nowitzki foremost for his playoff failures—not after 2011. They remember him as the player Cuban tearfully described.

17 Rolando Blackman

If Mark Aguirre embodied the Mavericks during the 1980s and Derek Harper gave them a heartbeat, then Rolando Blackman was the soul. Drafted eight picks after Aguirre in 1981, Blackman spent 11 seasons in Dallas and ended up as the team's leading scorer by the time he left.

Smooth as silk, with a killer jump shot. That's how he was described by those who watched him produce as the team's second star behind Aguirre. During the team's five straight playoff appearances from 1984 to 1988, the two were just about equals. From 1985 to 1987 and once more in 1990, Blackman was named to the NBA All-Star Game. With the West team down two with seconds left in the 1987 All-Star Game, Blackman was fouled, drained both free throws, and shouted, "Confidence, baby, confidence," as he returned to his huddle. (The West won in overtime.)

Blackman was drafted out of Kansas State University, where he hit an iconic jumper against top-seeded Oregon State in 1981. The two-time All-American spent four years with the Wildcats, scoring 1,844 points before Dallas nabbed him in that year's draft. Even though the Mavericks had won just 15 games in their inaugural season, Blackman quickly helped put them on a path toward success.

In 1984 Blackman posted a career high, averaging 22.4 points per game. It was his jump shot that forced overtime in the

A four-time NBA All-Star, Rolando Blackman averaged 19.2 points during his 11 seasons with the Mavericks.

unforgettable Moody Madness contest that led to Dallas' first playoff series win. He dropped 43 points in the first round of the 1985 playoffs, helping Dallas defeat the Portland Trail Blazers in a wild double-overtime Game 1 contest. However, the Mavericks lost the next three games to be bounced from the postseason.

After failing to win a championship with the Mavericks, Blackman spent the final two years of his career with the New York Knicks. It looked like he might get that ring in 1994, when the Knicks and the Houston Rockets played all the way to a Game 7. Pat Riley, then New York's head coach, says the worst call of his coaching career was not playing Blackman in Game 7 over an ice cold John Starks. Instead, Starks shot 2-of-18 from the field, and Houston won its first of two championships.

Blackman retired from the NBA after that, spending a few seasons overseas where he won an Italian League title. Blackman then returned to the Mavericks as an assistant coach. He served various roles within the team—from defensive coordinator to television analyst to eventually being named director of player development. One season he even worked as an assistant coach for the German National Team when Dirk Nowitzki was the team's star.

It's not just basketball that Blackman cares about overseas. Born in Panama until moving to Brooklyn to live with his grandmother when he was eight, Blackman has served as a goodwill ambassador for the United Nations while traveling through war-torn African countries, is on the board of directors for a foundation helping underprivileged youths in Dallas, and has also helped with the NBA's Basketball Without Borders program. Anyone you ask will tell you how great of a man he is—as if his resume doesn't speak for itself.

Now focusing on their community outreach rather than working on the basketball side, Blackman remains involved with the Mavericks. His perspective is an important one. "People always say it's a small world, but it's not," Blackman told the *New York Daily News* in 2009. "It's a huge world, and there are a lot of people out there who need help. You can help change their course, and that's a good thing."

18 The Late 2000s

It took willpower to remain emotionally invested in the Mavericks after 2006 and 2007. Both seasons brought fans up to a mountaintop before heartbreakingly pushing them off the steepest incline. Every fan had a different way of dealing with it. The most ostentatious supporters denounced their Mavericks fandom through the fledgling social media networks that existed or by constantly telling everyone they knew. Others grew apathetic, watching fewer games and spending less time with the team. "I literally stopped watching games in 2008 and 2009," said Austin Ngaruiya, an editor for SB Nation blog, Mavs Moneyball. "I knew what happened. But it was like, 'I love you, but it hurts too much.'"

Yet even with the playoff collapses, the Mavericks didn't fall apart. They didn't win as prolifically or advance very far once they made it to the playoffs, but they were there every year. It may have been a distressing time to be a fan, but some couldn't look away. "I probably followed the team even more closely," said Doyle Rader, a Mavericks contributor for the website of WFAA, the local ABC affiliate in Dallas. "It just hurt more every year."

If only fans knew what was coming to them, they could have seen the championship team slowly forming in front of their eyes. In 2008 the Mavericks dealt for Jason Kidd, welcoming the first true point guard since Steve Nash. Avery Johnson was fired shortly after the season, making way for basketball wizard Rick Carlisle. In the 2009 offseason, the team acquired Shawn Marion, whose lock-down defense and quirky offensive game gave them the two-way player they had desired for years.

During the season in 2010, Dallas swapped Josh Howard for Caron Butler, Brendan Haywood, and DeShawn Stevenson. No one could have predicted Stevenson would have been the most significant acquisition, but all three contributed. Finally, during the summer of 2010, the Mavericks traded for Tyson Chandler. Of course, Mavericks fans were hurt, but they soon realized this team was different.

19 Rick Carlisle

Rick Carlisle is a title-winning coach in the NBA, which already puts him in rare company. Add his 1986 Boston Celtics championship from his five years playing in the league, and Carlisle is one of 14 people who has won rings both playing and coaching.

The championship in Boston was a right place, right time moment. Carlisle will be the first to admit that he barely made it as a professional hooper, playing 188 games in his career and scoring just 422 points. His best season came in 1986, where he played 77 games while averaging just under 10 minutes. When Boston shortened its rotation in the playoffs, Carlisle was usually on the outside looking in.

Still, Carlisle was a person who always appreciated a challenge. He knew coaching was his future more than playing, but he still transferred from the University of Maine to the University of Virginia because he wanted to compete on a higher stage. "I decided I wanted to play at the greatest level of college basketball," Carlisle said.

At Virginia, Carlisle sat out for a year due to transfer rules and worked locally as a bartender. He chose psychology as a major, anticipating its usefulness for a future coaching career, and then averaged about 11 points in his two seasons. After Carlisle was part of a run to the Final Four in 1984 as a starting guard and co-captain for the Hokies, Boston selected him in the third round.

He spent three seasons with the Celtics, playing sparingly, before going to the New York Knicks. With the Knicks he played under coaching legend Rick Pitino and alongside Billy Donovan, another guard who ended up as a longtime head coach. In 1989 Carlisle played five games with the New Jersey Nets. Later that season Carlisle accepted an assistant coaching position with them, effectively signaling his retirement as a player.

It took a decade for Carlisle to rise through the NBA ranks. After five years with the Nets, he spent three seasons with the Portland Trail Blazers and three more with the Indiana Pacers under Larry Bird. When Bird stepped down in 2000, he thought Carlisle deserved the opportunity. Instead, the gig went to Isiah Thomas.

The Detroit Pistons hired Carlisle in 2001, and he won Coach of the Year as a rookie head coach and led the team to consecutive 50-win seasons. But the Pistons had high expectations, and the headstrong Carlisle clashed with team ownership—in part due to his unwillingness to play promising but inconsistent rookie Tayshaun Prince. Despite a run to the Eastern Conference Finals, Detroit fired Carlisle after that season, and longtime head coach Larry Brown, who replaced Carlisle, led the Pistons to an NBA championship the next year.

Thomas had flamed out in Indiana, and Bird was now the team president. This time, Carlisle did get the job, leading the Pacers to 61 wins his first season there. He might still be there, but the infamous Malice in the Palace brawl derailed the entire franchise. When the Pacers missed the postseason in 2007, Carlisle resigned.

That's how the Mavericks ended up with Carlisle in 2008. In a league where job security is nonexistent, Carlisle begins his 10th season in 2017. He's the third longest tenured coach in the league and one of just five active coaches to be hired before 2013. Notably, two other coaches who meet that criteria are Dwane Casey with the Toronto Raptors and Terry Stotts with the Trail Blazers. Those were Carlisle's two top assistants when the Mavericks won in 2011, and two people Carlisle personally vouched for when teams began calling that offseason. Although it wasn't in Carlisle's self-interest to lose high-caliber basketball minds like that, he called Bryan Colangelo—the Raptors general manager—on behalf of Casey. "Bryan, I want to know what it's going to take to get Dwane that job in Toronto," said Carlisle, per Colangelo. "It's right for him. It's right for you. It's right for the situation. You need to strongly consider it."

Carlisle excels at both in-game coaching and developing chemistry with players. Many pundits place him only behind Gregg Popovich as the league's best coach. If there's one position he exerts more control over, it's at point guard, where he played throughout his career. Notably, Rajon Rondo and Carlisle argued constantly about who had control of the offense, finally blowing up in the 2015 playoffs when Rondo was benched and dismissed from the team.

It wasn't known at the time, but Carlisle once had similar arguments with Jason Kidd early on. "Rick and Jason used to get into it about the exact same thing except Jason's demeanor was so quiet that a lot of times people didn't know that they were arguing," former Mavs center Brendan Haywood told ESPN in 2015. "They had an argument on the bench with four-letter words going back and forth."

Kidd eventually won him over. Carlisle used to call strict plays that often didn't allow improvisation, but Kidd pushed him into a more modern flow offense. Now, players in Dallas are inundated with basic offensive sets and actions that they'll run habitually, which trusts players to allow possessions to ebb and flow naturally. It increases randomness and makes it harder for defenses to game-plan against, and that is crucial in the increasingly calculated NBA. The change helped the Mavericks win in 2011, and it has been working ever since.

As Carlisle starts his second decade in Dallas, it's clear he loves it. He re-signed for five years in 2015, and it doesn't appear he wants any more front-office control than the current three-man power structure of him, Mark Cuban, and Donnie Nelson. Don't ask him why a certain player didn't suit up, or he'll icily inform you it was a coach's decision. (This has happened to me more than once.) But his relationship with the media is great, and everyone in Dallas loves him.

Off the floor, Carlisle is a man with diverse talents. He plays table tennis at a high level and is an even better pianist, performing in packed concert venues. In the 2014 offseason, he purchased a plane and began learning to fly. It was a practical decision that allowed Carlisle to visit his parents in upstate New York more frequently, but he also sees it as a parallel to his coaching career. "My great friend and mentor Chuck Daly once compared NBA coaching to being the pilot of an aircraft navigating through the turbulence that inevitably comes with any NBA season. 'An NBA head coach's job,' as Chuck so succinctly said, 'is at the end of the season to safely land the plane,'" Carlisle told ESPN in 2015. "I'm gonna keep working on my landings."

Carlisle accomplished the one thing the Mavericks asked of him: to win a championship before Dirk Nowitzki fell from the peak of his career. Although another one doesn't look imminent, Carlisle has earned himself as much goodwill as a coach can with an organization. He, more than any prospect or player, is the biggest reason to remain optimistic for the future of the Mavericks.

20 **2011 Regular Season**

No one remembers how good the Mavericks were in 2011. Dallas was often described as "out of nowhere," "lightning in a bottle," and almost always as "underdogs" when it made its championship run in 2011, but those descriptors are incorrect. Even in the regular season, there were signs that this year was different.

Dallas won 57 games that season, third best in the Western Conference, and it easily could have been more. They started the year at 24–5 and finished it on a 31–11 run. The Mavericks ended up third thanks to a terrible 2–9 midseason slump when Dirk Nowitzki went out with a knee injury.

In Dallas at the time, regular-season success didn't really matter. Understand the Mavericks had been a dominant regular-season team for a decade now, and everyone had seen it before. At the start of the 2000s, Dallas was young, exciting, and the future seemed to stretch out in front of them forever. By the middle the Mavericks had an NBA Finals appearance and the expectations from a 67-win season. Several early playoff exits later, though, and Dallas supporters had developed a malaise. "I think people were kind of hopeful but still needed to see some proof," said Eddie Sefko, longtime Mavericks beat writer for *The Dallas Morning News*. "They had seen enough labor pains. They needed a baby."

That's the main reason why the Mavericks didn't attract more attention when they started 24–5. Mark Cuban coined the nickname *streakbusters* as Dallas snapped two 12-game win streaks

(Miami Heat and San Antonio Spurs) by opponents in November and December, plus four more ranging from five to eight straight wins. It wasn't a veteran team coasting against an easy early schedule; the Mavericks were playing the league's best teams while they were playing great basketball and beating them all the same.

The highlight of that early season was easy: defeating the Heat. Since the 2006 NBA Finals, the Mavericks had beaten Miami in every regular-season matchup, but things were suddenly different when LeBron James and Chris Bosh joined Dwyane Wade in South Beach. The two teams' first meeting came on November 27, and the Mavericks exploded on a 13–0 run to start the second half to win the game. Controversy spilled over from the game: the loss dropped Miami to 9–8, television cameras caught James bumping into head coach Erik Spoelstra on his way to the bench, and the Heat held a players-only meeting after the game. Already, drama had overtaken the biggest story in the NBA that season.

Not surprisingly, the Heat figured it out. In fact, they won their next 12 games. But you remember we were just talking about streakbusting, right? After 12 straight wins, of course, Miami had its second and final regular-season matchup against Dallas.

The Mavericks beat the Heat again.

Dallas truly could do no wrong, and there was no sign that they would slow down unless something terrible happened. Two games later, a couple days after Christmas, it did.

In a game against the Oklahoma City Thunder, Dirk Nowitzki didn't do anything out of the ordinary. After shooting a fadeaway jumper out of the post, Nowitzki took a couple steps back to balance himself and collapsed without anyone touching him. He walked off under his own power, but the injury was diagnosed as a strained knee, and Nowitzki missed the next nine games.

Caron Butler went down with a knee injury three games later that turned out to be a ruptured patella tendon, which sidelined him for the season. Butler had long been an isolation scorer who sometimes hurt an offense's ball movement and rhythm, but that had totally changed through the first third of the season. He was hitting three-pointers, attacking the basket, and playing the most efficient basketball of his career. During an interview before the NBA Finals, Rick Carlisle said "it's unlikely, but I can't say no for sure," when asked if Butler could return from his injury. He didn't, and that series clearly worked out for the Mavericks anyway. However, it's a testament to Butler's drive to recover that he nearly made it back in time. Despite not playing in the postseason, Butler clearly deserved his ring.

It turned out Butler's injury allowed Shawn Marion to enter the starting lineup. Looking back—and this wasn't Butler's fault—that may have been a crucial piece to the puzzle. Marion's defense and timely shotmaking was a steady factor throughout the postseason. Still, at the time, Butler's injury seemed devastating. When the Mavericks dropped seven of the nine games that Nowitzki missed, he was furious. They lost two more games after he returned, and all the doubts from the past few years began rushing back. "I went back and looked at texts Dirk sent me in 2011," Mark Cuban said. "He said all kinds of not complimentary things about our squad as we were going through a 2–9 stretch. We were shooting 32, 33 percent without him."

Of course, Dallas righted the ship, winning 18 games out of 19 at one point shortly after Nowitzki's return. Despite their 24–5 start and 18–1 midseason run, though, the Mavericks still flew under the radar heading into the 2011 playoffs.

21 Mark Aguirre

Mark Aguirre was the Mavericks' first star. Drafted first overall in the 1981 NBA Draft, Aguirre arrived with high expectations and delivered on every one. Dallas had been embarrassed the year before when its first pick refused to even play for the team, but Aguirre took on the task with aplomb. He was the Mavericks' first All-Star, going in 1984, 1987, and 1988. During the 1983–84 season, he finished as the NBA's second leading scorer while averaging 29.5 points. When Aguirre departed from Dallas in 1989, he left as the team's leading scorer and still remains third overall.

Aguirre was one of the most talented offensive players of his generation, leaning heavily on a deadly low-post game, even though he only stood 6'6". The small forward was a stabilizing force for Dallas, leading the team in scoring every year after his rookie season. His midrange jumper was just as dangerous as his drives to the rim, and he could handle the ball better than the average forward of that era. "Very hard, tough basketball is what I like," Aguirre told NBA.com. "I like everything to be a totally exhausting type of basketball. I want guys to play extremely hard every second of the game. That's how I like to see basketball played. And then you learn how to play after that. I have no problem with making guys play hard."

You could compare Aguirre to Carmelo Anthony in the modern NBA, two gifted scorers who knew all the tricks for putting the ball through the hoop. Aguirre had a flashiness to his game, too, something that might have been appreciated more in the Internet age. The Mavericks traded Aguirre to the Detroit Pistons. Though he started on back-to-back championship teams there, he took a significant step back as a scorer.

NBA commissioner Larry O'Brien greets Mark Aguirre, who the Mavericks selected with the No. 1 overall pick in the 1981 NBA Draft.

Aguirre was an enormous reason why the Mavericks climbed from a 15-win squad in their inaugural season to five straight post-season appearances from 1984 to 1988. But when the Mavericks began melting down the following season—Rolando Blackman was injured, Roy Tarpley went into drug rehab, and the team missed the playoffs—Aguirre demanded a trade.

The request didn't come as a total surprise. Mavericks fans had long complained about their star's constant complaints about referees, and some had become increasingly annoyed with his antics. One *Los Angeles Times* columnist even wrote that season that his "selfish manner and deteriorating play are threatening to tear the franchise asunder."

That may have been a theatrical interpretation, but the Mavericks did deal Aguirre for Detroit's Adrian Dantley. They made the playoffs just once more before a 10-year postseason drought that lasted throughout the 1990s. Though Aguirre's messy departure puts a strange postscript, he's still remembered as one of the Mavericks' most important foundational players.

22 2011 Western Conference First Round

For proof that public perception had clearly swung against the Mavericks, look at ESPN's predictions prior to Dallas' 2011 first-round playoff series against the Portland Trail Blazers. In an eight-writer poll, four predicted an upset by the lower ranked Blazers. For a moment midway through the series, they briefly looked prophetic.

The Mavericks won Games 1 and 2 at home. Both games were close in the fourth quarter, but Dallas pushed past Portland with no major scares. Jason Kidd had his best two games of the entire post-season, scoring a combined 42 points and nine three-pointers, and even knocked down a pull-up dagger three to put Portland away for good in Game 1. He credited his shooting surge to Dirk Nowitzki and his mentor Holger Geschwindner, who had given him a tip to make sure the ball stayed straight.

All the goodwill and confidence built up during the Mavericks' first two games came crashing back down, though. Dallas lost Game 3 by five points, a tough defeat but hardly crippling. A win in Game 4 would put them right back on track to close this series out and it looked like that's exactly what was happening when the Mavericks led 67–49 headed into the final quarter.

Instead, Dallas gave up 35 points that quarter as Portland erased a 23-point deficit to win 84–82. Brandon Roy, whose career had been gutted with debilitating knee problems, had his final shining moment in the NBA when he scored 18 points in the fourth quarter, including the go-ahead bank shot. He even beat one-on-one man defense by Shawn Marion to do it.

It was an amazing effort from Roy, who only had scored six points entering the final frame. His 18 points came in every conceivable way: driving layups, pull-up jumpers, and even a four-point play, and it was a sad throwback to what he could have become if his knees hadn't betrayed him. Still, even after Roy put Portland up, there were 39 seconds on the clock. Dallas withered in the moment just like it had done the entire quarter, missing two three-pointers that could have won them the game.

Mavericks fans were speechless. The brutal loss had even the most optimistic fans doubting that the playoffs could lead anywhere but another heartbreaking loss. In some ways, Game 5 may have been the most important game the Mavericks played in that postseason. Dallas recollected themselves, Nowitzki scored 25 points, Tyson Chandler had a monster 20-rebound performance, and panicking fans finally exhaled. "[That game] set things right in that series," said Eddie Sefko, the Mavericks beat writer for *The Dallas Morning News*. "It was a different team after that. Their confidence shot up, they started rolling by people—pretty cool to watch them grow as a team in a very short amount of time."

Dallas finished off the series in Game 6 at Portland's home building. The team had relived all their playoff failures and disappointments after Game 4, but this year wasn't destined for the same sad path. As the Mavericks said throughout the playoffs, this year was different.

2011 Western Conference Semifinals

Dallas had no bigger rival in the 1980s than the Los Angeles Lakers, who ousted the Mavericks from the postseason thrice. The competitiveness faded over the following years, though. Despite both teams' success—thanks to Dirk Nowitzki and Kobe Bryant—they hadn't met in a playoff series until 2011 brought them together.

Los Angeles was a two-time defending champion as it entered the Western Conference Semifinals against the Mavericks, so, of course, the Lakers were heavily favored. In that 12-person ESPN panel, all 12 predicted the Lakers to prevail. Bryant, the Lakers' playoff history, and the Mavericks' recent disappointments were all factors too strong to predict anything otherwise.

One game. That's all the Mavericks realistically planned to steal from the series' opening two played in Los Angeles. After Dallas opened the second half of Game 1 with three straight turnovers and the Lakers began padding a double-digit lead, it looked like the "steal one in Los Angeles" strategy would have to live to fight another day.

Rick Carlisle responded by substituting Corey Brewer in not even 90 seconds into the half. When I asked him about this moment, Brewer instantly recalled every detail, including the lead: 16 points, with 10:37 on the clock. By the time Brewer subbed out about eight minutes later, the Mavericks only trailed by five as a result of his five points and extra energy.

Dallas completed that Game 1 comeback, going ahead on Nowitzki free throws and clutching on to its win for dear life when Bryant missed a way-too-open three-pointer as time expired that would have won the game. That was the win the Mavericks wanted on the road, but when Dallas also rolled through Game 2 for a victory, no one was complaining.

Whichever basketball god wrote the script for Game 3 must have plagiarized from the series opener because the two games played out almost identically. Los Angeles led for nearly 31 minutes of that game, including a quick start after halftime. With five minutes left, the Lakers were still up by seven points. This time, though, the spark plug off the bench wasn't Brewer but Peja Stojakovic, who scored 15 points off the bench against Los Angeles. Stojakovic's heyday came in Sacramento years before, where the Kings lost the most controversially officiated series of all time to the Lakers in the 2002 Western Conference Finals. (Call the 2006 NBA Finals a close second.) Although Kings fans still can't get over that, at least Stojakovic earned himself minor revenge. Nowitzki took the Mavericks home, hitting the decisive basket with his left hand over Pau Gasol to cap his 32-point evening.

Stojakovic's payback carried into Game 4, where the Mavericks tied a then-playoff record with 20 made threes. He hit six himself on six attempts while Jason Terry added nine more makes, and Dallas trounced Los Angeles in a game now known as the Mother's Day Massacre. The antiquated Lakers defense had left Dallas open behind the arc all series long while barely hitting shots from deep themselves, exposing the team's biggest flaw. Still, no one had seen a sweep coming, and for Mavericks fans who had refused to buy in after too many disappointments, this is when they all started believing.

24 2011 Western Conference Finals

This was the Dirk Nowitzki series. This is the one you cite to prove—without question—that he was on another level during the 2011 postseason. This is the one that erased any doubts that Nowitzki wasn't clutch, wasn't able to lead a team, or wasn't as good as everyone said he was. This was Nowitzki at his unparalleled best.

Nowitzki scored 48 points in Game 1, and it was one of the most brilliant playoff performances of all time. He opened the game 4-of-4 in the first four minutes and he proceeded to draw constant fouls against any Thunder defender who tried to guard him. None of them stood a chance. In that series it felt like the best defender in the world could have matched him up, and you'd still say Nowitzki had the mismatch.

When the debris settled, Nowitzki's line seemed farcical: 12-of-15 from the field, 24-of-24 from the free throw line plus six rebounds, four assists, and four blocks. No player has ever scored that many points on that few shot attempts, and no player has ever attempted that many free throws without a miss. Both remain NBA records—for both the regular and postseason.

The feisty, young Thunder drew real blood in Game 2, winning 106–100 at the American Airlines Center, but Dallas retook the series lead by winning Game 3. Whether the Mavericks were in for a quick series or a drawn-out war came down to the outcome of Game 4, and for a good part of the game, Oklahoma City held the upper hand. In fact, the Thunder led by 10 points with 2:22 left in the game.

That should have been it.

However, Nowitzki had other plans. He hit a three-pointer, then a contorted baseline shot, and then a turnaround jumper in the lane off a pump fake—all with ungradable degrees of difficulty. With seconds left he tied the game at the line. Jason Kidd knocked down the dagger three-point jumper from the corner in overtime, but Nowitzki's efforts—40 points on 12-of-20 shooting, including 14-of-15 from the free throw line—turned what could have easily been a tied series into a 3–1 lead headed back to Dallas.

The Mavericks won Game 5 with Nowitzki scoring 26 more points on 53 percent shooting. In the five-game series, Nowitzki averaged 32 points on 56 percent shooting. He shot 61 free throws, making 59 of them. It was a dazzling offensive showing that pushed Dallas to the NBA Finals. His teammates had been saying they only needed to do their parts, and Nowitzki would make sure they got where they were headed. This series made that even more clear.

1988 Western Conference Finals

Four years in a row, the Mavericks had gone to the playoffs without advancing past the second round. The Los Angeles Lakers eliminated them twice from the postseason. Three more times in the opening six games of the 1988 Western Conference Finals, the Lakers had beaten Dallas. None of that mattered when the series moved to a Game 7. The winner moved on, the loser went home,

Los Angeles Lakers forward A.C. Green defends Derek Harper, who helped guide the Mavericks to a 105–103 win in Game 6 of the 1988 Western Conference Finals.

and the Mavericks were only 48 minutes away from making it to the NBA Finals. Dallas didn't know it, but it was the best chance this team was going to get. "Anytime you get greatness on the brink, you've got to knock them out," Derek Harper told me. "You've got to get hit in the mouth a couple times, get hit in the mouth, and I had never thought we had been hit in the mouth enough."

The Showtime Lakers, as they were called, were indeed greatness. They had already won four championships that decade, including one the year before in 1987. They had Magic Johnson, James Worthy, and Byron Scott playing together in their prime, as well as a 41-year-old Kareem Abdul-Jabbar, who still averaged nearly 15 points per game. "They had a Hall of Fame roster, so to knock them off would have been a big deal," Harper said.

Dallas had a reputation for disappointing in the playoffs, especially after the previous season's first-round exit despite winning 55 games. But this year felt different, as the Mavericks handily beat the Houston Rockets in the first round before knocking off the Denver Nuggets in the semifinals. The Lakers had turned into somewhat of a rival after they knocked Dallas off twice before, and the team was ready for the challenge. "I think it's time for the Lakers and the Celtics to step aside," Mavericks head coach John MacLeod said in an interview leading up to the series. "And for Dallas and for some team in the East to be in the NBA championship."

Despite all the talk and the ease of the first two series for the Mavericks, the Lakers dominated the first two games of the Western Conference Finals, winning by a combined 37 points. Los Angeles, so good on its home court, scored 113 in the first game and 123 in the second with its dangerously high scoring offense. It looked like the series might be a sweep.

The tone changed back in Dallas, though, as the games played out in reverse fashion. Roy Tarpley did everything in Game 3 with 21 points and 20 rebounds, while in Game 4 Harper set his playoffs career high with 35 points. The Mavericks won both games by a combined 26 points and tied the series at two.

Still, the Mavericks needed at least one win in Los Angeles to carry the series, and Game 5 played out the same way as the first two games. After the Lakers' 119–102 win in Game 5, Mavericks fans weren't even confident they could win at home in Game 6. But Dallas surged back once more, staving off the Lakers in a 105–103 win to set up Game 7.

That's where Dallas finally fell short. If you looked at the 117–102 final score, you might assume the game was another blowout. In fact, the Mavericks trailed by only six when the unimaginable happened—Mark Aguirre went to the bench. Aguirre, the player who made the Mavericks offense tick, had hurt his wrist, and his departure doomed Dallas. After the injury the team was outscored by nine points the rest of the way, and the Lakers put away the series for good. They went on to beat the Detroit Pistons in the NBA Finals.

The Mavericks had three chances at Los Angeles over the years, and 1988 was no doubt their best shot. Still relatively young, Dallas was sure they would get another chance to knock the Lakers off their throne. Instead, they missed the playoffs the following year, and their team quickly fell apart. When asked, Harper said that's the series he'll always wonder about what could have been. "At that point in our careers, we were still learning. We started thinking, *Oh, we'll see 'em next year*," he said. "You can't take anything for granted."

26 Game 2 of the 2011 NBA Finals

It's the most important play in the franchise's history: Dirk Nowitzki catches the ball at the three-point line, his back facing Chris Bosh. He patiently runs a few precious ticks off the clock, starts one way, and then spins back the other way where the lane is open. His left-handed layup wins the game.

If the Mavericks had lost Game 2 and given the Miami Heat a 2–0 lead in the 2011 Finals, history probably would have been written differently. And when Dwyane Wade nailed a corner three to give the Heat a 15-point lead and LeBron James celebrated with Wade right in front of the Mavericks' bench, it looked like it would be.

The Mavericks hadn't trailed a series all postseason before losing Game 1 of the NBA Finals, but a Game 2 win would still give them home-court advantage headed back to Dallas. Though tied at halftime, an early fourth-quarter surge by the Heat pushed them ahead by double digits with about seven minutes to go.

Who knows if Wade and James flaunting in front of the Mavericks' bench after Wade's shot caused the comeback, or whether Dallas would have roared back to life anyway. Several Mavericks said it did spark them, including Jason Terry, who has always been a player who performed better when he felt he was being slighted. "Right at that moment, it was a turning point in the game," Terry told reporters afterward. "Obviously, we come out of that timeout and if we don't score then we were pretty much dead. We looked at each guy in the huddle to a man. I specifically looked at Dirk and said, 'There's no way we're going out like this.'"

Terry did just that, hitting two quick shots. Then Shawn Marion hit a layup. Jason Kidd nailed a three. Terry hit another jumper. Suddenly, a 15-point Miami lead was down to four, and a Nowitzki jumper made it two.

Why LeBron James—this generation's most dominant player who has proven his ability to be clutch a hundred times over—decided to shoot two long jumpers on the ensuing possession without even an attempt to drive the ball to the rim is something only he can answer. It's equally baffling why Wade did the same thing one play later. Nowitzki evened the score with a layup and with 26.7 seconds remaining he put the Mavericks ahead with an open three from the left side.

It took 2.2 seconds for the Heat to tie the game. Terry didn't guard Mario Chalmers in the corner. As Chalmers ran through a screen, Terry inexplicably peeled off to double team Wade at the top of the key. James' crosscourt pass hit Chalmers in the corner, and the player best known for a last-second shot in the 2008 NCAA Championship Game hit another tying three in a huge moment. (James' pass, by the way, was overlooked and one of the most incredible of his career.) If the Mavericks had lost, it's a moment Terry may never have been able to live down. But Nowitzki wouldn't let that happen.

Why the Heat didn't foul despite having one to give or why Bosh was guarding Nowitzki on that final possession instead of Udonis Haslem doesn't matter now. It isn't important that Nowitzki had a torn tendon in his left hand because he went straight to the basket and finished with that injured hand anyway. If the Mavericks had lost Game 2—if Nowitzki hadn't made that shot—then 2011 may have been all different. But Dirk wouldn't let that happen.

27 Game 4 of the 2011 NBA Finals

His hair mussed up and his demeanor quiet, Dirk Nowitzki slumped into his seat on a training table in the back of the Mavericks locker room. It was only hours before Game 4—the most important game of his career to date—and he was sick. The Mavericks had their backs against the wall after losing Game 3 at home. At the time, no team had ever blown a 3–1 lead in the NBA Finals. (The Warriors, of course, suffered that fate in 2016.) A win didn't guarantee the Mavericks anything, but a loss would be backbreaking. "I said, 'Ah no, no no no,'" said Jason Terry, remembering his reaction. "Not right now. Not in this moment."

Nowitzki had gone to bed shivering and cold, but he thought he could sleep it off. Instead, he woke with flu-like symptoms, coughing and sweating with a fever that reached as high as 102 degrees during points of the day. The players learned that as they filtered into the arena, but most television viewers didn't know until Doris Burke's sideline report after the first break in action. Fans at the arena went even longer without realizing Nowitzki had any sort of illness, though it quickly became clear he wasn't his normal self.

After a quick six points in the opening minutes, Nowitzki quickly began to wear down. His steps were slower, his appearance ragged. Nowitzki missed 10 of his next 11 shots, and the Mavericks were forced to take a timeout early in the fourth quarter when Miami went up by nine.

The Mavericks, to their credit, succeeded in turning the game into a slog. With their captain under the weather, they slowed the pace, refused to push the ball, and set up a half-court offense on every play. Miami fell into the same tempo, which went against the team's best qualities. Game 4 was one of the worst of LeBron James' life. Despite nine rebounds and seven assists, his eight points on 3-of-11 shooting simply wasn't enough.

Jason Terry immediately cut into that nine-point deficit, and then Nowitzki joined the fight. He first hit a pair of free throws before following up with a layup, his first field goal since the second quarter. With 2:16 left two more Nowitzki free throws made the score 82–78. With 30 seconds remaining, though, Miami pulled within one.

Cue Nowitzki. The Mavericks gave him the ball at the high elbow and cleared out of his way. With 12 seconds left on the shot clock—"he's going too early!" is Jeff Van Gundy's classic call from the broadcast—Nowitzki darted past his defender with a dribble and laid the ball in off the glass. It almost seemed like Nowitzki shocked Miami by not running the shot clock down further, but on a night where Nowitzki was a step slow, he needed every advantage he could get. Dwyane Wade's block attempt arrived a beat too late. Mike Miller's three-point attempt on the Heat's final possession came up short. "The average person, you know, has sick days and battling 100-something [fever], it's just tough to get out of bed," Tyson Chandler said. "This guy is playing against the best athletes in the world."

28 Game 5 of the 2011 NBA Finals

The turn game. That's what people around the league call Game 5 of any series tied at two. The reasoning is simple: whoever wins Game 5 and goes up 3–2 is the overwhelming favorite to win the series. In 2011 Dallas and Miami had reached the turn game. It was only a matter of which way the series would turn.

Dirk Nowitzki's fever had subsided from the game before, and with it went the low scoring nature of the series. Through four games both teams were averaging fewer than 90 points per game, and neither had hit the 100-point plateau yet. In Game 5, that changed quickly.

Miami led 31–30 after the first quarter thanks to a half-court heave from Mario Chalmers that went in. The Mavericks' backup center, Brendan Haywood, was injured and didn't play after Game 3, opening the rotation for two players: Ian Mahinmi, who played a huge role in the series finale, and Brian Cardinal, who had several crucial moments through the final two games.

One of those moments came just eight minutes into Game 5. With Dwyane Wade driving to the rim, Cardinal slid in front and shifted his weight when Wade tried to Eurostep past him. The collision was called a blocking foul, but the collateral damage cost Miami dearly. After making a pair of free throws, Wade exited shortly thereafter while wincing about his hip.

Though Wade returned later in the half, the nagging injury bothered him throughout the final two games. His first-half absence meant he played just 34 minutes in Game 5, his lowest of the series, and only shot 6-of-16 in the series' closeout Game 6. Cardinal had no ill intentions on the play—he had also taken a charge against

LeBron James in Game 4—but a slightly-less-than-100 percent Wade played right into the Mavericks' hands.

Like in their previous two wins, the Mavericks trailed late in the fourth quarter. But this time the largest lead Miami could build was a four-point one, going up 99–95 after a Wade three-pointer with slightly more than four minutes left in the game. Dallas had already beaten Miami in this series when trailing by 15 in the fourth quarter; it seemed clear this four-point lead simply wouldn't be enough.

But the Mavericks needed Jason Terry for it to happen. After Terry blew a defensive assignment and followed it up with a lazy screen on the other end, Rick Carlisle yanked him from the game. "Refocus," he told Terry. "I'm putting you right back in."

Terry did. When he subbed back in less than a minute later, the Mavericks made a decisive 16–3 run that closed out the game. Terry assisted or scored on 13 of those points, including a game-tying three and another one right in James' face that he launched with all the confidence in the world. It splashed in, and Terry ran back to the other side with his arms outstretched. For the Heat it was the backbreaker. For the Mavericks it was the turning point. They were up 3–2 but still needed one more win.

Game 6 of the 2011 NBA Finals

Dirk Nowitzki didn't blitz the Heat into a 50-point blowout in Game 6 while setting an NBA Finals scoring record or notch a triple-double in a chest-pounding feat of dominance. He never made a play we refer to with capital letters, like The Shot or The Block. What Nowitzki mostly did in Game 6 was struggle. He showed his

After coaching the Mavericks to a 105–95 victory in Game 6 of the 2011 NBA Finals, Rick Carlisle holds the Larry O'Brien Trophy aloft.

mortality—after a playoff run that was so perfect we wondered if this man was even human. And then, at the end of it, he won it all. There is no coda that could have been more perfect.

Nowitzki carried the Mavericks through three playoff series— without any discredit to his essential teammates—and then through three more wins in the 2011 NBA Finals. In Game 6 his teammates carried him. It was a relay race where Nowitzki had run the first three legs. When he finally handed off the baton, his teammates told him simply: *We got it from here.*

The Mavericks had won Games 4 and 5, back-to-back victories that put them up 3–2 in the series, but now the series shifted back to Miami for a conclusion. Nowitzki's worst half of the playoffs— maybe all season—came in those first 24 minutes of Game 6. He contributed three points, attempting 12 shots and making only one.

But Dallas led at the half anyway, withdrawing to the locker room with a 53–51 lead. His teammates had filled in everywhere Nowitzki had not. Jason Terry had 19 points, DeShawn Stevenson materialized to bury three triples, Ian Mahinmi beat the third-quarter buzzer with a jump shot, Shawn Marion and Jason Kidd, two veterans who must have known this was their best and last shot at winning it all, agitated the Heat all night.

The second half began with Nowitzki finally making a long jump shot. He wasn't his best self, but it was enough. In the last eight minutes, Nowitzki took six shots and made five. The second-to-last one—a fading baseline jumper with about two minutes left, a shot he drilled despite having Chris Bosh draped all over him—could not have been more Dirk. As the shot went in and the Mavericks went up by 10, the city of Dallas began celebrating— and wouldn't stop for days.

The cameras followed Dirk. As the seconds slowly ticked off the clock in that final minute, Nowitzki wasn't beaming like his teammates. The laser focus that had dominated his face for weeks now morphed into shock—or even incredulity. More than a decade chasing a single moment, and it had finally arrived. After 13 years figuring out how to get here, he had never considered what he would do when it finally happened. That look of confusion still planted on his face, Nowitzki hugged a couple teammates and then sprinted back to the locker room.

That's where he broke down. "I had to get away for a moment," said Nowitzki, sitting on the court during a postgame interview with NBA TV. "I went to the locker room, I had to go lay down. I cried for a second there and I had to get my composure back for a second there. If you put so much work into something and you finally achieve it, it feels amazing, and [I had to] be by myself for a few minutes and then I was able to make it through the trophy presentation."

As Nowitzki sat on that NBA TV set, you could see it had finally hit him. He cradled the NBA Finals trophy in his right hand. He wore a "2011 champions" shirt over his jersey, and a hat saying the same thing was perched on his head. Right there, in that moment, Nowitzki finally started smiling.

30 Derek Harper

In almost every way, Derek Harper was a perfect Maverick. Dallas drafted him in 1983, and he played his next 11 seasons with them. He averaged 14 points and six assists throughout his career with the team. All those cliches about hustling and heart apply to Harper. As of 2017 Harper was 23rd all time in career assists, proving his steadiness since he never averaged more than 7.9 in a single season.

For his first few seasons, Harper came off the bench while Brad Davis started for the Mavericks. It wasn't long until he supplanted the older Davis in the starting five, a spot he would fill until Dallas traded him to the New York Knicks in 1994. After a stint in New York, which included an NBA Finals appearance, Harper ended up back in Dallas for a year in 1997 before finishing his career chasing a ring with the Orlando Magic and Los Angeles Lakers. He was one year too early—the Lakers' run of three straight began in 2000, a year after Harper's 1999 retirement.

The other way Harper proved himself was defensively, where he was named to the all-defensive team in 1987 and 1990. Frequently, Harper ended up guarding Michael Jordan. Once, in an interview with the *Fort Worth Star-Telegram*, he recounted something Jordan told him while the two were going at it in a game. "Harp, I've got a couple of things to say," Michael Jordan told him. "You're a pretty good defender. The other thing is right now it doesn't matter because you know when I'm hot it doesn't matter."

Maybe not against Jordan—but to most players—Harper was a total nuisance. He knew when to put his hand on his man's hip or grab jersey when the referees weren't looking and he was a top notch trash talker. But with reporters Harper was always gracious with his time. The Derek Harper Assist Award, presented by the Pro Basketball Writers Association, was named after him and is presented to the player who exhibits "outstanding professionalism" dealing with the media during the season. Today, Harper is the color commentator for the Mavericks' television broadcast, coming back to the franchise that was home for him.

31 Tyson Chandler

In 2014 I asked Tyson Chandler if he knew who the greatest center in the Mavericks' history was. "Me," he replied with a grin.

You could argue semantics with him if you really wanted, but he has a point. Chandler didn't need the complete history of the Mavericks to know the team has never had a great center. When he arrived with the Mavericks in 2010, Chandler turned out to be the big man that Dallas had been looking to put next to Dirk Nowitzki for years. "The addition of Tyson Chandler finished the team off," Rick Carlisle said.

But the Mavericks didn't acquire Chandler with those expectations when he arrived from Charlotte. In fact, Dallas thought he would back up Brendan Haywood, who they had traded for at the previous deadline with excellent results. Chandler, on the other hand, was coming off injuries and his worst season, playing only 51 games. "It's [Haywood's] job to lose," Carlisle said that preseason. "I don't see it as a battle."

By the third preseason game, though, Chandler was starting. He was healthier than he had been in a couple seasons and springier than anyone the Mavericks had rolled out at the five. Quickly, he became an alley-oop favorite of Jason Kidd, finishing around the basket much easier than the stockier, more ground-bound Haywood. Just as importantly, Chandler's defense was unbelievable. He not only defended the rim, but also moved his feet on the perimeter against pick-and-rolls.

Chandler started all 74 games he played that year, averaging 10 points and nine rebounds while making 65 percent of his shots. If you could carve a center out of stone to be a perfect complement to Nowitzki, it might just be Chandler. His defense picked up for Nowitzki's flaws, and his vocal leadership meshed well with Nowitzki's more subdued style.

To a franchise that had seen a turnstile at center over the past decade, Chandler was a godsend. The team had run out Shawn Bradley, Raef LaFrentz, DeSagana Diop, Pops Mensah-Bonsu, and Erick Dampier, but none of them fit as well as Chandler did. "Seriously, six weeks into his first run with the Mavericks, and we were already comfortably referring to him as the best Mavs center of all time," Bob Sturm, a midday radio host on 1310 The Ticket, told me in 2015. "It's partially a compliment to Tyson that he's been the best center here, that he won a Defensive Player of the Year, that he fit so perfectly with Dirk that it's almost like he was genetically designed to fit with [Dirk]. On the other hand, it does illuminate the issues the Mavericks have had at that position forever."

Sure, James Donaldson and Sam Perkins both were capable players in the 1980s, but you could argue neither was ever quite as good as Chandler in 2011. Since then, the position had always been in flux. Dallas fans were convinced a really good big man next to Nowitzki would push the team over the top. As it turned out, they were right. And with Chandler, it felt right.

It really was no surprise Dallas fell in love with him so quickly. When the Mavericks decided not to bring back the title team after the championship in 2011, it looked like Chandler would only have that one magical season in Dallas. Instead, with a year left on the lucrative contract he signed with the New York Knicks, the Mavericks dealt for him in 2014. At media day a few months later, it felt like Chandler had never left. "I spent one year, and everyone thinks I spent my whole career here," Tyson said that day. "Even guys around the league, they ask me how long I played in Dallas, and I tell them one year, and they said, 'What?'"

On opening night that season, the roar for Chandler when he was introduced in the starting lineup before the game may have equaled the applause for Nowitzki. For months afterward, even the public address announcer stuck "welcome home!" into Chandler's introduction. But as the season churned along, and especially after the Mavericks made an ill-fated trade for Rajon Rondo, it became clear that Chandler wasn't quite the player he was in 2011, and the Mavericks certainly weren't that same team. "Personally, I took a lot of it on," Chandler told me at the end of the year, "just a lot of long nights, trying to figure out how to push this team and really how to bring this team together."

When Mark Cuban said he "learned from his mistakes" early that season, we all assumed Chandler would be re-signed that summer. But the trying season, plus a first-round loss to the Houston Rockets, cast doubt on that. When the Mavericks instead chose to pursue DeAndre Jordan that summer—beginning their courting process while Chandler was still in uniform—it didn't sit well with the two-time Maverick. His harsh words for the front office the following season made that clear. "I saw the bullshit they put out," Chandler said. "It's just bullshit, just saving face. It was what it was. It was clear. The whole process was going on while I was basically still in the jersey."

In so many ways, Chandler deserved to retire in Dallas. His championship came here, and the city still reveres him. He was the best big man the Mavericks ever put next to Nowitzki and probably the best one in franchise history, a title solidified by his second season here. He still greets the Mavericks' staff by name when he comes back for games and he gave Rick Carlisle a bearhug when they passed each other in the tunnels before a game in 2017. They chatted briefly before parting ways, but reality set back in when Chandler headed the other way toward the visiting locker room.

None of that takes away from the time Chandler did spend in Dallas, though. He was undoubtedly the catalyst for the title run in 2011 and for that he will always be beloved in this city. But if there's any player you wish had been paired with Nowitzki sooner, or for longer, it's him.

32 Free-Agency Failure

When the Mavericks broke up their title team in 2011, they did it with noble intentions: they wanted to give Dirk Nowitzki a true second star. It was a great plan if they could execute it—Dallas had talked about getting a player who could be Nowitzki's equal. But actually attracting that free agent was an entirely different challenge. Every offseason from 2012 to 2015, Dallas tried. They aimed high, even requesting meetings with LeBron James. They touted their cap space and Nowitzki as a superstar. Despite two close calls, it never worked. Here's a breakdown.

Deron Williams

The Dallas native, who ended up with the Mavericks years later, was still a bonafide superstar in 2012. Two seasons earlier at the trade deadline, the Utah Jazz had dealt him to the New Jersey Nets. When free agency began, it quickly became apparent that Williams would either stay with the Nets or make the decision to return to his hometown. Williams was coming off his highest scoring season, having averaged 21 points and nearly nine assists for the Nets. There were some warning signs—the 27-year-old's turnovers were up, and his efficiency was declining as he frequently played through nagging injuries—but Dallas set their sights on the point guard anyway. Though ridiculous in retrospect, arguments had raged for several years whether Chris Paul or Deron Williams was the best point guard in the league. The Mavericks, knowing his ties here, went all in.

The Nets offered the allure of the big city and the potential of a team who had an owner, Russian billionaire Mikhail Prokhorov, willing to spend lucratively. Dallas countered with its proven track record as 2011 champions, a chance to play with Dirk Nowitzki, and a homecoming. When the Mavericks contingent met Williams, Mark Cuban was notably absent. He had a scheduling conflict with his television show *Shark Tank*, and the always-involved Cuban left the recruiting visit to his coach and general manager.

Later on, after he picked the Nets, Williams said Cuban's absence was a factor in his decision. The extra $24 million the Nets could offer was likely an even bigger one. With the way Williams declined from his superstar days into an average guard, the Mavericks may have ended up better off without him signing here. But the trend of Dallas missing out on big name stars was just beginning.

Chris Paul and Dwight Howard

That same summer in 2012, two superstars could have permanently changed the Mavericks. After spending time on the 2008 Olympics gold medal-winning USA Basketball squad, Chris Paul and Dwight Howard had talked about teaming up since 2009. After Paul failed to recruit Howard to New Orleans, and Howard couldn't convince him to join him in Orlando, they discussed meeting in Dallas as an alternative.

Cuban could have cleared cap space for them both, and Paul was "all in for joining the Mavericks as a free agent in 2012," according to Yahoo! Sports, but Howard couldn't make up his mind and give Paul a commitment. Paul was traded to the Clippers before the lockout season and ended up picking up his player option for the next year, putting to rest the two players' plans of joining forces.

By 2013 Paul was committed to the Clippers. Howard was a free agent, however, and an unhappy season with the Lakers had many people expecting him to leave. Howard met with the Mavericks—along with the Los Angeles Lakers, the Houston Rockets, and two other teams—in the opening days of free agency. It was reported that Dallas had a real chance, which turned the city into a circus. When a chicken strip chain in Houston offered Howard free chicken fingers for life if he signed with the Rockets, at least 34 Dallas businesses and groups responded with counteroffers. Some highlights: a signature drink in an Uptown club, a free acoustic show from North Texas punk band Bowling for Soup, free Zamboni rides whenever the Allen Event Center's ice rink was open, a guest feature on a local rap group's album, and a Saturday morning radio show called *The Superman Hour with Superman Howard*. (Please try to imagine Howard listening to Bowling for Soup to get pumped up for a game and not laugh. You laughed, didn't you?)

Despite those tantalizing offers, Howard narrowed the choice to Houston or Los Angeles before deciding on the Rockets. The Mavericks rebounded with another wave of one-year veterans, including Monta Ellis, Jose Calderon, and Samuel Dalembert.

LeBron James and Carmelo Anthony

Once again, the Mavericks aimed high. They were one of five teams who spoke with LeBron James' agent, supposedly a prerequisite to earn an audience with the man himself. They met with Carmelo Anthony on July 2, but it was much shorter than planned after Anthony's meeting with the Rockets in Houston ran so long. Ultimately, Dallas had no real shot at either free agent. James went home to Cleveland while Anthony re-signed with the Knicks. The Mavericks, meanwhile, didn't even wait until those two made decisions before extending an offer sheet to the Rockets' Chandler Parsons.

Free agency is the hardest way to acquire superstars. All superstars have to be drafted, and they don't have a choice if they're traded, but free agency requires them to choose your team over 29 others. We've occasionally seen generational players change teams over the past decade, but it usually involved them joining another young superstar (like Howard to Houston) or two players on their level. In the case of Kevin Durant, he decided to join the Golden State Warriors and their preexisting Big Three.

The Mavericks' free-agency pitch centered on the Big German had two problems. The first was Nowitzki's age, which meant the team's cloudy future once Nowitzki retired grew closer each summer. Superstars don't leave uncertain situations in free agency only to join another one, and despite Dallas' winning culture, that's what the team appeared to be. You could argue the second was Nowitzki's lack of relationships with other players. Chumming it up with the other NBAers in the offseason was never Nowitzki's style, nor did it need to be. But having those personal relationships (often ones built through mutual Team USA experiences) wouldn't have hurt.

33 DeAndre Jordan

DeAndre Jordan never really wanted to leave the Los Angeles Clippers. Looking back, that's pretty clear. But on July 3, 2015, Jordan decided to leave anyway. With Mark Cuban and Chandler Parsons stopping by his house, Jordan verbally agreed to a maximum contract with the Dallas Mavericks to have him leave the only team he had ever known. The media reported it instantly, and for five days, Jordan was publicly a member of the Dallas Mavericks.

And then he changed his mind.

Jordan was the closest the Mavericks came to a max contract free agent in the five years following the 2011 championship, so close he actually agreed to sign with them. Because the league needs time to calculate the salary cap before each season, NBA free agency has always had a moratorium on officially signing free agents during the opening days. In 2015, free agency began on July 1, but the moratorium lasted until July 8, meaning no official contracts could be signed between those two dates, and every "signing" existed only as a verbal agreement between the player and the team.

Dozens of players verbally agreed to contracts in the opening days, just like they do every year. At midnight on July 1, a Mavericks contingent involving Cuban, Parsons, and Dirk Nowitzki met with Jordan at a sushi restaurant in Los Angeles. In the days leading up to free agency, Parsons had dined with Jordan almost nightly, which didn't break the league's tampering rules since Parsons was a player, and their dinners were viewed merely as a couple friends out for the evening. (Obviously, though, this was pushing the boundaries of a major gray area.) But the talks became very serious once the calendar rolled over to July 1 and free-agency chatter turned legal. The Mavericks made it clear to Jordan they wanted him.

While Dallas pampered him, Jordan felt slighted by the team where he had played his first seven seasons. Jordan wanted a bigger role in Los Angeles after averaging less than one post-up per game, and his concerns were being ignored. When he met with the Clippers, Chris Paul skipped the meeting to go on vacation. And so three days after free agency, Jordan made the biggest decision of his life after contemplating everything the Mavericks told him—and what Los Angeles hadn't. "I love that," Jordan reportedly told Cuban. "I love that. I'm going to Dallas."

Jordan, his family, Cuban, and Parsons celebrated the moment with tequila. Not even 24 hours later, Jordan was having second thoughts. The Clippers knew right away they were in trouble.

The Most Ridiculous Day in Mavericks History

Dallas didn't want to be the biggest story in sports on July 8, 2015. They just wanted DeAndre Jordan to sign with their team—like he had verbally agreed to days before. Instead, the Mavericks and the collective sports world slowly watched the 12-hour saga of Jordan decommitting from Dallas and rejoining the Los Angeles Clippers unfold through tweets, emojis, and a steady stream of reports that painted a more and more depressing picture for Mavericks fans still holding out hope that it would work out.

What follows is my best attempt to document exactly how many ridiculous things happened that day.

- Chandler Parsons tweeted the emoji of an airplane. At the time it was assumed he was headed to Houston to talk Jordan back into signing with the Mavericks. Later on, he revealed that wasn't it. He was actually just flying to Las Vegas for his girlfriend's birthday. ("At this point, it was already over," he told the Dallas radio station 105.3 The Fan months afterward.)
- Just nine minutes after the airplane tweet, J.J. Redick followed up Parsons' emoji with a car emoji. Redick lives in Austin, Texas, during the offseason and drove down to Houston, a three-hour trip.
- About 10 minutes later, Blake Griffin tweeted the plane, helicopter, and car emoji all at once. It's still unclear whether Griffin actually owns a heliplanecar.
- Days before the saga, Chris Paul had been photographed on a boat shaped like a banana along with LeBron James and Dwyane Wade. When the tweets started flying, Paul tweeted the banana and boat emojis. It was arguably the best joke made that day.
- Unintentionally, Paul Pierce created the funniest moment of the night. Instead of joining the trend of tweeting emojis, Pierce tweeted a grainy image of a rocket ship. If you didn't follow that, just understand that you finally have something in common with a future NBA Hall of Famer.
- Trying to get the then 37-year-old Pierce to understand emojis is a lost cause. "Paul Pierce reveals he has no idea how smartphones work," read an SB Nation headline from

that day. "Paul Pierce just tweeted with his Game Boy color lol," tweeted Utah Jazz big man Rudy Gobert. Pierce still gets clowned on to this day for not knowing how emojis work.

- Even Mike Woodson, an assistant coach for Los Angeles who was 19 years older than Pierce, correctly tweeted out an emoji. (It was the emoji of a man swimming, so apparently he was vacationing in the Bahamas and used the breaststroke to come into town.)
- Tyson Chandler, who had already signed with the Phoenix Suns after a season in Dallas, sent a tweet that was a sun emoji and a peace sign emoji. (It was clearly a not-so-subtle shot at the Mavericks.)
- Kobe Bryant tweeted five championship trophies, and many other teams' social media accounts tweeted our their best ones.
- Later in the night, after reports that the Clippers weren't allowing Jordan to leave before the moratorium ended and he could officially sign with Los Angeles, Griffin tweeted the photo of a chair in front of a door. At the time, everyone assumed Griffin had actually placed a chair in front of Jordan's door, preventing him from leaving (presumably for the Twitter joke, but who knew). In reality, Griffin later said he just Googled that image.
- One reporter claimed Mark Cuban was driving around Houston "distraught" since he didn't know where Jordan lived. Neither of those things were true, of course, and the reporter eventually apologized.
- Jordan's mom eventually got like 50 bags of Raising Cane's Chicken Fingers and brought it back to the house where all the Clippers were gathered, waiting so he could officially sign his contract after the moratorium expired at 11:00 PM. (Well, at least I can defend one decision made by Jordan. Raising Cane's makes really great chicken.)

For most people it was the greatest entertainment sports could provide, and no actual basketball was even involved. For Mavericks fans it was drawn-out torture on a national stage. Still, hopefully looking back, you can see the humor in an absolutely ridiculous day.

Even if they didn't view Jordan as a valid post presence, his role as the backbone of their defense, and his ability to throw down alley-oops were crucial to their team. Once a player verbally agrees to a contract during the moratorium, there's an unwritten rule that you don't continue courting him. But the Clippers caught wind that Jordan was rethinking his decision, and someone—either Doc Rivers to Jordan or the other way around—reached out.

Meanwhile, there were signs from the Mavericks that not all was right. It was a small thing, but Jordan didn't announce his decision on Twitter. His silence started on July 3 and lasted for days. Second, Cuban stopped receiving texts from the big man, according to ESPN. Even Parsons—already friends from Team USA and someone who had become even closer in recent months as Parsons ramped up his recruiting pitch—stopped hearing from Jordan with the same frequency. Still, nobody in Dallas knew for certain that Jordan was considering flipping his allegiance to the team until July 7.

Jordan had ended up in Houston. He had a house there, and Blake Griffin flew out to join his longtime frontcourt partner. Cuban traveled down to Houston, too, but he couldn't get a meeting with Jordan. It all escalated on July 8, more than a week into free agency, when everyone had assumed all the major NBA storylines had been settled. Until that moment they had been. And then it broke. "DeAndre Jordan having second thoughts as Clips, Mavs battle for center," read the headline on the story from ESPN's Marc Stein. It was the first moment that Mavericks fans had any indication that something was wrong. But quickly, disbelief and denial gave way to bewilderment and anger.

It was the most ludicrous 12 hours I've ever covered in this sport. The Mavericks had made the biggest free-agent signing in the team's history—only for it to turn into the most embarrassing moment of the franchise. DeAndre Jordan's "Indecision" was the biggest story in sports on that day in July, and it wasn't even close. As league reporters slowly added details to the developing Jordan situation, players flooded Twitter with emojis and jokes. Eventually, Jordan, Clippers coach Doc Rivers, and several teammates all ended up at Jordan's house in Houston, and he officially re-signed with the Clippers.

In that moment, it was heartbreak for the Mavericks. For five days Dallas thought they had a new franchise center. Articles had already been written about what he meant for the twilight of the Dirk Nowitzki era. Instead, eight days into free agency with half the market already signed, the Mavericks had to go back to square one.

Jordan eventually apologized over Twitter to Mavericks fans. It didn't stop the entire American Airlines Center crowd from booing him in his first game back since November, a game the Mavericks unexpectedly won despite Parsons having to sit out. Jordan has been booed in every Dallas game since and, while he technically didn't break any rules, he'll never receive a warm welcome in Dallas to the day he retires.

34 Dirk's Twilight Years

The free agency failures for the Mavericks put the most pressure on Dirk Nowitzki. Dallas tried their damndest to put a second star next to Nowitzki, but it ended up filling up its roster with one-year contracts and unwanted veterans. The common thread was the Big German, who was asked to bring the roster together every year.

Nowitzki, fortunately, was usually good enough to do just that.

Even successful NBA players need a special mix of skills to play late into their 30s, but Nowitzki barely missed a beat. Nowitzki was never the most athletic player, of course, and he began to slow down every year after the championship. But at seven feet and armed with a timeless jump shot, Nowitzki aged like wine. In the five years following the championship, he averaged 19 points on 47 percent shooting. No wonder he's a soon-to-be Hall of Famer.

It still wasn't the easiest path. Twice, Nowitzki started the season with injuries that caused him to miss a chunk of games. His best teammate during those years was...Monta Ellis? Vince Carter? Harrison Barnes? Either way, it was a constant shuffling of parts on the Dallas roster. Every training camp began with new faces and a new challenge for Rick Carlisle. As the iconic luminary on the roster, some of that weight fell on Nowitzki, too.

Still, the Mavericks made do. Every time Dallas missed on their first free-agent target, some fans called for the team to tank. That was never going to happen with Nowitzki on the roster, though. They owed him that much—especially after Nowitzki continually took discounted contracts to help Dallas fill out its roster. For the 2017–18 season, he signed for just $5 million.

Finally in 2017, Dallas gave up the dream of acquiring a second star through free agency. Instead, the Mavericks began bringing in young players who could bridge the game between Nowitzki's final years and the era that begins as soon as he retires. In the closing months of the 2017 season, Dallas often closed games with a lineup of players all under 26 years old, including Harrison Barnes, Seth Curry, and Nerlens Noel. In the ensuing draft, the Mavericks selected Dennis Smith Jr. ninth overall, and the team has high hopes for the athletic point guard.

Nowitzki will play at least until 2018. If he stays healthy and remains effective—and if Dallas has a successful team that might be going somewhere to pair with Nowitzki—then that's the perfect recipe to keep him around even longer. Even if it's just one more season, that's worth it. Nowitzki is the greatest Maverick of all time and one of the best players, too. Savor every final moment that he grants us.

35 Why the Title Team Broke Up

The months following the 2011 championship were joyous—and then strange. Unable to reach terms on a new collective bargaining agreement with the players association, the NBA went into a lockout. It stretched into November, threatened to shut down the entire season, and was resolved at the last minute. The shortened season began on Christmas.

With all that going on, the Mavericks had to decide whether they would bring back their roster in its entirety or break it up. Tyson Chandler, J.J. Barea, DeShawn Stevenson, and Caron Butler were all free agents, and Dallas was leery of paying that group of aging veterans as much as they would have commanded. "I wanted to bring the whole team back," Rick Carlisle told me. "That's no secret. Look, this is a decision that's an owner's decision, and in my view, Mark [Cuban] had earned the right to do what he wanted to do."

For a number of reasons, the Mavericks decided not to. For one thing the team was old, and most of the players were at or near their 30s. They weren't sure the window that was cracked open perfectly in 2011 would exist in 2012 because of the crammed season and fewer off days, thanks to the lockout. Each conference had rising contenders in the Miami Heat and Oklahoma City Thunder, teams that Dallas had beaten in 2011 but wasn't sure they would be able to again. And, of course, there was the money. To commit to bringing back the team, Dallas would have needed to pay everyone an extra "championship fee." "When you win a championship," Donnie Nelson told me with a laugh, "you think your value is triple."

The logic was sound, but inflexible. No title team in recent memory had ever broken up a championship roster before they had a chance to prove themselves again. Dallas robbed themselves the ability to defend their crown by gutting the roster, and players who won in 2011 will never forget that. "There's no doubt in my mind that we would have repeated and gone back-to-back," Tyson Chandler said. "We, for sure, would have been in the Finals… Oklahoma City, nothing against them, but we had their number. And we had Miami's number."

Chandler went to the New York Knicks instead, where he was named Defensive Player of the Year in 2012. Barea, Stevenson, and Butler, though, struggled elsewhere, and even Chandler was eventually traded back to Dallas for a small return. "In hindsight, I think they could have kept Chandler and moved another player and still had cap room, and it would have served them better," said Jeff Wade, a local radio host and Mavericks announcer. "But that's hindsight. At the time, I understood that with the way this team is structured, Dirk needs somebody else to help him score."

Dallas was also certain one of the upcoming free agents would go their way. In fact, behind the scenes, Cuban may have been convinced that Dwight Howard, at least, could be obtained in the summer of 2012. "Dwight opting into the last year of his deal in Orlando [in 2012] absolutely blindsided the Mavericks, frankly blindsided his agent, shocking everybody," said Tim MacMahon, Mavericks beat writer for ESPN. "I think [Cuban] expected to get Dwight, hoped to get [Chris Paul], and considered [Deron Williams] a solid fallback option."

Instead of defending the title, Dallas limped through the lockout year and spent several seasons chasing big names with nothing to show for it. The plan was idealistic and bold, and sometimes, those plans don't work out. Given what actually happened, gunning for one more championship with that group would have at least been the more enjoyable option. But at least for those running the Mavericks, they were sure they made the right call. "We were good and we were lucky," Nelson said. "If we brought the same group back together, I'm not going to tell you that we would have another championship trophy in that case and I don't think that we would have anyone worth their NBA salt that would disagree with me."

36 A Texas-Sized Rivalry

The first game the Mavericks ever played was against the Spurs. It shouldn't have been a contest for playoff-bound San Antonio. It faced a brand new franchise, whose top pick Kiki VanDeWeghe was refusing to even play for them, but Dallas stunned San Antonio in a 103–92 upset anyway. You could say the two team's rivalry was born then.

Since that day, the Mavericks and the Spurs have been the best rivalry in basketball outside of the Los Angeles Lakers and the Boston Celtics. (You can argue for a few others, but I'll still take this one.) The rivalry has proximity; the two cities are separated by a construction-filled five-hour drive on Interstate 35. It has longevity; the Spurs have won the most games of any franchise since 2000, and the Mavericks have won the second most. It has pettiness and figurative shots below the belt—and one infamous literal shot below the belt, too. It has one of the greatest playoff series of all time, the 2006 Western Conference Semifinals, which Dallas won in seven games.

The Mavericks and the Spurs also respect the hell out of each other. Everything else helps make the rivalry what it is, but the mutual admiration is the best part about it. That comes from Dirk Nowitzki and Tim Duncan, two gentle legends who steered the franchises through their battles against each other with virtue and grace.

The two first faced each other in the postseason in 2001. The Mavericks, who hadn't been to the playoffs since 1990, advanced past the Utah Jazz on a last-second Calvin Booth layup to meet the Spurs in the semifinals. San Antonio won the series in five games, but their championship hopes were shattered when they lost Derek Anderson, their second leading scorer, to a separated shoulder caused by a hard flagrant-two foul by Mavericks center Juwan Howard in Game 1. (The Spurs were swept by the Los Angeles Lakers in the next round.)

Another injury marred the two teams' next playoff meeting, but this time it was Nowitzki. With the series tied at a game apiece, the Mavericks' star hurt his knee in a Game 3 loss during the Western Conference Finals. Dallas was already on their way to a loss that game—they trailed by 14 in the fourth when Nowitzki exited—but there's no telling whether a healthy Nowitzki could have led the team to a series win. Instead, the Mavericks fell in six games, and the Spurs ended up beating Jason Kidd's New Jersey Nets for the franchise's second championship.

The Mavericks and the Spurs were seeded into the same division when the NBA reworked its conference structure in 2004. The move guaranteed the two teams four matchups per year, and the two teams share 11 of the 13 division titles since its inception. (To be fair, the Spurs have nine of those 11.)

By 2005 the two franchises had flipped two huge figures in Avery Johnson and Michael Finley. Johnson was beloved in San Antonio for his 10 seasons with the team and he joined the Mavericks as an assistant in 2004. When Don Nelson resigned in 2005, Johnson took over as a head coach in Dallas. Meanwhile, Finley left the Mavericks after nine seasons to play for San Antonio. Adding familiar figures only made the team's duels even more interesting.

The culmination of the rivalry was the 2006 Western Conference Semifinals. In 2013 ESPN.com's John Hollinger—now the vice president of basketball operations for the Memphis Grizzlies—ranked the series as the third greatest of all time. Terry was suspended for Game 6 of that series after punching Michael Finley in his Finleys.

After 2006 the rivalry turned more one-sided. The Mavericks beat San Antonio in the first round of the 2009 playoffs, but the Spurs ousted them from the playoffs in 2010 and 2014. The 2010 first-round series was an upset—the Mavericks had won 55 games but saw a No. 7-seed Spurs team trounce them in six games. In 2014 the eighth-seeded Mavericks actually forced a Game 7 against San Antonio before the Spurs ended up winning en route to their fifth championship.

The two teams' stars fostered a culture of respect, but it was mainly because of how much they appreciated the other. "Say it ain't so. Greatest power forward ever," Dirk Nowitzki tweeted when Duncan announced his retirement in the summer of 2016. "I am sorry to see Tim retire," Nowitzki told *The Dallas Morning*

News afterward. "I have so much respect for him. He was so good. He could do it all: pass, score on both blocks, drive, rebound, block shots. He wasn't flashy and always put the team first. I will always appreciate that he was about winning and never worried about the limelight. The league will miss him."

As his tweet indicates, Nowitzki can admit Duncan is somewhere ahead of him on the all-time list. In their 90 head-to-head matchups, Duncan leads 53–37. That includes a 35–22 edge in the regular season and an 18–15 advantage in the postseason. (Nowitzki's injury in the 2003 series robbed us of what could have been another all-time great seven-game series.) And, of course, Duncan's five championships with the Spurs is the ultimate tiebreaker. They're both all-time greats, but one clearly has an edge.

Always cordial, Nowitzki and Duncan weren't necessarily friends. Their relationship consisted of handshakes and head nods during their half dozen meetings throughout the year rather than long conversations or offseason hangouts. "We're not going to go over there and hug each other or anything, but it's good to see guys like that still out there," Duncan told the *San Antonio Express-News* in 2015. "We're a dying breed."

It would be heartwarming if Nowitzki took trips down to Duncan's auto shop in San Antonio during the offseason or if Duncan made appearances at Nowitzki's celebrity baseball game, but it makes more sense this way. What Nowitzki most appreciated about Duncan was that he cared about winning before anything else, never caring to market himself as a brand or constantly appear in commercials. That same mind-set made both of them fiercely loyal to their teammates but meant they only cared so much about extending relationships around the league.

For nearly 20 years, the two brought their best against each other every time they stepped on the court. That, more than anything, is what their rivalry should be remembered as.

37 Shawn Marion

Shawn Marion embraced Dallas as much as Dallas embraced him. Now retired, he still owns his home here and lives in the city, staying close to the franchise where he won his lone championship. Best known for his years with the seven-seconds-or-less Phoenix Suns, Marion is one of the most unique and eccentric players to ever compete in the NBA. But his five years in Dallas are the ones that stand out to him now. "I love the Mavericks," Marion told the *Fort Worth Star-Telegram* in 2016. "I bleed blue, baby. I bleed that [Suns] purple and orange, too. That's where it started at. You never forget where it started, but Dallas is home."

The Matrix joined the Mavericks in the 2009 offseason, signing a five-year deal worth $39 million. (The transaction was technically a four-team trade, as Marion was a sign-and-trade, but the point is he chose Dallas and ended up there.) It signaled the end of Josh Howard, who was dealt midseason, and laid the foundation for the team's championship defense.

The first thing that sticks out about Marion is his jump shot, a bizarre, low-angled flick from his chest. He barely shot it in Dallas, making just eight three-pointers his first two seasons, but Marion finished his career with 791 made threes on 33 percent shooting, including 58 made shots from deep his final year with the Mavericks.

Although he could make open threes, Marion's jump shot limited him inside the arc. He rarely if ever shot pull-up jumpers; it was too easy to block his low-release point. Instead, Marion's offense came with an odd variety of flip shots in the post and runners from inside 15 feet. During his five years in Dallas, Marion actually took more than half of his shots between three and 16 feet from the basket, a ridiculously high percentage. For reference, Dirk Nowitzki—midrange extraordinaire—never even took 40 percent of his attempts from that part of the floor.

It's a damn shame that Marion never made an all-defense team because he was brilliant on that end. While with the Suns, Marion could guard every position effectively. You wouldn't want him guarding the quickest point guards or the bulkiest centers, but at 6'7" and 220 pounds, Marion had the size and overall athleticism to match nearly anyone on the court. Through his nine years in Phoenix, Marion averaged 1.9 steals and 1.4 blocks. In the 2005–06 season, Marion recorded 2.0 steals and 1.7 blocks per game. Only eight other players have ever averaged that over an entire year.

Though his raw numbers declined somewhat in Dallas, the Mavericks relied on Marion extensively as an elite defender on the wings. Adding Tyson Chandler in the middle and DeShawn

Why Marion Never Made an All-Defense Team

Marion never making an all-defensive team feels sacrilegious. After all, his career defensive win shares, one advanced defensive metric touted by basketball-reference.com, is 27th best all time. No one doubts he was one of the very best.

The biggest problem was his competition. Marion was a forward, and during his prime, three forwards—Tim Duncan, Kevin Garnett, and Ron Artest—were basically locked into the team every year. Bruce Bowen and Andrei Kirilenko, both noted defensive specialists, made the team over Marion a couple seasons, too. By the time Marion made it to Dallas, LeBron James had started joining these teams regularly.

The other problem was that his best years came on the seven-seconds-or-less Phoenix Suns. Because head coach Mike D'Antoni pushed Phoenix at such a quick pace and because Steve Nash and Amar'e Stoudemire both lacked defensive chops, their raw defensive numbers were always poor—even if a player like Marion was not. The Suns' reputation during those years surely hurt Marion's chances.

Stevenson as a hard-nosed guard for the 2010–11 season turned the Mavericks into a top 10 defense. In consecutive series during the championship run, Marion kept Kobe Bryant from going off, frustrated Kevin Durant, and helped spook LeBron James into the worst playoff series of his life, including James' eight points on 3-of-11 shooting in Game 4 of the 2011 NBA Finals.

Marion was technically a role player with the Mavericks, but he took that "role" to the highest possible level. He never had plays called for him but scored 4,170 points in a Dallas jersey—thanks to his constant hustle and a knack for being in the right place. He accepted the nights where he only took five shots and instead led the team in rebounding or drew the toughest defensive assignment for 35 minutes at a time. Marion's wacky shots occasionally drove fans batty in the heat of a game, but, looking back on his time in Dallas, no one has a bad word to say about the Matrix. "He's one of the all-time great Mavericks," Rick Carlisle told ESPN Dallas in 2015. "There's no question about it. His contributions over five years were gigantic to a championship, to a consistent level of success. He's a guy who's a special guy. He's building a home here in Dallas to live after his career. That's cool that a guy feels like he wants to make his permanent home here, and I know that he'll be very much welcomed by the people of Dallas."

Too many great moments stand out from Marion's time here, but I'll try to name a few: his signature catchphrase, "that's what's up," which he used frequently in postgame media sessions; his wonderfully awkward dancing during the Mavericks' ring ceremony after winning the title; the way one of his pinkie fingers was (and still is, as far as I know) permanently bent at a 40-degree angle after being dislocated too many times; the way he carried out a WWE-styled Mavericks championship belt during the parade, beaming with a smile, not even realizing he was carrying it upside down; his manner of saluting in a celebratory way. And there are hundreds more.

Whether Marion deserves to make the Hall of Fame is a fascinating debate, and there are valid arguments both ways. His raw numbers are lacking, and he was never the best player at his position. Basketball-reference.com's Hall of Fame probability lists him at 0.75, which makes him a fringe case but equal to players like Joe Dumars and Dennis Rodman, who did make the hall. Because the Basketball Hall of Fame generally sides with a player rather than against him, I'd guess Marion eventually sneaks in.

There is no debate, though, about what Marion meant to the Mavericks. Without him, the Mavericks never win a title, and without the Mavericks, he never gets his ring. It was a symbiotic relationship in the best possible way, and Dallas is forever grateful for the funky, loveable forward who ended up one of their own.

38 Holger

Dirk Nowitzki looks ridiculous. He's bending with his knees all the way to the ground before springing up to shoot and taking long lunges from one side of the free throw line to the other. It's a training method far outside the norm in professional sports, but it's the one that made Dirk the basketball player he is. And for that, he can thank Holger Geschwindner.

It was Holger who spotted Nowitzki as a gangly 16-year-old playing pickup basketball in a gym and it was Holger who declared he would coach him upon learning the teenaged Nowitzki had no one instructing him. It was a chance encounter: Geschwindner had showed up for an adults league, and Nowitzki's team was playing in a game that had run long. Right away, Geschwindner saw the teenager as an unpainted canvas who just needed guidance.

Dirk Nowitzki stands next to his mentor, Holger Geschwindner, during the German premiere of the documentary, Nowitzki: The Perfect Shot.

Geschwindner had been the captain of the 1972 West German National Team in his day and was well-known in Germany. He promised Nowitzki's parents he could turn their son into the best basketball player in the country, but he also told them he could reach even further—to the NBA.

Nowitzki did just that. Geschwindner turned into Nowitzki's closest mentor, one whom he trusted beyond basketball. After all, it was Holger who accompanied Dirk to Australia for weeks after the 2007 first-round collapse when Nowitzki just needed to clear his head. As Nowitzki adapted to the NBA, a completely different culture in America, and life on his own all at once, it was Holger who was a steady influence. He was like a second father.

As Nowitzki's career progressed, Holger settled into a steady schedule where he would visit the U.S. twice per season—once early on, staying in hotels or later Nowitzki's guest rooms, and a second time during the playoffs. He traveled with Nowitzki for the entire 2011 NBA Finals, always watching from a seat in the stands a dozen rows behind the Mavericks' bench, always seemingly wearing the same plaid shirt and leather jacket. Those who have sat near him describe him as completely emotionless, never cheering or even standing when his star pupil made a big play. But during timeouts he'd gesture at Nowitzki, the two communicating nonverbally about something Nowitzki was doing right or wrong.

Geschwindner's philosophies often seemed mad, but they were heavily based in science. He has continued running basketball camps in Germany, which he calls "The Institute of Applied Nonsense," where he emphasizes learning to control your body and to master it. Nowitzki's "perfect shot" was mathematically calculated early on. Geschwindner used calculus to determine the optimal trajectory and release point. (Using his background in physics, Geschwindner found it's 60 degrees.)

Geschwindner worried about the effect of constant weight-lifting on a growing teenager's joints. Instead, he put Nowitzki through natural strengthening exercises: rowing with his teammates or bailing hay at a local farm. He encouraged Nowitzki (and any pupil he has coached since) to develop skills outside basketball like learning an instrument, likening the connected nature of a jazz band to organized team sports like basketball. Geschwindner assigned required reading, too, all meant for well-rounded development.

Not every habit Geschwindner instilled persists with Nowitzki today. He stopped playing the saxophone, for example, after getting a tooth knocked out during the 2001 playoffs. Nowitzki tried to keep a journal a decade back, but it felt too much like a chore. A young Nowitzki could do the splits and walk to half court on his hands, something an older one knows better than to attempt. But many more of Geschwindner's obsessive teachings have continued, helping mold Nowitzki into a 13-time All-Star. "I realized that he was not just developed by an average coach out there," Donnie Nelson said in the 2014 Nowitzki documentary, *The Perfect Shot*, "that this was a coach with a very high IQ."

It's probably not an approach that would have worked in the United States. American basketball demanded that big men rebound and work out of the post, and shooting was viewed as a gimmick or niche. "If he was born in the United States, there's a pretty good chance with all of the specialization of our kids that a guy like that would be taught to rebound the ball, get it to a point guard, and then get it off the glass on the other end," Nelson said.

Nowitzki's teammates have marveled at the duo over the year—both at how long the two would work after a practice and how different it looked from what any of them were used to.

"You just watched it. It was like he was rehearsing," former teammate Corey Brewer told me. "And he'd go out there and kill everyone with the same moves he was just doing in slow mo."

With his work ethic and seven feet of athleticism, Nowitzki was the perfect pupil for Geschwindner's teaching. Holger couldn't have created a basketball assassin like Nowitzki out of thin air. But the student himself is quick to heap credit on the teacher. Nowitzki understands he was just a gangly 16-year-old needing direction when Geschwindner found him. That chance meeting changed his life. "I have no idea if I would have even stuck with it [without him]," Nowitzki told me.

There's one moment immediately after Game 6 of the 2011 NBA Finals that cannot go unmentioned. As Nowitzki fought to control his own emotions on the court, a camera found Geschwindner in the stands. The normally stoic mentor was smiling—well, almost—as his mouth twitched upwards in spite of himself, his eyes not quite as dry as usual. You could see his pride in watching his understudy finally reach his zenith.

39 Visit the American Airlines Center

The American Airlines Center is a spectacle. That's what Mark Cuban wants. If you're a traditionalist who only cares about the basketball, this might not be the best viewing experience for you. But with the flashing neon and bouncing pop music reverberating off the walls and the digital shorts involving players against green screens playing at every timeout, the AAC will attempt to entertain everyone who walks through its doors. You don't have to be a Mavericks die-hard or a basketball expert. You just have to want two-and-a-half hours of enjoyment.

The Mavericks moved into the $420 million arena in 2001 along with the Dallas Stars. It was a state-of-the-art arena in downtown Dallas, located in the Victory Park area, and it has since become the premier venue for many major acts that come through

What to Know About AAC

Dining

The area around the American Airlines Center has slowly been building up over the past few years. It's not on the same level as Deep Ellum or Bishop Arts, but if you're interested in going to dinner before a game, there are a few spots to hit up. I can personally recommend Olivella's for great pizza or BuzzBrews for more traditional American bar food, while Happiest Hour is good if you're only looking for a drink. (It fills up after games, but it's also huge.) You don't have to go too far north into Uptown to find more spots either. You could even visit the Perot Museum—which is excellent—and walk over to the AAC when you're done for the game.

There are plenty of food options inside the arena, of course. The two standouts are a couple Taco Bueno locations and two 7-11 Slurpee spots located around the concourse. Old No. 7 Club and other restaurants/bars are located around the premises, too, though, like everything in the arena, you'll be paying extra for the convenience.

National Anthem

I've heard a hundred different versions of it and I can confidently say the best ones are sung briskly with some heart. Michael Borts is a Dallas native whom the Mavericks frequently enlist and he's great.

The Rafters

Find the 2011 championship banner because that's forever. There are also ones for Western Conference and Southwest Division championships. The Stars hang their banners, too, and the 1999 Stanley Cup banner is a nice sight. There's often a blimp that flies around the arena before the game because marketing never stops. It took me at least three years covering the Mavericks to notice there's two disco balls hanging from the ceiling, too.

T-Shirt Cannon

The Mavericks have a number of activities they run through during timeouts. The best is when they just play a video on the board or when two contestants battle off in the Whataburger Fry Toss. The worst is the kiss cam, but hey, I've been saying that for years, and pro sports arenas are still trotting it out there at every game.

Watch out for the T-shirt cannon, though, when the Mavericks have a pump-up team parade onto the court and throw rolled-up T-shirts into the crowd. I often sit in the press box and you'd think I'd be safe there—about as high up in the arena as you can be—but no. At least a dozen times, my life has flashed before my eyes when a shirt carries all the way from the floor and hits the wall right behind or below me. It's not as bad as the time a foul baseball destroyed someone's laptop sitting next to me—since T-shirts fortunately are more pliable—but it's close.

Halftime Entertainment
I hope, for your sake, that it's Red Panda, Quick Change, or something involving dogs. Those are by far the best halftime acts. Otherwise, be prepared for some sort of wild gymnastics act.

Mavs ManiAACs
Most basketball teams have a dance crew, but the Mavericks double down with another dance crew of ManiAACs. Basically, it's a bunch of big dudes with better-than-average dancing skills that are always loved by Maverick fans.

MFFLs
It's a nickname—or slogan? Rallying call? Motto?—that has survived since the early days of Mark Cuban's ownership. Literally short for Mavericks Fan For Life, it means be rowdy, proud, and loud all game. When an opposing player goes to the line for crucial free throws, yell your butt off. When Dirk Nowitzki hits yet another clutch shot, holler for joy like it's the best day of your life. If you enter the American Airlines Center, this is your one sworn duty.

town. The venue has hosted 2016 election campaign rallies; four UFC events; concerts like Rihanna, Lady Gaga, and Kanye West; and All-Star games for both the NBA and the NHL.

Until late 2016 the team practiced at the AAC, too. There's a single practice court located under the arena that still gets used by players shooting on off days and sometimes before or after games. However, the team's primary practice facility has moved a few hundred yards across Interstate 35 to a standalone location.

Before starting the 2018 season, the Mavericks boasted the longest active sellout streak in the NBA. It began on December 15, 2001, and it has now spanned 637 games. It's a misleading figure, to be honest. Of the 19,200 seats available, all but a couple thousand are already "purchased" by season-ticket holders. For some games the Mavericks have less than 1,000 actual tickets to sell to reach the sellout. Still, that speaks to how good the Mavericks have been over the past decade.

40 Jason Kidd's Second Stint

Jason Kidd and Dirk Nowitzki met as teammates wearing different uniforms at the 2008 All-Star Game. A deal between the Mavericks and the New Jersey Nets centered around Kidd had been agreed upon, but it wouldn't be officially completed until that Monday. Instead, a Western Conference All-Star and an Eastern Conference All-Star joked around on the court in New Orleans, knowing they would soon be on the same side.

The Kidd deal was polarizing when it happened; essentially, the Mavericks gave up two draft picks to swap 24-year-old Devin Harris for the 34-year-old Kidd. Many fans hated dealing Harris, a good young player with a bright future. But when Kidd turned out to be a perfect cog at point guard for their championship team, no one was complaining.

In May 2008 after the Mavericks were eliminated, Mark Cuban wrote a blog post explaining his thought process behind making the Kidd-for-Harris swap. "We went back and forth about whether or not we should trade Devin. We knew he was a good point guard, with the potential to be amazing. What we didn't know was how long that would take," he wrote on blog-maverick.com. "In Jason Kidd, we felt we would get a player that would make it easier for Dirk, Josh, Jet to get open shots. That Avery would no longer have to scream to push the ball, that JK was the best in the business at pushing the ball in the open court. Plus, our rebounding had suffered this year vs last, JKidd is a great rebounder, and the presses that had caused us problems, would no longer be a problem."

Kidd's numbers weren't flashy, and his play was less so, but he fit those Mavericks squads perfectly. As a versatile defender, his presence allowed smaller backcourts involving Jason Terry or J.J. Barea (and sometimes both) to thrive. His basketball IQ gave Rick Carlisle— a former high IQ point guard who demanded more from that position than any other—someone whom he could trust.

That trust didn't come immediately, mind you. Kidd and Carlisle often clashed in the early days of their relationship, mostly about the offense. Carlisle had always preferred to control the pace from the sideline by calling frequent plays, something Kidd couldn't stand. He just wanted to play ball and let the results speak for themselves. "I think they both respected each other, but they didn't agree too much," teammate J.J. Barea told ESPN's Tim MacMahon in 2015 for an article that detailed much of the previously unreported power struggle with the Mavericks.

Eventually, Kidd's arguments reshaped how Carlisle viewed offense, and it was a "flow offense" led by Kidd, one that mostly avoided set play calls, that won Dallas the championship in 2011. That Kidd could fundamentally change the mind of one of the NBA's most stubborn coaches speaks better than anything else about his understanding of the game.

A poor shooter most of his career, Kidd also turned into a reliable sharpshooter during his time with the Mavericks—perhaps none more than the first two games of the 2011 playoff run.

Despite never scoring more than 21 all season, Kidd dropped 24 in Game 1 before scoring 18 more in Game 2. Without those abnormal scoring bursts, you can wonder if the Mavericks would have even advanced past the first round.

An odd ending—Kidd told the Mavericks he'd re-sign during the 2012 offseason before abruptly bailing to the Knicks—doesn't take anything away from Kidd's second stint. That he was drafted by the team years before only adds another wrinkle to what he was able to accomplish here. Kidd never played his best years in Dallas, but he bookended his Hall of Fame career with the Mavericks both times. Before long, that will send his jersey into the rafters.

41 Boneheaded Plays

In some ways basketball is a simple game. Two baskets, one ball, 10 players. You try to score and you do everything you can to prevent the other team. Oh, and dribble the ball.

But basketball grows exponentially more complicated as you reach higher levels. For every second a player is on the court, there are a hundred different outcomes. Most of the decisions are made instantly and compartmentalized into some part of the brain that just knows the correct choice. But occasionally, at the worst possible time, these decisions short-circuit. These are those Mavericks moments.

Antoine Wright's Phantom Foul
It was the final seconds of Game 3 of the 2009 Western Conference Semifinals. The Mavericks trailed in the series 2–0 but led the Denver Nuggets 105–103 at home and were defending on final

possession. Antoine Wright was a journeyman who ended up in Dallas for two seasons after arriving during the Jason Kidd trade. That year, he started 53 games for the Mavericks, filling in the empty two-guard spot while Jason Terry came off the bench. Although his offense appeared only sporadically, Wright had carved out a role that season playing hard-nosed, smart defense that first-year head coach Rick Carlisle loved. He earned the assignment guarding Carmelo Anthony on that play.

The Mavericks could commit one foul without putting the Nuggets onto the free throw line, and as Anthony dribbled on the right wing, Wright started to take that foul. He bumped Anthony, started to wrap his arms around, and then for reasons unknown, he stopped. Wright even took a step back, throwing his hands up in the air in the universal "I didn't do it" symbol. The whistle didn't blow. Anthony stepped around him and knocked down a three, giving Denver a one-point lead with a second left on the clock.

It was bizarre. In fairness to Wright, there was contact. He fooled the ESPN play-by-play announcer calling the game. "And there's the foul," the announcer said, before realizing, "They didn't call it!" It's especially mystifying, considering the context of the game, where the referees had called 61 fouls, and the teams attempted 89 combined free throws in that game. Given how quick the whistles were all game, it's very surprising that Wright's actions were ignored.

But Wright still should have bear-hugged Anthony, completely wrapping around him to make sure the foul was called correctly and eliminating any doubt. The Nuggets would have needed to inbound the ball with just two seconds on the clock and hit a winning shot instead of casually stepping into one like Anthony did. Denver won the game, went up 3–0 on the Mavericks, and won the series in Game 5.

Josh Howard's Invisible Timeout

Let's just say it right now: it wasn't really Josh Howard's fault. Dwyane Wade had just hit the first of two free throw attempts, tying the game at 100 each. With 1.7 seconds left in Game 5 of the 2006 NBA Finals, another made free throw meant Dallas was in trouble. They had already lost twice after taking a quick 2–0 lead in the series. Now, they were on the verge of going down 3–2.

Dallas did have one timeout remaining, which would allow them to advance the ball from their own baseline to half court. If Wade made the second foul shot, they could call it, regroup, set up a play, and hopefully win on a buzzer beater. They had a real chance. They didn't need a desperation buzzer beater.

As Wade approached the free throw line for his second attempt, though, a referee stopped him. Dallas called a timeout, the official says. More specifically, Howard called the last one, and now the Mavericks were out. Josh Howard said he didn't call for a timeout after the game. In the television footage of the game, an animated Avery Johnson makes the timeout gesture—one hand crossed perpendicular over the other to from a capital T—on the sideline. Johnson admitted to doing that but said he thought it was clear he wanted a timeout to be called after Wade's attempt—not before. Perhaps the referee saw Johnson's quick signal, or perhaps Howard passed along the timeout reminder incorrectly. Either way, the Mavericks were whistled for the last one against their wishes. They could really only hope that Wade missed.

Wade didn't. The Heat went up 101–100, the Mavericks' desperate full-court heave fell short, and the Heat went up 3–2 in the series. As unfair as it is, the moment lives on as one of the NBA's biggest gaffes and one that is always attributed to Josh Howard.

Derek Harper's Nonexistent Lead

Through 12 seasons and 872 games, Derek Harper is one of the most important players in the Mavericks' history. In the 1984

Western Conference Semifinals, though, Harper was just a rookie playing in the postseason for the first time. And with seconds left in regulation in Game 4, Harper forgot the score. The game was tied at 108 with 12 seconds left when the Mavericks rebounded a missed sky hook by Kareem Abdul-Jabbar. Rolando Blackman grabbed the shot and passed it along to Dale Ellis. The ball ended up in Harper's hands.

But the rookie thought the score was 109–108 and that the Mavericks were up one, rather than it being a tied game. Instead of attempting a game-winning shot, he held the ball until the buzzer sounded. The game went to overtime, where the Mavericks lost 122–115 and the Los Angeles Lakers took a 3–1 lead. Los Angeles eliminated Dallas in the next game. In the years following, Harper often roasted the Lakers when the two teams played. And yeah, his career obviously ended up okay. "It was a mistake, and I think I learned from it," Harper told the *Los Angeles Times* in 1988. "I didn't expect to go jump off a roof after it. But I don't think a lot of people expected to hear from me again. I think they thought it would ruin my career."

42 Dirk's Australia Getaway

Dirk Nowitzki had gone to Australia because there no one cared who he was. Nearly 10,000 miles separated Nowitzki from the first-round humiliation at the hands of the Golden State Warriors in 2007, but Nowitzki couldn't stop thinking about it. As the Mavericks swept through the regular season on their way to 67 wins, it looked like a revenge tour. They were mad at the Miami Heat, at the referees, at Dwyane Wade's unrelenting procession to the free throw line, and at their own failings that caused them to blow a 2–0 lead in the 2006 NBA Finals. Nowitzki was the best player in the league that regular season, and that postseason was supposed to continue his excellence and make up for any shortcomings the season before. The Mavericks were expected to play into May and June that season because of a lengthy playoff run that vindicated everything that had come before it. That's where Nowitzki was supposed to be.

Instead, he was in Australia.

Nowitzki had wilted against the Warriors—the only team the Mavericks hadn't beaten that regular season—and his team followed his lead. Looking back, blame can be assigned to everyone involved. Once it was over, Nowitzki just wanted to get away, but he was made to wait two more weeks because he had to attend his own MVP ceremony. He barely left the house before giving that subdued speech and fleeing to a continent as far away from his home as he could go.

Nowitzki's lone traveling companions were his mentor, Holger Geschwindner, and a bottle of whiskey. Nowitzki spent most summers with Geschwindner over the years, but it was usually squirreled away in a gym making countless jump shots and fine-tuning a lethal game even more. But the 62-year-old German agreed with Nowitzki—he needed to get away. "It seemed like Australia was the best spot to go," Nowitzki told ESPN's Marc Stein a couple months after he returned. "Nobody cares about the MVP down there."

They flew into Dubai before starting the sojourn in Sydney, where they experienced Beethoven's symphonies in the city's world famous opera house. They went to Melbourne and Adelaide before moving out toward the Outback, where they slept in youth hostels and in a car. They visited Uluru, the enormous sandstone rock formation in the Northern Territories, and made several trips to Tahiti and New Zealand. Nowitzki strummed a guitar around a campfire and read German novels on the seashore near the Great Barrier Reef. He had always wanted to see Australia, though certainly not under these conditions.

Sometimes, Nowitzki and Geschwindner talked about basketball. Other times, they talked about everything but. A few times, Nowitzki said they never exchanged more than a few words for an entire day. Nowitzki didn't bring a razor, letting a full beard grow out and his shaggy blonde locks get more unkempt than ever. It was an appropriate metaphor for his emotional state, and you can imagine the thoughts about that series that must have run through Nowitzki's mind.

Cell service went in and out intermittently, and Nowitzki said he only watched a single half of the NBA Finals that year. But while he was separated from fans and media members who criticized him or cast disbelief, he couldn't escape his own critical thoughts. Nowitzki is one of the greatest competitors the league has ever known. To lose on that stage, against a team who had barely scraped its way into the playoffs, in a year that was supposed to redeem all the Mavericks' past failings, versus a former coach who helped turn him into the player he was, must have emotionally wrecked him. Certainly, he blamed himself for it more than anyone else at first.

But the trip—going weeks without even touching a basketball—was exactly what Nowitzki needed. "Actually, I feel pretty good right now," he said in an ESPN interview. "I think I got over the worst of it. The two months I took off were the longest I haven't touched a ball in 10 years or more."

After five weeks on the other side of the world, Nowitzki began to realize he didn't bear the individual weight of that playoff loss on his shoulders. He talked about the absurd shots the Warriors hit frequently and how that team was uniquely suited to beating the Mavericks. Although 2007 will always rank as one of Nowitzki's biggest disappointments, he accepted that in Australia.

43 The Biggest Fan of Them All

Pink noisemakers. A bedazzled, flamboyant Mavericks championship jacket. Custom-made boots from a shop in Fort Worth. Sunglasses and sometimes dyed hair. A front-row seat whether he's attending a game at home or on the road. Don Knobler, the Mavericks' biggest superfan, is impossible to miss.

You have probably seen Knobler on television or spotted him near the floor if you've attended a game. He's not a heckler or a screamer because his outfit does the talking for him. He has 500 different outfits, and that doesn't include the many he has donated to his church.

Knobler and his wife, Damaris, first bought Mavericks season tickets back in the 1990s when Ross Perot Jr. still owned the team. They haven't looked back since, regularly attending home games and working with the Mavericks to make special, team-sponsored trips on the road with fans who are lucky enough to win trips. "We like to be an active participant at what we do, either in our church or here with the Mavericks," Knobler told DFW.com in 2015. "In life you really need something to occupy your free time, and for us it is the Dallas Mavericks."

The local broadcast knows how to find him for B-roll footage as they cut to break, and the Knoblers are known by virtually everyone within the Mavericks organization. Knobler, a real estate magnate, acquires most of his outfits in Las Vegas, where he visits twice a year. His Mavericks championship jacket was a $5,500 investment. But Knobler's most prized possession is his 2011 championship ring, which the team gifted to him. You can't assign a value to that.

44 Some Good Dirk Stories

When writing, researching, and reporting this book, I definitely learned that everyone who has spent time around Dirk Nowitzki has a good story to share. Here are a few of my favorite ones that didn't fit neatly into another chapter.

Charles Barkley about playing a teenaged Dirk at an NBA Global Game in Germany.

"[It was me,] Michael, Scottie, a bunch of guys, NBA players. Dirk's like 18. This is when Scottie was 'the best defender' in the world. So Dirk is kicking our ass, he has like 25 at halftime, and me and Michael are like, 'Scottie, you've got to pick it up a little bit.' And he's like, 'Man, I'm gonna lock him down in the second half, I'm gonna lock him down in the second half.' Dirk ends with like 52. So I was like, 'Dude, who the hell are you?'

"And he starts talking, he's like 18 or 19, and I asked, 'Where you gonna play at?' He says, 'I have to go in the army,' and I say, 'Dude, you can't go in the army playing like that.' So I'll tell you what. I called Nike and I told them, 'Find out about this kid, tell him I'll give him anything he wants to go to Auburn. Just tell him, anything he wants, we'll get it done…The next year, the Mavs—actually, Milwaukee drafted him, so I was like, 'You should have gone to Auburn, we would have a few banners up right now.'"

Ian Mahinmi, former Nowitzki teammate (2010–12)

"I've gotta watch what I say, man! I have so many good stories. The thing about Dirk that I respect so much—for him to be one of the greatest power forwards ever, he was such a humble guy, such a

Plenty of good stories exist about the beloved Dirk Nowitzki, who has spent nearly two decades playing for the Mavericks.

great teammate. He goes from one to 15 guys in the locker room, he likes to joke with everybody, likes to make everybody feel like they're a part of something. When you have your leader showing that type of character, it carries a ways. It's something that always sticks out. It's funny. Throughout my career, I've been around a lot of great guys. I've been around the greatest, [Tim Duncan], David West, a bunch of good guys, and a bunch of guys who are going to be Hall of Famers or finishing their careers as one of the best. And that's like one trend that always comes back, the great guys, the great leaders, how they always care about everybody else and how they always make you feel like you're an important piece of everything they do. And to be honest with you, in that Game 6, I made two shots—the buzzer beater and I took a one-legger like Dirk. Believe it or not, messing with Dirk every day, being with him, seeing him, all that stuff participated in me being confident enough to do stuff like that on the biggest stage ever. Dirk is just one of those guys, a great leader, great character, just a great champion."

Scott Brooks, longtime NBA coach who faced Nowitzki in the 2011 Western Conference Finals

"There's so many [stories]. I've been able to coach him in an All-Star Game, and just being around him then, that was special moments not only for myself, but the staff. We came away from that game just understanding that is one good dude, and he loves the game, and you can talk basketball with him, and he was gracious enough to not put any pressure on me. He wasn't interested in playing any big minutes, getting a lot of shots. He just wanted one five or six-minute stint. He's going to go down as one of the greatest players of all time and rightfully so. The guy is, if not the best, one of the top two or three shotmakers in the game's history. Oh, and the 24-for-24 free throws in that game [Game 1 of the 2011 Western Conference Finals against the Mavericks], whatever it was...That's a memory."

Ben Rogers, longtime Dallas sports radio host

"My favorite thing is the Dirk shirt. This was during the playoffs. A friend of ours named Jordan Rogers, he was a T-shirt guy. He had made this artwork of Dirk's face. He made these stickers and signs and during that playoff run. They were everywhere. During the playoff run, he made a shirt of Dirk's face and he asked us to help him define what Dirk is, and it was something like, "German, workhouse, with wide shoulders. Unstoppable." It made it look like it was a Webster's definition. He wasn't selling them. He was just making them, some for us and some for him. He wanted to get one to Dirk, and since we were going on the team plane when the [2011] playoffs started, I gave one of the shirts to Al Whitley, equipment manager, and asked him, 'Can you show this to Dirk and see if he likes it?' And he went up to the front of the plane, came back, and gave me the shirt back, and said, 'Dirk said it's trash.' And I was like, 'Ah man, he doesn't like it?' I thought the shirt was pretty cool.

"We can't wear team gear in the locker room. We might lose our credential. But I decided to wear the shirt under my shirt to one of the first games. After the game I was like, 'Dude, you didn't like this shirt?' And there was no one around. He said, 'Nah, that shirt's tight. I love that shirt.' I think he just didn't want to—in front of everyone as he's holding it up—say, 'Oh, this shirt saying I'm unguardable, I'm the best, is amazing.' But he secretly liked it. So I told him, 'Dude, I'm going to wear this shirt under my shirt at every game because it's good luck.

"After the next game, I'm interviewing or talking to him or whatever, and he said, 'Let me see it, you're wearing the shirt?' And I'm like, 'Yup.' So he checked for the shirt. We went to Los Angeles, I show him the shirt, all good. They win the second game, they beat L.A., and I only had one shirt. I didn't do laundry, so I didn't wear it. We're in the locker room, and he says, 'Let me see it!' and I say, 'Dude, I'm not wearing it.' And he acted like he was so sad. They're on this epic run and they're kicking ass, and he goes and sits down over at his locker, looks down on the ground, looks back at me dejectedly, and looks back down shaking his head like it's the most devastating thing that happened. The rest of the way, regardless of how clean it was, I wore that shirt. And that night when we celebrated the championship, I was wearing that shirt as well."

45 Calvin Booth's Layup

Calvin Booth suited up for seven teams in 10 seasons but only played 366 games. His 6'11" height kept him in the league as a backup center. He rarely started and often only played in emergency situations or during blowouts. He finished with career averages of 3.3 points and 2.8 rebounds. But Booth has a permanent place in the history of the Mavericks, thanks to one night in 2001. Fittingly, the moment that secured his legacy in Dallas was an ordinary layup.

It was May 2001, and the Mavericks had made the playoffs for the first time in a decade. Down two games to zero to the Utah Jazz, an experienced playoff team led by their wizened stars Karl Malone and John Stockton, Dallas didn't seem to have a chance. Honestly, the Mavericks were just happy to be there. Then, out of nowhere, the young Mavericks squad tied the series in Games 3 and 4 at home. In a best-of-five series, the next matchup was win or go home.

Game 5 was a slog. Steve Nash was scoreless through three quarters, and neither team cracked 80 points until there was minutes left in the fourth quarter. Twice, the Mavericks trailed by double figures before fighting back into the game. Shawn Bradley had started at center, but Don Nelson tried Booth in the fourth quarter. As each minute passed, Booth wondered when Nelson would finally pull him from the game in favor of his starting five. Instead, he remained on the floor the entire fourth quarter, grabbing six rebounds and blocking two shots. With less than 30 seconds remaining and the Mavericks trailing by one point, though, Booth still hadn't made a shot.

Dallas had the ball, Michael Finley found himself guarded by Stockton and took him into the post, where the Jazz were forced to double team. Booth, seeing the double team, came running from the far side of the floor to help Finley. The pass was made, Booth caught it under the basket, and he easily laid it in on the right side. "I never thought I would be a hero," Booth told reporters after the game. "I just wanted to give us a little boost."

Malone missed a potential game-winner as time expired, and Booth will always be remembered as the player who helped the Mavericks win their first of many playoff series in the Dirk Nowitzki era.

46 Fan Favorites

If you're a Mavericks fan, of course, you love Dirk Nowitzki. You grew up watching Rolando Blackman or Jason Terry. You lived and died with each Mark Aguirre or Michael Finley shot in the postseason. All these players have unforgettable memories. Occasionally, a player who isn't a star, and who might have only spent a few seasons in Dallas, captures your attention. Here are some players who won't be remembered in the grand narrative of the Mavericks, but deserve recognition all the same.

Nick Van Exel

There are a million great Nick Van Exel stories. The best one was when Van Exel was playing for the Los Angeles Lakers, and they were down 3–0 in a playoff series. During a timeout in the second half, it was clear Los Angeles wasn't coming back—and even if they were, it's not like they were going to win the series. The team typically broke the huddle by shouting, "1-2-3, team!" Van Exel, instead, yelled "Cancun!" The Lakers lost the game, but Van Exel took his summer vacation to Cancun.

It was years after that story that Van Exel joined the Mavericks, and he was only in Dallas for a season and a half—briefly in 2002 and then for the entirety of the 2002–03 season. Still, that's all it took for Van Exel to become a fan favorite. After all, his wild shot selection and never-give-a-shit attitude were impossible to dislike.

Darrell Armstrong

There's a reason Armstrong has been an assistant coach for years with the Mavericks since his retirement: players love him. You can't mistake his voice on the practice floor or in the hallway under the American Airlines Center. When a player hits at least 20 threes shooting around the arc after a practice, he's usually the one who runs to a bell the Mavericks have hanging up and rings it furiously. It's a longtime team tradition.

Armstrong was infectious as a player, too. Just six feet tall, he played like his personality: brash, confident, always in your face but somehow in a way that makes you laugh, even as he's scoring on you. Once with the Mavericks in 2005, Armstrong was fined $1,000 for grabbing a live mic before a game in Dallas and yelling, "How 'bout those Redskins?" to the crowd because Washington had just beaten the Cowboys in an NFL game earlier that day

Eduardo Najera

Najera got the most out of his ability. He was a scrapper, making up for moderate athleticism by exerting incredible effort around the rim. The first Mexican to ever be selected in the NBA draft and just the second to ever play in the league, he was also a trailblazer for his country. When Najera retired, he returned to Dallas, where he has worked for the organization in a number of roles over the years.

Brian Cardinal

Would the Mavericks have won the 2011 NBA Finals without Cardinal? Well, okay, probably. But his small but crucial role in Games 4, 5, and 6 of the Finals can never be forgotten. Perhaps his biggest contribution came in the locker room at halftime of Game 6, when he walked up to a struggling Dirk Nowitzki with a big, goofy grin and told him, "You've got them right where you want them!"

"What the hell is wrong with you," Nowitzki replied. But Cardinal went on to explain that Nowitzki had got all his misses out of the way, and a frustrated Nowitzki couldn't help but break a smile. Of course, in the second half, Nowitzki hit six straight shots to put the Miami Heat away in the final seven minutes and finally win his championship.

Yogi Ferrell

It's impossible to say how long the undrafted rookie will stick with the Mavericks. But after two great performances and improbable wins against the San Antonio Spurs and Cleveland Cavaliers in 2017, the player, who is listed at 6'0" and has the cool nickname, scored 32 points against the Portland Trail Blazers on February 3rd and tied a rookie record with nine made three-pointers. The next day, Dallas announced they had signed him to a two-year contract. Dallas embraced "Yogimania" that week.

47 Reunion Arena

One thing that helped Don Carter and Norm Sonju bring the Mavericks to Dallas was the opening of Reunion Arena. The new stadium broke ground in Dallas in 1978, a full two years before the Mavericks would be brought into existence. But with all of North Texas booming, the arena was built knowing business would come.

Owned and operated by the city of Dallas, Reunion Arena was located right next to Reunion Tower, Dallas' iconic observation tower that identifies its skyline more than any other building. With the arena's odd, flat-topped square design accented in red, the dark-glassed roof certainly stood out from the buildings around it. Originally, the arena received criticism, especially after Dallas mayor Robert Folsom avoided bringing the building to a public vote. But just two years after it opened, Folsom was bragging how it was the "most successful building the city owned."

It was hard to argue with him at the time. Reunion Arena opened in April 1980, the Mavericks were playing there by October, and the capacity for basketball games maxed out at 18,187 spectators. Their attendance failed to get near that mark for the first few seasons, as the Mavericks had the sixth worst attendance in the league their first season while averaging fewer than 8,000 fans per contest. But by the franchise's fourth year—the 1983–84 season—Dallas began filling out Reunion Arena on the regular. More than 580,000 fans came to see the Mavericks that season. With an average slightly over 14,000, that mark ranked as the fifth best in the league.

All the largest events in Dallas came to Reunion Arena. It had the biggest musical acts, including Queen, Prince, Michael Jackson, Whitney Houston, and Madonna. It hosted major sporting events:

the WCT Tennis Tournaments in the 1980s (which forced the Mavericks out of the building and caused Moody Madness), an NCAA Tournament Final Four, and the 1986 NBA All-Star Game. When the Dallas Stars of the National Hockey League moved to Texas in 1993, they made their home in Reunion. In 2005 the arena and the Dallas Convention Center next door hosted many of the Hurricane Katrina refugees who had been evacuated from New Orleans.

As the attendance rose and the Mavericks' success along with it, so did the fanbase. The best way to develop fans is to win a lot, and the team's six postseason appearances in seven years did just that. From 1984 to 1991, Dallas saw attendance hold steady between 680,000 and 700,000 fans per season. For three straight years, it was good enough for the second best mark in the league. But it wasn't just thousands of casual fans who flooded into Reunion Arena, but die-hards. Meet the Reunion Rowdys. "It was one of the loudest buildings I ever played in," former Mavericks star Brad Davis once said. "It got so loud sometimes that you couldn't even hear yourself think."

The Mavericks described any fan who came out to see them play as Reunion Rowdys, but it especially resonated with the most loyal fans. The atmosphere was both loud and electric, most notably during the 1988 Western Conference Finals. Facing the Los Angeles Lakers in Game 6 on the brink of elimination, fans cajoled the team to "Beat L.A." with chants and shouts all game. The sound was recorded at 121 decibels, the same level as a jet engine, and Dallas did indeed beat Los Angeles in a 105–103 victory.

By the 1990s the arena's flaws—most notably a lack of lucrative luxury boxes—began to be overwhelming. Reunion Arena's most memorable tenant underwent the same decline, suffering through the '90s with losing seasons and finishing with a 428–417 overall record while at Reunion Arena. (To be fair, the Dallas Stars went to the Stanley Cup Finals twice, including a win in 1999. The stadium wasn't totally devoid of good times.)

With a move to the new American Airlines Center pending the next season, Mavericks fans had one final hurrah in the 2001 playoffs when Dallas beat the Utah Jazz in a first-round series. In the game-clinching Game 5, Mark Cuban offered free tickets to any Reunion Rowdy who wanted to make the trip up to Utah, ultimately handing out 400 free ones. In 2008 after losing millions of dollars over the past six years, the Dallas City Council unanimously voted an end for Reunion Arena. The city held out briefly, hoping to lure Hollywood into imploding the arena for a big-budget movie shoot and thus footing the bill. When no one was interested, the site was officially demolished in November 2009.

48 Avery Johnson

It was April 2006 when Avery Johnson learned he was being awarded the NBA Coach of the Year. After replacing Don Nelson halfway through the previous season, it was only his first full season as a head coach and it seemed like the Mavericks had found their coach of the future. Instead, as it turned out, Johnson's career only went downhill from that moment forward. Two years later, he was fired.

Johnson's coaching career features what is one of the most sudden rises to success and falls from grace in the NBA's history. It's certainly up there. With his distinctive Southern drawl and a close connection with the locker room, thanks to his long and relatively recent playing career, Johnson was well-liked. But there's a lot more to a head coach than that, which Johnson learned over the course of his five seasons in Dallas. Too often, he pushed the wrong button—and lost his job because of it.

It was March 2005 when Coach Nelson stepped down in the middle of the season. The timing was abrupt, but the split had been brewing for more than a year. There were fundamental differences in philosophy between Nelson and Mark Cuban, ones that pushed their relationship to a breaking point. Though both sides remained friendly, it was clear to Nelson that his time with the team had expired. Nelson, also the Mavericks' general manager, named Johnson as his replacement. Johnson had carved out a 16-year career as a point guard over the previous decades, most prominently playing and winning a championship with the San Antonio Spurs in 1999. He had played backup guard under Nelson from 2001 to 2003 and when Johnson retired in 2004 he returned to Dallas as an assistant coach with the understanding that he was being groomed for the lead position.

It was all roses for Johnson at first. Nicknamed "Lil General" for his fiery temper, Johnson pushed Dirk Nowitzki to develop his low-post game and led the Mavericks to a 60–22 record in the 2005–06 season. Not only did Johnson win Coach of the Year, but the Mavericks pushed through the first three rounds of the playoffs for the first time in franchise history.

Everyone knows how the 2006 NBA Finals ended. Of the hundreds of decisions you can second-guess from that playoff series—like Johnson's decision to double team Shaquille O'Neal instead of Dwyane Wade—one stands out above the rest. After a heartbreaking Game 3 loss, where the Mavericks blew a 13 point lead in the game's final six minutes, Johnson quickly pulled the Mavericks away from their downtown Miami hotel to Fort Lauderdale, nearly an hour away from the arena. "And that's when Avery kind of lost it after the game on the bus," Dirk Nowitzki recalled in an ESPN interview. "He announced on the bus that we're moving tomorrow. And then the next day after practice is when we moved to Fort Lauderdale or wherever it was, that Marriott…He completely lost it, yelling and screaming, 'There's too much family here, too many distractions.'"

The hastily thrown together plans meant the Mavericks had to share rooms. Dirk Nowitzki roomed with Darrell Armstrong, while Jason Terry was bunking with Erick Dampier. It wasn't an ideal scenario, but even after the fact, the players don't blame the loss on it. "People will say what they will about Avery, but I thought it was the right strategy," Terry said in the same ESPN article. "I may have sent the family members to that hotel and not us, but that's just me. But I think he was doing the right thing—just trying to get refocused and realize the opportunity ahead of us."

Still, the Mavericks blew that two-game lead, and blame for that fell on Johnson. After the Mavericks bounced back with a 67-win season, Dallas ran into the one team they couldn't beat, the Golden State Warriors. Johnson chose to adjust his starting lineup to the Warriors' small-ball lineup despite being the top seed. It clearly should have been the other way around.

You could see the writing on the wall for Johnson by 2008. Devin Harris regressed under Johnson's leadership, and then the Mavericks swapped him for Jason Kidd. Johnson sparred with Kidd, playing him off the ball and not giving him control of the offense. Johnson relied heavily on Eddie Jones and Devean George that season, using them as veteran crutches despite mediocre returns at best. When the Mavericks had another first-round exit in 2008, it was clear. "But now, if and when Johnson oversees another painfully disappointing playoff failure, Cuban must fire him. I know I would," the *Dallas Observer*'s Richie Whitt penned after the first two games of that series. The fanbase had turned against him, too, even launching fireavery.com in protest.

That first-round loss to the New Orleans Hornets doomed him. The Mavericks fired him shortly afterward, just two years after his Coach of the Year award, and that's how the Johnson era ended.

After a couple seasons as a broadcaster, Johnson was hired as head coach of the Brooklyn Nets in 2010. He was fired by the end of 2012 and is now the head coach at the University of Alabama, where he had the No. 3-ranked recruiting class, heading into the 2017 season.

49 Vince Carter

Vince Carter knew the ball was coming his way. "Get ready," Rick Carlisle told him in the huddle. "It's going to be there. You're going to knock down this shot."

It was Game 3 of the 2014 first-round series, and the Mavericks were down two points to the San Antonio Spurs with 1.7 seconds left. Dallas was here after a late rally that tied the game, only to see Manu Ginobili answer back with a shot that spun around the basket painfully long before dropping in. Now it was down to Vince. Jose Calderon inbounded the ball. As Monta Ellis sprinted one way, Carter crashed the other—straight to the corner and straight toward a painful memory more than a decade old.

In 2001 as a member of the Toronto Raptors, Carter had missed a shot from the left corner in Game 7 of the Eastern Conference Semifinals. There had been two seconds left, and the Raptors were down by a point, a made shot away from his first NBA Finals. Carter caught the pass, pump faked once, and fired away—only to see it narrowly clank off the back iron. It was a miss that Carter said still haunts him to this day.

Thirteen years later, the ball came back to Carter, now in Dallas home whites. He caught the pass and pump faked once, letting Ginobili fly past him. Had he put his heels down, they would have landed on the out-of-bounds line, but he never did. Carter fired away, and with the ball halfway to its destination, the clock hit 0.0 and the buzzer sounded.

Swish.

Mark Cuban considers that three-pointer to win the game 109–108 as one of the five best shots ever hit in the team's history.

The Bizarro Near-Upset in 2014

This 2014 first-round series will confuse NBA historians in a few decades. It's confusing even right now. The San Antonio Spurs won the championship in 2014, sweeping through the final three rounds in an absolutely dominating show of offensive execution and defensive pride. Why they needed seven games to dispose of the No. 8 seed Mavericks—nearly losing—will never make sense.

San Antonio fans often blame Carter's shot, but the Mavericks had already won Game 2 in a blowout. They could have won Game 1, too, after leading by 10 points with eight minutes remaining before managing just four points the rest of the way. And no matter what you tell me, I'll always believe they would have won Game 4 if DeJuan Blair wasn't ejected.

Blair was a reserve who barely played in the first three games, but he completely changed Game 4 when he entered in the third quarter. By the time there was three minutes left in the game, Blair had 12 points and 11 rebounds in 16 minutes. After being knocked to the floor, Blair kicked his legs out without clear intent and hit Tiago Splitter in the head. He certainly deserved a flagrant foul but instead was questionably ejected and thus suspended for the rest of the game.

At that moment the Mavericks were leading by a point. They ended up losing 93–89. San Antonio won Game 5, Dallas returned serve in Game 6, and the Spurs finally started clicking in Game 7, and that 119–96 victory propelled their championship run. They deserved it, of course, and life moves on. But how they nearly lost that first-round series, we'll never know.

It's even more powerful, considering the backstory from Carter's career behind it. Carter may still regret that miss in 2001, but in at least a sense, this one provided *redemption*.

That's the best word to describe Carter's entire Mavericks tenure. Carter goes down as one of the best players in NBA history to never appear in the NBA Finals, and whether it's completely fair or not, much of that is blamed on him. It's true that Carter struggled in the postseason at times, averaging fewer points and worse shooting percentages than his regular-season marks.

There was also Carter's unhappy departure from Toronto, one that caused him to get booed on every trip back for years, and a reputation he didn't play hard. Carter had played for four teams when he joined the Mavericks in 2011. At the time many fans weren't even sure if they wanted him around. Instead, Cuban turned everyone into fans. "Let me just say that right now—Vince is a warrior. All these things I heard about him being soft, not playing hard, fuck that," Cuban told me in April of 2013. "That dude comes out to deliver every fucking night. I'm proud that he's on the Mavs, and he's one of the guys I want to retire…You guys talk about doing it for Dirk? Doing it for Vince is just as important."

In three seasons Carter became a consistent scorer off the bench, making plays for the second unit and occasionally turning back the clock to dunk on some hapless defender who didn't realize the 36-year-old Carter was still capable of making posters at the rim. He was always an encouraging teammates and team leader. He developed a great relationship with Nowitzki.

When his three-year deal ran out in 2014, the Mavericks wanted to bring Carter back. After spending money early, though, they simply couldn't offer Carter enough money. He opted for a richer deal with the Memphis Grizzlies. Carter ended up playing 234 total games in a Dallas uniform, and the culmination of it all was that shot in Game 3.

That one shot from the corner was something Mavericks fans will never forget. The bedlam following is nearly as memorable. Calderon started sprinting the wrong way. Brandan Wright stood in shock, still trying to process what had happened. There's one photo that sums up the moment better than any other I've seen. Taken mere seconds afterward, Nowitzki has his arm wrapped around Carter as he's screaming something into the roaring stadium. Ellis' hand is grabbing at Carter's head. Shane Larkin is jumping onto him on the other side to start a dogpile. And in the middle is Carter, a stone-faced assassin staring right into the camera, just pointing up to the scoreboard.

50 Donnie Nelson

On a June evening in 1998, the Mavericks acquired two unproven international players who both eventually turned into league MVPs. Professionally, it has to be Donnie Nelson's finest moment. Nelson held the assistant general manager title for the Mavericks in 1998, and his father Don Nelson served as the head coach and general manager in Dallas. But it was the younger Nelson who facilitated both moves, vouching for Steve Nash and personally scouting Dirk Nowitzki. Those two, along with Hakeem Olajuwon, remain the only international MVPs in league history.

Now Donnie is in his 18th season with the Mavericks, outlasting his dad and an ownership change, with no end in sight. He never imagined it working like this when he joined his dad in the Dallas front office in 1998, and it seemed even more unlikely when Mark Cuban bought the team from Ross Perot Jr. in 2000. In fact,

Donnie and the coaching staff assumed it was only a matter of time before Cuban cleaned house to install his own people. "We went out for what we called 'The Last Supper,'" Donnie told me. "We all got the news, and my dad got the call from Ross, and then I got the call from Ross. First thing out of his mouth is, 'I sold the team,' and my blood runs cold. And the second thing, 'I think you're going to be alright,' and when you hear that, it's usually because you're not. I think, *You're going to be alright?* [I'm] like, 'Okay, now I'm definitely gone.'"

One of the architects of the Mavericks, Donnie Nelson shakes hands with his father, Don Nelson, in 2002 after Don appointed him president of basketball operations.

With a father like Don Nelson, Donnie Nelson couldn't escape basketball if he had tried. Donnie didn't, embracing the sport and playing collegiately at a Division-III school, where he traveled internationally during the summers with a religious basketball outreach group. It was on these trips that he developed his passion for making basketball into a global game.

Donnie spent his first decade out of school working as an assistant wherever his dad was coaching. In 1995 he broke from him, however, to join the Phoenix Suns as an assistant. He was a major influence on their decision to draft Steve Nash, a Canadian point guard wrecking opponents at a small California university.

In 1998 he rejoined the elder Nelson, who had taken over as the Mavericks' head coach and general manager. In 2001 Donnie even coached Dallas to a 15–8 record while his dad recovered from cancer surgery, but his future had been firmly set in the front office. In 2002 he was promoted to team president, and when his father resigned, Donnie officially took over as the team's general manager.

He has drafted players from Greece, Lithuania, and Croatia. In 1999 Dallas selected Wang Zhizhi, the first Chinese player in the league. Especially early on, Donnie constantly traveled overseas to watch international prospects and scout for potential steals. Though some prospects never panned out, like Zhizhi, he proved he had an excellent eye for talent evaluation. Donnie endorsed budding superstar Giannis Antetokounmpo in the 2013 draft, but Cuban traded down in pursuit of cap space.

His time overseas, though, hasn't just been spent scouting, though. In 2004 he was honored by the Lithuanian government for his help with their national team, where Donnie worked for free as a coach in 1992 and for whom he helped raise sponsors throughout the following decade since Lithuania had just gained independence and couldn't rely on public funding. "That's what I take the most pride in," he told the *Fort Worth Star-Telegram* in 2003. "At the end of the day, to me, it's how many lives you've touched, how many people you've had a chance to help."

51 Best Celebrations

Basketball celebrations are becoming more creative than at any time in the past. Here are the best ones from the Mavericks.

Jason Terry

You have to put the JET first. Based off his initials—Jason Eugene Terry—the JET nickname fueled itself. When he hit a backbreaking three, we all demanded he spread his arms out, running back down the court, cruising back on defense like a skyliner coasting down to the runway after another successful passage across the ocean. I can't tell you how many times announcers declared, "The JET is on the runway." It was a flawless nickname/celebration combo.

Wesley Matthews

No one stole Terry's outstretched airplane celebration, but the same can't be said for Matthews' bow-and-arrow routine. Dozens of college and high school players have adopted it, whipping an invisible arrow from behind the back and firing it at their bench in celebration after hitting a three.

Dirk Nowitzki

Hold up three fingers. If you're an American, you probably just held up your second, third, and fourth fingers, tucking the thumb and pinkie beneath. Maybe you made the "OK" sign, with the thumb and index forming an "O" and the other three fingers sticking up. Nowitzki doesn't do either of those. Instead he raises his thumb, index and middle finger together after nailing a three.

Indicating a three-pointer in that way is a European trend, especially in Germany. That's just how Nowitzki does it, and he has turned that into a signature celebration. If you see him back-pedaling after burying a three from the top of the key, chances are those are the three fingers he stuck up in the air.

Vince Carter

Carter is proof that celebrations have evolved. Early in his career, he didn't need elaborate celebrations; his absurd soaring highlights spoke for themselves. But somewhere along the way, Carter picked up a signature routine: revving up like he was on a motorcycle, usually after an absurd dunk he shouldn't be capable of at his age.

DeShawn Stevenson

Stevenson was famous for the I-can't-feel-my-face routine, waving his hands in front of his head when he was "unconscious" shooting the ball behind the arc. He had mostly retired it by the time he came to Dallas, but it's an all-time one.

52 Study the Rulebook

James Naismith is credited with inventing the sport of basketball in 1891, but you would hardly recognize the game he originally created. It wasn't until the mid-1940s that basketball took on a recognizable form, adding fundamental rules like goaltending (1944), unlimited substitutions (1945), and in-game coaching (1949). Since then—even with the advent of the three-point line in

1979—the evolution of basketball has come gradually. Look back at more recent rules and strategies that have changed the game, and you'll see the Mavericks are involved in several.

Hack-a-Shaq

In his first year coaching the Mavericks during the 1997–98 season, Don Nelson wanted to test a theory. When there was a poor free throw shooter on the floor, wouldn't intentionally fouling him and making him take shots from the line yield fewer points than if his team played defense straight up? In a game on December 29, 1997, Nelson tried it out.

Nelson subbed in Bubba Wells deep off his bench and had him intentionally foul Dennis Rodman six straight possessions. It didn't work. Despite entering the game as a 38 percent foul shooter, Rodman shot 9-of-12. Wells' six fouls in just three minutes remains the record for the quickest an NBA player has fouled out of a game.

Nelson set that strategy aside for a couple years until his team played Shaquille O'Neal. It made sense; O'Neal scored more than 28,000 points in his career, but his 5,317 missed free throws ranked as the second most in the history of the NBA. As other coaches began employing the same strategy on O'Neal, it was eventually coined "Hack-a-Shaq."

One day soon, the NBA probably will ban Hack-a-Shaq. After all, free throws are the most boring part of this sport, and the NBA is an entertainment industry at its core. There's no reason for them to encourage such behavior, even if the strategy itself is valid. But for at least two decades, the NBA occasionally has used a strategy that was pioneered by Nelson and the Mavericks.

The Jerry Stackhouse Rule

Oh, Jerry. Come on, man! All you had to do was not let the secret slip. This is a two-part rule: it was first called the Gary Payton rule, but when the rule was expanded, so was the name. In 2005 Payton was traded from the Boston Celtics to the Atlanta Hawks, who intended to waive him for salary cap relief. Three days later Payton rejoined the Celtics. The NBA didn't love that, adding a 30-day waiting period before players traded from a team could re-sign with them.

That's alright, the Mavericks thought. As they planned to trade for Jason Kidd in 2008, they wanted to include Jerry Stackhouse, knowing he would be waived and they could just wait 30 days. Stackhouse, though, was a little too friendly about offering up details. "I get 30 days to rest, then I'll be right back," Stackhouse told the Associated Press at the time. "I ain't going nowhere."

Uh oh. Opposing team executives quickly complained, causing the NBA to tell the Mavericks they wouldn't be able to re-sign Stackhouse if he was included in the trade. Later, the rule was formalized: after a player is traded, if he is waived, he must wait one calendar year before he can rejoin a team who traded them. The Mavericks ended up trading for Jason Kidd with a different combination of players, and Stackhouse remained in Dallas. But now Stackhouse's name lives on whenever fans ask about re-signing players their team dealt away.

The Stepien Rule

Ted Stepien wanted to win games badly, but he also wanted to win games now. From 1981 to 1983, Stepien owned the Cleveland Cavaliers and decided to trade five consecutive first-round draft picks for veteran players who he thought would turn the franchise around. Every trade was a complete disaster, and Stepien was quickly run out of town.

Several of the first-round draft picks went to the Mavericks, including Derek Harper in 1983, Sam Perkins in 1984, Detlef Schrempf in 1985, and Roy Tarpley in 1986. Those picks helped turn the club into a playoff team just four seasons into its inception.

Today, thanks to the Stepien Rule, NBA teams cannot trade future first-round draft picks in multiple seasons, and all trades must be approved by the league office.

53 Where Dirk Stands All Time

Kareem Abdul-Jabbar sparked a controversy in early 2016 when he called Dirk Nowitzki a "one-trick pony" and said he wasn't "dominant" throughout his career. Abdul-Jabbar deserves utmost respect for his storied basketball career. The NBA's all-time leading scorer helped popularize the sport and has used his influence to push for positive change both in the NBA and in social issues off the court. But speaking in an hour-long conversation at George Mason University, Abdul-Jabbar voiced a few indisputably bad opinions about Nowitzki, a fellow living legend.

"Has there been an unstoppable move in the NBA since the sky hook? And I bring up Dirk's fadeaway," an audience member asked.

"You asked about Dirk Nowitzki," Abdul-Jabbar replied. "Dirk Nowitzki's shot is very hard to block, but I don't think that he was able to have a dominant career because he couldn't do other things. If he could have shot like that and rebounded and played defense and blocked shots, then he would have been all-around and he would have gotten more credit. He was like a one-trick pony. You want guys that can shoot like that on your team. I'm not saying that he lacked value, but he would have been considered at a higher level if he had done more on the court other than just shoot the ball."

Nearly everyone universally disagreed with Abdul-Jabbar's comments. Nowitzki diplomatically responded, telling ESPN, "I guess he's not a big fan of my game, which is okay. But I like to think I was dominant at some point—especially on the offensive end—of my career in my prime." Mavericks teammates and media members alike stuck up for him in the following week before the hullabaloo petered out. The reasons are clear.

Nowitzki isn't considered a top 10 all-time player like Abdul-Jabbar, but he's close. In a 2016 all-time ranking, ESPN put Nowitzki as the 17th best player in the league's history. He's the first and only player in league history to record 25,000 points, 10,000 rebounds, 1,000 blocks, 1,000 steals, and 1,000 three-pointers. That's a lot more tricks than one.

Let's repeat his accolades: 13-time All-Star, 12-time All-NBA selection, NBA champion, NBA MVP, and NBA Finals MVP. Only 14 players (at the start of the 2017–18 season) have been voted to the All-Star Game 13 or more times. Nowitzki also remains one of just four players to average 25 points and 10 rebounds in the playoffs—a list that Abdul-Jabbar isn't on, mind you.

Abdul-Jabbar criticized Nowitzki's rebounding, but Nowitzki is the No. 8 all-time defensive rebounder in NBA history. His offensive rebounding is much lower, but that's because Nowitzki constantly lived on the perimeter offensively and was never asked to crash the glass. Even defensively, Abdul-Jabbar's criticisms fall short. It's true: Nowitzki was never an elite shot blocker or defender, but he was consistently average on that end throughout the prime of his career, especially when paired with a defensive-minded center that could relieve him of the most taxing man-on-man assignments. One good example is Dallas' championship season, where the Mavericks were on average six points better defensively with Nowitzki on the floor than with him sitting, and that was by far the best on the team. Tyson Chandler's defensive impact in the same setting was only three points.

So where does Nowitzki really deserve to rank? ESPN's all-time ranking referenced earlier is a good place to start. Does everyone in their top 10 have a clear case over Nowitzki?

- Michael Jordan: yes, the greatest ever
- Kareem Abdul-Jabbar: yes, despite his comments
- LeBron James: yes
- Magic Johnson: yes, even with an early retirement
- Wilt Chamberlain: yes
- Larry Bird: yes, even without Nowitzki's longevity
- Bill Russell: yes, with more championship rings (11) than fingers
- Tim Duncan: yes, and even Nowitzki agrees
- Shaquille O'Neal: yes
- Hakeem Olajuwon: yes, given his two championships and two Defensive Player of the Year awards in addition to nearly 27,000 career points

It's hard to argue Nowitzki over the next five, too. Oscar Robertson also has an MVP and a championship and was the first player to ever average a triple-double. Nowitzki himself puts Kobe Bryant, ESPN's 12th ranked player, ahead of him, and his five championships speak volumes. Jerry West once averaged 40 points during an entire championship run and is the NBA logo. Julius Erving's NBA career is incredible (including an MVP season) even if you don't count his first five years dominating the ABA.

There are incredible players that come after that—Moses Malone, Charles Barkley, John Stockton, Karl Malone, David Robinson—and you can compare Nowitzki favorably to every one of them. I call Nowitzki a top 20 player of all time. If he's not in your top 30, please reevaluate.

54 Rick Pitino's Dirk Story

The Boston Celtics wanted Dirk Nowitzki long before he was a perennial All-Star. It's often said no one knew who Nowitzki was when the Mavericks selected him in the first round, but that's not true. It's best to let Rick Pitino—the legendary college basketball coach who was briefly the head coach of the Celtics—tell it. "I was over in Italy on vacation with my brother-in-law and his wife, and we did all our [draft] workouts and we took off for Rome," Pitino said in 2011. "We were on an Italian tour. And I got a call from the general manager Chris Wallace, and he said, 'Look, can you work this German kid out?' And I said, 'Chris, we've already finished all our workouts.'

"He said, 'No, I think this kid might be special. I want you to work him out.' And I said, 'Okay, so where am I going to work him out?' And he said, 'Okay, so we can't let anyone know you're working him out.'"

The workout was totally legal within the NBA's draft rules, but the Celtics wanted to hide it nevertheless. Despite one notable standout performance in the U.S. at the Nike Hoops Summit game, Nowitzki was still an overseas prospect who had relatively little exposure, and Boston thought it might be the only team who was seriously interested in him. "He came in with his trainer [Holger], his shooting coach, the guy you see on TV," Pitino said. "We find this place where we have security outside, and literally my brother, a Wall Street broker, is getting in gym shorts. I had to buy him shorts and sneakers and everything, and he was gonna be the guy who had to pass the ball while I worked [Dirk] out. And I worked him out for a good, hard hour and I was shaking after the workout and I met with both of them at lunch."

The Celtics had the 10th overall pick in the draft that year. Publicly, Nowitzki was supposed to spend another season overseas to fulfil his German military requirements, but Boston had learned there was actually a chance he could come over that following season. "I called Red Auerbach and I told him, 'Coach, we've got to keep this between you, me, and Chris,'" Pitino said. "Outside of that, I want nobody to know about this kid. And I said I found the next Larry Bird. Red was laughing, and he said, 'Are you kidding me?' And I said, 'No, he's different in a lot of ways because he's taller, but he jumps higher. I don't know about his passing skills or anything like that because I just worked him out [one on one], but this kid's going to set Boston on fire.'"

Pitino was beyond impressed. "You don't see it now, how high he could jump and run," he said. "I put him through some running and jumping drills back then, and [he] was amazing. Our mouths were open, and I'm running my brother-in-law up and down, and [Dirk's] putting on this shooting show like the likes I've never seen. So I was so, so pumped up."

The Mavericks had the sixth overall pick in the 1998 NBA Draft, but they knew they wanted to trade down. When Dallas called the Celtics to ask them about a potential swap, Pitino immediately had a sinking feeling it was about Nowitzki. "I hung up the phone and I said, 'Fuck, they know about Nowitzki. They know about him,'" Pitino said. "And prior to this, it wasn't even mentioned."

Instead, the Mavericks selected Robert "Tractor" Traylor. Or so it seemed. Minutes later, the rumors started circulating that Dallas had traded down three spots, and the Milwaukee Bucks selected Traylor while the Mavericks ended up with their real prize, Nowitzki. "It was so disappointing when all of a sudden that was pulled off, and we no longer had Dirk," Pitino said. "He said he was staying in the military, everything was all set, and we were getting him. And then it was all blown away, and we're stuck with nobody to draft."

Still, this story turns out alright for Pitino and the Celtics. Left on the board was another future Hall of Famer: Paul Pierce. "Now we're scrambling because Pierce was supposed to go second or third in the draft," Pitino said. "We were very excited that Paul Pierce slipped to 10. Everybody always asks me the question now, when I tell them that story: who would you rather have had, Pierce or Nowitzki? And Pierce has won a championship, obviously, with Boston, and it's an interesting debate of who's the better basketball player between the two of them. But it was an incredible day as I look back on it—my brother-in-law running around for one hour throwing to this unbelievable basketball player. So that's my Dirk Nowitzki story."

55 To Draft or Not to Draft

For two decades the Dallas Mavericks built their teams—successful or not—through the draft. The front office made trades and occasionally pursued players through free agency, but the star players leading their rosters were homegrown talent.

Mark Aguirre and Rolando Blackman both came to Dallas in 1981 as the first and ninth overall picks, respectively, of that year's draft. Dallas selected another key player, Jay Vincent, with its second round selection. In 1983 the Mavericks drafted Derek Harper in the first round, and in 1984 Sam Perkins, Detlef Schrempf, and Roy Tarpley followed consecutively in the two following drafts. After the success of the 1980s had passed and the Mavericks were struggling through the 1990s, they once again retooled through the draft. The Three J's came together in three straight seasons. First came Jim Jackson—followed by Jamal Mashburn and finally Jason Kidd.

Drafting players is an inexact science, and things can fall apart even when you select the right ones. That's what happened with the Three J's, unfortunately, as their personal relationships crumbled, and they were all traded out of Dallas within a couple months. It was recently hired Don Nelson who shipped Jackson and Mashburn out of town before the 1997 trade deadline, and this was weeks after he was brought on as general manager.

With Nelson's hiring came his trade and free-agency-driven approach to team building that the Mavericks would employ for the next two decades. However, one more crucial draft pick had to be made: Dirk Nowitzki, of course, who was selected in 1998 by the Mavericks. Although Nowitzki was the star, his two costars—Michael Finley and Steve Nash—had joined the team through trade. A few years later, the Mavericks re-signed Jason Terry in free agency. During the 2011 championship run, the entire starting five outside of Nowitzki had been acquired through one of those two means—and not by an original Mavericks draft pick.

Dallas has slowly shifted its philosophy back toward the draft. It's not that the Mavericks aren't opportunistic about free agency or the trade market, but the draft is too valuable to be ignored. From 2000 to their current roster, the Mavericks have only signed a single player to a second, multi-year deal. Before sounding too critical of the Mavericks, there are two things to consider.

- The Mavericks won 50 games in 11 straight seasons and went to the postseason nearly every year since 2001. Good, winning teams can rarely obtain valuable draft picks. Selecting between 21st and 30th in the first round isn't the most beneficial way to find, say, a superstar to put next to Nowitzki.

• The front office's best skill over the past decade or so has been finding individuals who have been discarded by the NBA and turning them into fantastic role players. They excel at talent evaluation and acquisition for the third tier of the NBA—players who aren't superstars or stars but can provide valuable minutes.

During this time Dallas saw first-round picks as assets to help make trades rather than a way to bolster its bench with cheap, young talent. They didn't have first-round draft picks in 2001, 2002, or 2005; they dealt away their 2008 and 2010 picks in the Jason Kidd deal; and they shipped away the 2016 first rounder due to the shortsighted Rajon Rondo acquisition.

Early on it worked because the Mavericks struck gold several times. Drafted 29th overall in 2003, Josh Howard was the one player who signed a second, multi-year deal with the Mavericks. That same year Dallas snagged Marquis Daniels, who went on to have a 10-year career in the league, as an undrafted free agent. Two years later with a rare top five selection, the Mavericks selected Devin Harris with a pick acquired from the Washington Wizards.

After that, though, disappointment began to sink in. Maurice Ager and Nick Fazekas, drafted in 2006 and 2007, quickly fell out of the league. A calculated gamble for Rodrigue Beaubois in 2009 was worth taking, but the French sensation regressed after a wonderful rookie year. Dominique Jones, Shane Larkin, and Jared Cunningham spent a combined four seasons with Dallas. At least 2015's Justin Anderson is still around and showing potential—even if he hasn't carved out a steady role in the league yet.

The Larkin decision stands out most. The Mavericks had missed the playoffs that season for the first time since 2000 and held the 13th overall pick. Instead of selecting Giannis Antetokounmpo, who Donnie Nelson loved, the team traded down five spots for Larkin.

Antetokounmpo is a budding superstar, Larkin is out of the league, and the half a million dollars the Mavericks saved by trading down still didn't allow them to sign the superstar they wanted.

After seeing how a decade spent neglecting the draft has hurt them, it, though, appears the Mavericks' philosophy is shifting back toward valuing first-round selections.

56 Sam Perkins

Sam Perkins shares an award with Michael Jordan. Who cares about the context? That's something to brag about. It's the 1984 USA Basketball Male Athlete of the Year, an honor that was bestowed upon Perkins and His Airness back when Jordan was only known as a promising college athlete. In 1984 Team USA still fielded teams with amateur athletes from college. Led by Perkins, Jordan, Patrick Ewing, and Wayman Tisdale, Team USA was so strong that future Hall of Famers John Stockton and Charles Barkley were left off the roster and it still easily won gold.

A month after earning the gold medal, Perkins showed up in Dallas for training camp. The 6'9" power forward had been drafted fourth overall in the 1984 NBA Draft by the Mavericks. Jordan had gone one pick before, and both had played at North Carolina, winning the national championship together in 1982. Now the two were selected into the NBA in back-to-back selections. Dallas had chosen the big man to round out its frontcourt rotation.

Perkins started his first six games in Dallas and moved into the starting lineup permanently in the team's 48th game. He averaged 14 points and nine rebounds through the end of the season. He

Mavericks big man Sam Perkins throws down a dunk during the first round of the 1985 playoffs.

started all but eight games during his next five seasons with the Mavericks, spending most of his time locking down the power forward spot next to James Donaldson. Due to an 18-year career, he only played a third of his NBA tenure with the Mavericks, but his presence was instrumental to the mid-1980s teams. In a close-out Game 6 against the Denver Nuggets in the 1988 semifinals, Perkins dropped 23 points, 11 rebounds, and four assists. But Perkins couldn't duplicate those efforts against the Los Angeles Lakers in the next round, as the Mavericks ended their playoff run short of the NBA Finals.

As it turned out, despite 1,286 games played, Perkins would never win in the NBA Finals, losing in the 1991 NBA Finals with the Lakers. He next joined the Seattle SuperSonics, and they lost in Game 7 of the 1993 Western Conference Finals and then came up short against the Chicago Bulls in the 1996 NBA Finals. In 2000 Perkins went once more while playing for the Indiana Pacers only to lose to a budding Lakers dynasty. He, though, not only played in three different NBA Finals with three different teams, but he also enjoyed one of the longest, most productive careers ever for any NBA player. His contributions early on for the Mavericks can't be understated.

57 Don Nelson

Without Don Nelson, Dirk Nowitzki would not be the Mavericks star he has become.

It was Nellie, as he has been affectionately nicknamed, who drafted Dirk Nowitzki in 1998 and it was Nellie who was the perfect person to coach him in his formative years. Serving as both the Mavericks' general manager and head coach at the time, Nellie saw Nowitzki as the unique talent he was. Instead of pushing Nowitzki into the role of a traditional American big man, Nelson encouraged him to shoot threes and dribble the ball up the floor like he did in Europe. Not every coach would have done that. "He knew to put Dirk at power forward and some at center and let big guys run around the perimeter trying to chase him," Rick Carlisle told the *Fort Worth Star-Telegram* in 2014. "And it was tough to do. Nellie was the right coach at that time."

After joining the Mavericks in 1997, Nelson was immediately tasked with a dysfunctional roster and a team that hadn't made the playoffs since 1990. So he went to work. He shipped off Jim Jackson and Jamal Mashburn, notably bringing back a young guard named Michael Finley. In 1998 he dealt for Phoenix Suns backup Steve Nash while selecting Nowitzki in the draft.

It was Nelson at the helm as the Mavericks finally made the playoffs again in 2001 and when they won 60 games in 2003. That season ended two games short of the NBA Finals, in part because of a Nowitzki knee injury in Game 3. Nowitzki wouldn't play the rest of the series with Nelson insisting he sit out while Mark Cuban wanted him to play. The fallout from that disagreement began fracturing the relationship between the coach and owner, who briefly went to court against each other. "I'm not even going to go there," Cuban told me. "You can read the transcript of my trial with Nellie on that one."

The next offseason, it fully splintered when Cuban failed to bring back Nash. Nelson had demanded Cuban bring back his star point guard pupil and he had little interest in continuing once Nash signed in Phoenix. Nellie resigned in March 2005, naming Avery Johnson as his replacement and his son, Donnie Nelson, as the team's new general manager. Looking back, Nelson certainly arrived in Dallas at exactly the right time, and maybe his departure then was necessary for the Mavericks to keep moving forward.

Their 2006 NBA Finals appearance came in Johnson's first full season coaching the team, after all.

Of course, the strange coda to Nelson's interactions with the Mavericks came in 2007 after Nellie had taken a new job with the Golden State Warriors. Facing a David vs. Goliath battle in the first round against Dallas, the "We Believe" Warriors prevailed in six games. Nelson thoroughly outcoached Johnson in that series, putting his onetime student on a path that eventually cost Johnson his job. Nelson and Cuban's relationship remained terrible for years, but the two parties eventually reconciled. Cuban told me they're on great terms now, at least. That's good since it's doubtful the Mavericks could have been nearly as successful as they've been since 2000 without Nellie's initial guidance.

58 Missed Superstars

Who is the best player Dirk Nowitzki ever played with? Steve Nash, you might say, but remember he was never a two-time MVP until after leaving Dallas. Michael Finley, maybe, early in Nowitzki's career. If it's not either of them, the only other option really is Jason Terry, right? Maybe even peak Tyson Chandler in the 2011 playoffs? It's a disappointing list.

Nowitzki is far from the first superstar to toil away with little help. Most end up leaving their original team to join a contender somewhere else. Amazingly, Nowitzki actually won a championship despite never benefitting from another true star around him. That's still the most undervalued part of Nowitzki's legacy.

This isn't to say that the Mavericks never tried, though. In fact, they often disregarded good players to chase great ones, a strategy

153

that could be argued hurt the team more than it helped. On the other hand, with the number of times they came close to acquiring a bonafide star, maybe they were just really, really unlucky. Here are a few of the most notable moments where Dallas just missed out on a superstar—both before and after Nowitzki's arrival.

Shaquille O'Neal

The Orlando Magic were the second worst team (21–61) when they won the lottery and the first overall pick for the 1992 NBA Draft. The draft was considered the deepest in years with Shaquille O'Neal, Alonzo Mourning, and Christian Laettner all considered sure things. Orlando grabbed O'Neal, and Mourning and Laettner both went on the board next.

The Mavericks had the third worst record in the league that year at 22–62 but only because they won their final two (and three of their last five) games. It's impossible to say the ping-pong balls would have bounced the exact same way, but ending the season with a loss instead of a win would have given them the same odds as Orlando. If it's any consolation, O'Neal's Magic tenure didn't end the way Orlando would have hoped. Who's to say the Mavericks would have been any different?

Shaquille O'Neal and Tracy McGrady

There was another missed opportunity for Shaquille O'Neal to join the Mavericks, and this time he reportedly wanted to bring Tracy McGrady with him. "We talk all the time about it," McGrady said in the summer of 2004, according to a *USA TODAY* report. "Me and the Big Fella are trying to get to Dallas together now."

O'Neal had started his career with the Magic, and McGrady was preparing to leave them that offseason, but the two were neighbors in Orlando. However, O'Neal was traded to the Miami Heat instead, and McGrady ended up with the Houston Rockets. There's no proof it was ever actually close to happening either—beyond the two players toying with the idea. Still, even with McGrady's injury history, it has to make you wonder what could have been.

Karl Malone

The Mavericks went from an expansion team to a playoff contender in four years, and their superb drafting is directly responsible for how quickly the team turned things around. Still, if there's a singular moment you can criticize, it's the team's 1985 NBA Draft.

It's not who the Mavericks selected: Detlef Schrempf with their eighth overall selection, and Bill Wennington, a solid pick at No. 16 who eventually was part of the Chicago Bulls' second three-peat. It was the player they passed on at 13—Karl Malone. And more specifically, it was why they passed on him. "I just don't think Malone is a rebounder," general manager Norm Sonju told the *Miami Herald* in 1986. "I have a problem with big men who like to shoot outside. I like a man to be where a man belongs."

Malone had been convinced the Mavericks were going to draft him and said he grew up wanting to play for them. (Malone grew up in northern Louisiana, closer to the Mavericks than any other professional basketball team.) "I must admit that for my first 10 years playing against the Mavericks I wanted to beat them really bad," Malone said on 105.3 The Fan in 2015. "I got to say that and get it off my chest."

Malone ended up as the NBA's second all-time leading scorer, and with 2,136 points scored against Dallas, he put up more points against the Mavericks than any other franchise in the NBA except the Denver Nuggets.

Kobe Bryant

The Mavericks came so close to trading for Kobe Bryant that Mark Cuban began spreading that word to stagehands on *Dancing with the Stars*, the reality television program he was participating in 2007. That's how confident he was that the Los Angeles Lakers were ready to swap Bryant for Josh Howard and Jason Terry. Los Angeles eventually came to its senses when a member of the front office talked Lakers owner Jerry Buss out of that idea. Still, it's fun to imagine the Big German and the Black Mamba on the same team. With the level of respect each player has expressed for the other over the years, you have to think that it would have worked seamlessly.

Paul Pierce

The two best players in the 1998 NBA Draft, who went off the board in consecutive picks, almost teamed up together at the 2013 trade deadline. In fact, Dallas believed the three-team deal they had lined up was going through, but the Boston Celtics got cold feet in the final moments.

Both players were past their prime by then, of course, so this wasn't a dynasty in the making. Pierce was still really good that season, though, averaging nearly 19 points in 77 games. It would have been fascinating to see the two stars close out their careers together, though you could debate for ages how successful that merger would have actually been.

Chris Paul and Dwight Howard

Like O'Neal and McGrady, two more superstars once briefly saw Dallas as a location where they could join forces in 2013. But like all the free agents the Mavericks pursued after the championship, it never materialized.

59 Michael Finley

Michael Finley's jersey should be retired by the Mavericks one day. He has the fifth most points in team history, scoring more than 12,000 in his career, and he's one of nine players to represent Dallas in an All-Star Game. Finley went twice, earning his way in 2000 and 2001. In 2002, when another Maverick went instead, Finley didn't pout and grumble. Instead, he told Dirk Nowitzki exactly what he needed to hear: it's your team now.

Finley came to Dallas from the Phoenix Suns, changing sides in the Jason Kidd trade. When you look back at the breakup of the Three J's, Finley was by far the most significant part Dallas received in return. Arriving in December 1996, he played his next nine seasons with the Mavericks and probably doesn't receive enough credit for helping the Mavericks climb out of their '90s doldrums—at least compared to Nowitzki and Steve Nash.

Finley was a workhorse. In the season he was traded to Dallas, he played 83 games because the Suns had played one more game than the Mavericks when the deal went down. He was known for his durability. Finley played every game the next four seasons before his consecutive-games streak finally ended at 490 games, and that was compiled over six seasons. Later in his career with the San Antonio Spurs, Finley twice played 82 games and suited up 81 times in another.

The hard-nosed 6'7" swingman had a great jump shot and more finesse than you'd think when he bullied his way into the lane. In the locker room, Finley was lauded as a leader. The classic example, of course, was the way he allowed Nowitzki to step into the top role on the team as the young German developed into a superstar.

The beginning of the end for Finley came when Dallas drafted Josh Howard in 2003. When Finley missed a stretch of games with an injury in December, Howard replaced him in the lineup without missing a beat. He played well enough that head coach Don Nelson said Howard had "definitely carved his way into the rotation, whether Mike is playing or not." It was enough to garner a buzz on the radio airwaves and leave fans to wonder if Finley's time with the Mavericks was winding to a close.

That speculation was premature; Finley finished out that season, starting every game he played that season and the next one. But as Howard kept emerging, Dallas took advantage of an amnesty provision to waive Finley and his massive contract in the summer of 2005. It gave the Mavericks crucial salary cap savings while opening up a spot for the younger Howard to take his place, which he did splendidly for his first few seasons.

It hurt that Finley ended up in San Antonio with the Mavericks' most heated rival, but the move allowed Finley to finally win a ring with the Spurs in 2007. In 2013, three years after retiring, Finley phoned Mark Cuban and told him he wanted to take him up on an offer the Mavericks' owner had made years ago, that he could have a job with the team. After two seasons in the front office in an internship role, as Finley himself described it, he was officially named the team's assistant vice president of basketball operations in 2016.

60 Huge Scoring Games Against Dallas

Ninety-one times. That's how often an opposing player has passed the 40-point plateau against the Mavericks. It happens about three times per season and it might surprise you that Dallas has won a majority of those games. The Mavericks have won more than they've lost over the franchise's history, so it actually makes sense. An opponent scoring 40 or more points, especially facing the historically good offenses in Dallas over the franchise's history, has by no means been a guaranteed loss. Not all of the memories are fond ones, but they're all rather historic. It's worth diving into some notable moments where individuals scored 40-plus points against Dallas.

Kobe Bryant's Three Terrifying Quarters

The score after three quarters said it all: Kobe Bryant 62, the Dallas Mavericks 61.

In December of 2005, Bryant recorded the most absurd statistical performance of his career to date. Playing nearly 33 of the game's opening 36 minutes, Bryant scored his 62 points on 18-of-31 shooting. No matter what the Mavericks did, they could neither keep him away from the paint nor stop his parade to the foul line. Bryant went there 25 times, knocking down 22 of the freebies.

Bryant didn't play the fourth quarter. It was an act of mercy akin to a prize-winning boxer who doesn't push for a TKO in the final round, knowing he's already won by decision. Not only did the Los Angeles Lakers know they were winning, but they also knew it so clearly that they didn't even bother putting Bryant back in the game. In retrospect, maybe the Mavericks should be thankful they didn't put up a fight. The next month, the Toronto Raptors did, so Bryant had his notorious 81-point game against them. That easily could have been the Mavericks.

Andre Miller's Out-of-Body Experience

Without a fateful evening in early 2010, Andre Miller would have never even scored 40 points. The 6'3" point guard, aptly nicknamed "the Professor," was always known best for a passing and basketball IQ. He scored sparingly by cleverly outmaneuvering defenses to the rim or with an excellent midrange jumper to average 12 points in his career. But one night against the Mavericks, he scored 52 points. It's the most out of character, Twilight Zone performance I've ever witnessed. The then-Portland Trail Blazers guard started quick and never looked back, pouring in midrange shots and layups all evening.

Miller forced overtime with a running hook shot at the end of regulation and he even opened the extra period with a three. (Miller only hit 193 threes in his 17-year career.) Despite sharing the court with Dirk Nowitzki, Jason Terry, and his own teammate LaMarcus Aldridge, Miller was the best scorer in the game. It'll be a while until we see a performance this bizarre again.

The Only Time Tim Duncan Scored 50 Points

Tim Duncan's only career 50-point game came against the Mavericks. It happened in December of 2001, the San Antonio Spurs' final season at the Alamodome. (The first thing that stands out watching highlights is the striking turquoise-and-purple colors still used by the Spurs that made up the painted area, and the game was delayed twice when a bat flew onto the court.)

Duncan was sitting at 25 points headed into the fourth quarter, but he took over from there, scoring 21 points in the fourth. It all happened out of the post, where Duncan hit turnaround jumpers and tossed in fading floaters like it was the simplest thing in the world. San Antonio still trailed by three with 15 seconds remaining, but Terry Porter knocked down a shot to send the game into overtime. All seven Spurs points in that frame came from Duncan, and that was matched by seven points from the Mavericks, leading to a 123–123 tie with 17 seconds left. Dallas had the last laugh, winning the game on a pull-up three from Steve Nash.

Stephen Curry Roasted the Mavericks with 10 Threes

There's nothing you can do when Stephen Curry starts cooking. The baby-faced assassin cooked the Mavericks in early February of 2015, scoring 51 points while knocking down 10 shots behind the arc. His last three was absurd: a stepback three-pointer that flew over Raymond Felton's outstretched hands. That jumper from at least five feet behind the three-point line pushed him to exactly 51.

The Splash Brothers love playing the Mavericks. Curry's 10 made threes is tied for the most the Mavericks have ever given up in a single game. The player he's tied with is Klay Thompson, of course, who had games with nine and 10 made threes against Dallas in the span of a week in March 2016.

Jason Terry and Dirk Nowitzki's Shootout

Jason Terry actually scored the most points of his career against the Mavericks. Back as a young guard with the Atlanta Hawks, JET rattled off 46 points in a shootout against Dirk Nowitzki, who dropped 40 points on his own. Dallas won the game despite Terry's best efforts, but you have to wonder if his showing that game originally put the idea of trading for him into the Mavericks' minds. Whether or not it did, the Mavericks did trade for him two offseasons later.

Purvis Short Scores 45 and 44

I had never heard of Purvis Short until I researched this book and I've decided that's a real shame. He averaged 28 points with the Golden State Warriors one season, and his nickname was

"Rainbowman" because his jumpers had such a high arc. Anyway, he scored 45 points against the Mavericks in March 1981 and he followed it up with a 44-point game in January 1986. I will never forget him again.

Michael Jordan Drops 43

The greatest hooper of all time broke the 40-point plateau against the Mavericks three times. His best showing, a 43-point outing in April 1990, came during a sensational game.

The Mavericks led by three after Derek Harper nailed a long jumper with 14 seconds remaining. Michael Jordan already had 40, but Dallas inexplicably left him open in the corner on the next possession. His three was money, tying the game at 106 within seconds. Mavericks center Sam Perkins—and Jordan's former college teammate—answered back with a quick drive, which earned him free throws, and he hit both, but it left too much time. For the final laugh, Jordan didn't score on the Mavericks. Instead, he found Bulls guard John Paxson in transition, who hit the game-winning three-pointer as the buzzer expired.

The Tracy McGrady vs. Dirk Nowitzki Shootout

If there's a better one-on-one duel between two players in the NBA's history, I haven't seen it yet. On a random December evening in 2004, Tracy McGrady and Dirk Nowitzki engaged in a ridiculous try-and-top-this, back-and-forth that still holds up to this day. McGrady was 25 and absurdly athletic before the injuries began affecting him. He also was fresh off back-to-back seasons leading the league in scoring. The 26-year-old Nowitzki was on the verge of his best season yet, combining unprecedented quickness for a seven-footer with his impossible-to-guard jump shot.

It was McGrady who answered first, dropping 25 points in the first half with an array of contested jump shots. Nowitzki matched him slowly at first before ramping it up in the second half.

Naturally, the game went to overtime, where Nowitzki scored the opening 10 points. He finished with 53 points while McGrady's final tally was 48—a 101-point performance for the two superstars combined.

61 J.J. Barea

No one knows how J.J. Barea's official height ended up listed at six feet. He says he never asked someone to fudge the number, so maybe a coach or agent suggested it when the NBA officially recorded the measurement. All we know for sure is Barea's not six feet, and it's not particularly close. The diminutive point guard from Puerto Rico says he's "5'10" on a good day," while his mother thinks it might be a half inch over 5'10". Whatever the real measurement is, Barea continues to chuckle whenever his "official" height is mentioned by someone. It certainly hasn't affected his career.

The decisive coaching maneuver in the 2011 NBA Finals came in Game 4, when Rick Carlisle inserted Barea into the starting lineup with his team down two games to one. Dallas, of course, won that game, the next two, and the championship. Carlisle made that move despite the fact that Barea had struggled in the first three games and he stuck with it even after Barea had a mediocre Game 4. In Games 5 and 6, Barea scored a combined 32 points and 10 assists. Without him, the Mavericks don't win the Finals.

Yes, the maybe-not-even-5'10" Barea was a crucial cog to a championship team. That's not something anyone would have predicted for him coming out of college at Northeastern, where he played four great seasons but understandably went undrafted. The

NBA isn't a welcoming place for undersized guards. To make the league while standing under six feet, you need a perfect blend of skills to make up for it: quickness, smarts, a great jump shot, and a unique, unteachable knack for getting shots off over bigger players. Most players like this get chewed up and spit out by the NBA. They're unable to adapt to constantly being the smallest player on the court, but there's a few success stories that give the others hope.

Barea's one of those success stories.

The Mavericks nabbed him as an undrafted free agent in 2006, and he played sparingly his first two seasons. Once during his rookie year, Dallas sent him to the D League for eight games, a relatively new phenomenon at the time. Barea averaged 27 points and nine assists, quickly proving that competition wasn't a challenge for him.

After only playing 651 combined minutes during his rookie and sophomore campaigns, the Mavericks re-signed Barea to a three-year deal. Barea made up for his size with quickness off the dribble and a good sense how to manipulate a defense to free himself around the basket. Carlisle became enamored with three-guard lineups involving Barea playing with Jason Kidd and Jason Terry, which sometimes drove fans batty but notably won the team several games.

While Barea technically played shooting guard in these lineups, the 6'4" Kidd enabled the move by switching onto the larger guard and sometimes even defending small forwards. During the championship season, Barea had his best season yet, playing 81 games while averaging about 10 points and nearly four assists per game.

That change to the starting lineup was bold, but it helped the Mavericks start quicker and break 100 points in Games 5 and 6 for the first time in the series. Barea had lit up the Los Angeles Lakers in Game 4 and scored 21 points in Game 1 vs. the Oklahoma City Thunder, but his efforts in the last two NBA Finals games were his best two performances. He torched the Miami Heat with timely shots and broke down their defense constantly. It was the perfect move from Carlisle, though he was exceptionally modest about it after Game 4. "I never had any thought that it could be genius," Carlisle said. "This is a move that we've made several times in my three years, starting Barea. And we've done it in a lot of instances where there have been big games. He has always stepped up and competed at an extremely high level. So I had no doubt that he would."

After the championship and the decision not to bring that team back, Barea signed with the Minnesota Timberwolves. On a mediocre team, he was asked to do too much without enough talent around him to really thrive. In 2014 the Timberwolves bought out his contract, and he returned to the Mavericks within days.

It's hard not to love a player who succeeds in a sport designed for men much taller than him. His chemistry with Dirk Nowitzki in the pick-and-roll is topped only by Steve Nash and Terry, and Barea has an uncanny knack for getting the Mavericks' superstar the ball. He may have dribbled too much at times or taken a few too many threes, but there's a reason Barea has been a permanent fixture in Dallas' offense for so long.

62 Visit the Gym Dirk Used Growing Up

The gym is small enough that the three-point line has no corners. From one side to the other, the room isn't wide enough to fit the full line, so it just runs into the wall and ends. Maybe that's why throughout his career Dirk Nowitzki was never a prolific three-point shooter from the corners. Connected to a German high school named after the local German and Nobel Peace Prize winner who discovered X-ray radiation, Röntgen Gymnasium was where Nowitzki spent hours growing up in Wurzburg, Germany. He and his mentor, Holger Geschwindner, trained there, studiously crafting his jump shot and his basketball game as Nowitzki developed into a star. As Geschwindner puts it, "This is the place where he shot the first baskets."

Nowitzki nicknamed it the "summer or winter gym." He called it that because it always felt like one extreme or the other and was often almost unbearable. "There was no A/C in there, so it was literally 110, 120 degrees in there [during the summer]," Nowitzki said in the *How Dirk Became Dirk* documentary. "Dying on every step, sweating, and then in the winter when we practiced, there was no heating system in there either, so I would literally practice with gloves that were cut off, so I could just feel the ball. I had two pairs of long pants, a shirt, a sweater, and a jacket over it, and that's sometimes how we practiced in there."

Although Geschwindner wasn't the pupil, he experienced it, too. "Dirk called it the 'summer gym,'" he said, "simply because in summer when the sun is on the roof we had close to 100 degrees in here, and sweat was a part of the job without practicing."

There was no seating for an audience, no corner threes, and no clear out-of-bounds markers. Instead, out of bounds simply meant touching the wall. "The gym was more there for other sports," Nowitzki said in the documentary, "volleyball, or chasing each other as kids, or kicking the soccer ball around a little bit."

Still, even though the two baskets had wooden backboards instead of the usual glass, they were there. The gym may not have been ideal, but it's a crucial part of his origin story. If by some chance you ever get to Germany, you must visit it.

63 The One-Legged Jumper

Dirk Nowitzki is never more recognizable, and never more iconic, than when he leans back on one foot. With the basketball cradled high above his head even as he fades away, the seven-footer launches a shot that is virtually unblockable, one that feels like it always goes in.

That signature pose will be encased in bronze when the Mavericks decide to erect a statue outside the American Airlines Center, and it's the shot that has spawned a hundred imitators. It's the reason 16-year-olds yell "Dirk" at the local YMCA when they sneer at using two feet while shooting.

When I asked him about it for this book, even Nowitzki admitted he didn't remember exactly when he started using the shot. He thinks it was right around when he turned 30—a couple seasons before the championship—though someone digging through old video may even be able to find earlier glimpses of it.

In Nowitzki's own self-deprecating words, he created the signature move that works perfectly with his shooting touch. "I came up with a shot where I just have to basically lean back, don't be athletic at all, and just hoist it up," Nowitzki said after passing Hakeem Olajuwon in all-time scoring in 2014. Olajuwon is famous for the Dream Shake, an iconic, unstoppable move in its own right. Nowitzki joked: "I came up with my own Dream Shake, I guess, the white version."

LeBron James. Kevin Durant. Carmelo Anthony. Kobe Bryant. Russell Westbrook. The list of modern superstars who have broken out the move in an NBA game could go longer. Some of the legends have used the move against Nowitzki himself as an homage. "It was a show of respect," James told reporters in 2013 after making a one-legged fadeaway against the Mavericks. "Dirk is one of my favorite guys. I love the way he approaches the game, the way he plays the game. He's amazing, obviously. We all know that, but I took that from him. I don't do that as well as him, though. He's been doing it a lot longer than me." Nowitzki responded to the imitation via ESPN Dallas: "I looked at him and gave him a smirk. It was a heck of a shot…I didn't think he'd shoot a one-legger. It looked pretty smooth. I've got to give it to him. He made it look easy."

And who can blame them? The shot really is unguardable when you shoot it right. An ESPN Sports Science segment dug into the release in 2011 and found that when Nowitzki usually releases the basketball on his average jump shot, it is nine feet above the court. On the one-footed fadeaway, he leans back 20 degrees, putting up his right leg to shield it even further, and creates two-and-a-half feet more space. With a release point that absurd, all you can do is hope Nowitzki misses.

Good luck with that.

Nowitzki may have been using the shot before 2011, but he told me and others that the championship popularized it. "Before then I think people kind of viewed it as this crazy shot," Nowitzki told *The Wall Street Journal* in 2016. "But when we won it all, you saw more and more people try it."

Fellow players have come to Nowitzki asking for help. Kristaps Porzingis and Giannis Antetokounmpo have both expressed interest in working out with Nowitzki over the offseason. Nowitzki doesn't want to give up all his secrets before retirement, but he'll eventually work with them if they insist. "I may be more willing to help once I'm done," Nowitzki told *The Journal.*

Still, Nowitzki didn't need the imitators to turn the one-footed fadeaway into an iconic shot. No matter who pays homage to him with it—and many will for a long time—Nowitzki will be the one who created it and the one who is the most recognizable when you see his silhouette fading back with the basketball over his head.

"Anytime you lift one leg and shoot it, everyone took that from Dirk," James said.

Olajuwon has the Dream Shake. Jerry West is on the NBA logo. Kareem Abdul-Jabbar's sky hook is still the most unguardable shot in NBA history, James said, but Nowitzki's one-foot fadeaway is second. Regardless, it is iconic. "It already is," Rick Carlisle told ESPN Dallas in 2013. "You've got those guys [James and Durant] emulating it and basically going out of their way to learn to shoot it as a tribute to him. I can make a case that Dirk has changed the NBA game as much as any player in history with his shooting ability."

64 Monta Ellis

The reason Monta Ellis was beloved by fans during his two years in Dallas, and the reason the Mavericks had no choice but to let him go, can be represented by a single game from March 2015. Ellis had been bothered by a hip injury for a few weeks, but he wouldn't consider sitting out an evening to rest it. As headstrong a player as he was, Ellis saw himself responsible to play all 82 games, every season, no matter what. He had played 234 games in a row coming into that March matchup, and there was a certain matter of pride that went along with that streak for Ellis, too. All this led to a limited Ellis, clearly not 100 percent, insisting on playing through the pain against the Phoenix Suns.

It backfired. Ellis made only four shots in 22 shot attempts that night, missing seven straight in the final minutes of a game that the Mavericks only lost by six points. Nobody in the Mavericks organization publicly blamed Ellis for the loss, and he came back two days later to score 38 points in a win. But nobody was surprised when Dallas finally forced him to sit out and rest that injury the following week.

Ellis was always stubborn to a fault. It was easy to love him while he fearlessly drove into the teeth of a defense or when he decided to take over in crunch time. After Mavericks fans spent years complaining about how the team never drove to the rim, Ellis was the dynamic attacker everyone had wanted to see in Dallas.

But Ellis' other antics rubbed the Mavericks the wrong way—his stubbornness with injuries and his moodiness when the Mavericks finally did make him sit down. Ellis had flaws as a player, too, as he fell in love with his midrange jumper more and more during his tenure in Dallas. While Ellis recorded a high number of steals, it came at the cost of constant gambling, something that hurt the team defense severely, and was a habit that the obstinate guard refused to break. When Ellis opted out of his three-year deal during the 2015 offseason, everyone around the team understood the Mavericks wouldn't be bringing him back.

Even though the partnership only lasted a couple seasons, it's easy for Mavericks fans to remember Ellis fondly. In the first-round series against the San Antonio Spurs in 2014, when Dallas pushed the eventual champions to a tightly contested seven games, Ellis had sensational moments. In the final seven minutes of Game 3, Ellis scored 12 points on impossibly difficult shots to keep the Mavericks in the game, which ultimately set up Vince Carter's unforgettable final shot to win it.

Other Ellis moments stand out like his buzzer beater to beat the Portland Trail Blazers about a month into his first season in Dallas, his maybe-it-was-a-travel-but-hey-they-didn't-call-it game-winning jumper against the Milwaukee Bucks, or the 26 points he averaged during the 2015 playoffs after Chandler Parsons was lost for the year and Rajon Rondo was dismissed from the team.

Most memorable was Ellis' fearlessness. It's a trait that caused Mavericks fans to love him during tight games and when facing fearsome defenses, but it's also ultimately the reason the team had to let him go.

65 Casey Smith

It was July 2010. The Mavericks were poised to make a trade for Charlotte Bobcats center Tyson Chandler, but they were concerned about Chandler's injury history and that he only played 51 games for Charlotte the year before. The question about Chandler's health came to Casey Smith. Thankfully, he gave a thumbs up, and, of course, the Mavericks were champions a year later.

It was an easy decision for Smith, who has been the Mavericks' head athletic trainer since 2004. As the lead trainer for Team USA Basketball as well—a role he filled from 2008 to 2012—Smith was already working with Chandler. With a firsthand look at how healthy Chandler looked, it was easy for him to sign off on the decision. "He had a clean bill of health at the time because he's playing for Team USA," Smith told me. "A lot of that plays into not just his injury—but what type of person, what type of worker—those type of things all played factors, and we felt comfortable with Tyson at that point as well."

Still, it wasn't guaranteed. Just a year prior at the trade deadline, the Oklahoma City Thunder had traded for Chandler at the deadline only to rescind it after he underwent a physical. They didn't like what they saw, expressing concerns with his left big toe injury, and killed the deal they had made with the New Orleans Hornets in 2009. Later that summer, the Hornets dealt him to the Bobcats.

You can imagine how things might have been different if the Thunder had let that trade go through. If Chandler had regained his health, like he did for the Mavericks in 2011, he would have been the perfect player to fill out Oklahoma City's young and talented starting five. In turn, Dallas never could have acquired the final puzzle piece for a championship. "We talked often about that," Casey said. "Obviously, he would have never ended up here if he had passed that. It's just ironic for us but fortunate. We were happy that it went down for us."

Signing off on the Chandler acquisition stands out from Smith's already exemplary body of work. Since joining the team in 2004, the Mavericks have consistently helped players recover quickly and prevented injuries for veterans whose career had been slowed down by nagging ailments. It's no surprise Smith spent time with the Phoenix Suns before joining Dallas since Phoenix has been cited as the gold standard among training staffs.

Especially in the last 10 to 15 years, training and especially injury prevention has taken huge leaps into the future. Smith has been responsible for keeping up with that and he's done so with aplomb. The Mavericks' front office greatly respects his voice.

66 Shawn Bradley

Shawn Bradley is best known for two things: being really tall, and getting dunked on.

Search his name on YouTube, and you'll get back dozens of videos featuring players dunking on him. *SportsCenter* once ranked the top 10 times Bradley was posterized. ("Keon Clark posterizing Shawn Bradley," the anchor joked, "but then again, doesn't

Shawn Bradley towers over the Milwaukee Bucks' 6'11" center, Ervin Johnson, during a 1997 game.

everyone?") The most famous one is probably Tracy McGrady's baseline jam in the 2005 playoffs. Even McGrady's coach, then-Houston Rockets head coach Jeff Van Gundy, has an affinity for that one. "It was in front of our bench," Van Gundy said. "It was in Dallas. They were playing 2-3 zone, and McGrady went in with such speed and force when he went at Bradley. And he got up before Bradley got up? One of the greatest plays I have ever seen."

Bradley stands 7'6" to tie Yao Ming as the third tallest player in NBA history. As he joked once in a television interview early in his career, he probably never had a conversation with anyone where his height didn't come up. Dunking on the third tallest player in league history earned any player instant bragging rights. Of course, the league and the media sometimes only portrayed Bradley as a basketball accomplishment, someone the league's top athletes needed to dunk on so they could check him off their list. But we didn't hear the other side often enough.

Though he was born in West Germany, Bradley grew up in a small Utah town with a population under 1,000. A devout Mormon, Bradley spent one season playing college basketball at Brigham Young University before taking a two-year mission trip overseas. In 1993 he declared for the NBA draft and was selected second overall by the Philadelphia 76ers. Bradley was expected to dominate the league for a decade with his height, but that never materialized. Instead, he was traded to the New Jersey Nets after a couple seasons and then to Dallas in 1997. Bradley spent his next nine seasons with the Mavericks before retiring in 2005.

Sure, Bradley got dunked on. As many times as he challenged opponents at the rim, it was bound to happen. Much more often than not, Bradley won those battles, averaging 2.5 blocks for his career and more than three per game five times. Having finished with 2,119 blocks, only 13 players have ever blocked more shots than Bradley has in his career.

ESPN Films produced a delightful 13-minute short documentary on Bradley in 2014, spending a year chasing an interview with the elusive Bradley before finally convincing him to participate. These days Bradley spends his time as a vice principal at a private school for at-risk youths and has traveled to Afghanistan and India on outreach trips. He has been married to his wife since 1993, and they now have six children. Bradley even ran for the Utah House of Representatives in 2010, losing by just a few hundred votes. "I got criticized a lot because people would say basketball isn't your No. 1 thing," Bradley told ESPN. "And I've never apologized for that because it's not. It never has been, it never will be. I value my family and my religion as No. 1. I hold those in almost the same light."

Bradley will always be remembered most as the guy who was dunked on. As the second overall pick in 1993 with expectations as high as he is tall, you can call him a bust. But Bradley did have a 12-year NBA career before launching an impressive post-basketball career. "Look at all he's accomplished!" Van Gundy told ESPN. "You're judging him on a 12-year period. He should be judged over the course of his life and what he's able to bring to this world."

67 Mark Cuban's Beginnings

Mark Cuban was a billionaire when he bought the Mavericks from Ross Perot Jr. in 2000, but he was basically broke when he first sputtered into Dallas in 1982. Recently graduated from Indiana University, Cuban only had a sleeping bag, a two-seat 1977 Fiat, and an invitation to crash with some guys he knew from school. For six months Cuban—nicknamed "Slobbins" and "Cubano"—and five roommates lived in a three-bedroom house. Cuban crashed on the living room floor. It wasn't a terrible arrangement at least until the tenants started raging parties every other week.

Cuban's money comes from two companies he created. The first was MicroSolutions, a systems integrator that helped other companies build the computing systems they needed by finding existing software from various clients. In 1990 Cuban sold MicroSolutions for $6 million, making a $2 million profit after taxes. Later that decade Cuban began funding Audionet, which became Broadcast.com. The company was 330 employees strong while bringing in $13.5 million one quarter in 1999, which is when Cuban sold it for $5.7 billion in Yahoo! stock during the dot-com boom. Just like that he was a billionaire and bought the Mavericks just months later.

Cuban now spends most of his time as an investor, funding nearly 100 deals through the reality television program *Shark Tank*. The Mavericks, whose majority stake he bought for $285 million, were ranked the ninth most valuable NBA team in 2017 by *Forbes* and listed as being worth $1.4 billion.

The first Mavericks game I ever covered, Cuban asked who I wrote for and introduced himself. I'm sure the gesture was mostly made so that Cuban knew which media members were covering him—and why they let some nerdy teenager into the room. Still, if you're wondering why Cuban has been so successful, his charisma left a clear impression. Cuban would have been successful in any era, and his timing allowed him to take full advantage of the Internet boom.

68 Josh Howard

Dirk Nowitzki played with four All-Stars in his career. First was Michael Finley, who went to the game twice in Nowitzki's first three seasons. Next was Steve Nash, who was rewarded with two trips in 2002 and 2003 after his fateful departure from Dallas. Later in Nowitzki's career, Jason Kidd made a single All-Star appearance based mostly on his reputation.

And then there was Josh Howard.

Howard's career is hard to neatly tie together in a few sentences. Selected 29th overall by Dallas in 2003, he was barely a first-round draft pick. In only his second season, though, he started every game he played and snuck into the 2007 All-Star Game after two players ahead of him dropped out with injuries. Three years and a torn ACL later, Howard had been traded from Dallas, and his career was basically over. Howard played 72 games over his final three years and attempted a comeback through the D League and NBA Summer League in 2014. He now coaches the basketball team at a tiny private college in North Carolina.

You often hear athletes described as having a meteoric rise and fall. Howard's wasn't. After the Mavericks drafted him, his role slowly increased—from an energetic defensive specialist off the bench, to a full-time starter, to a reliable scorer and an All-Star, to a player who didn't make the All-Star team but was arguably even better than the year before—for five straight seasons.

That last season was 2008. Howard averaged career highs in points (19.9), rebounds (7.0), and minutes (36.3), but the Mavericks declined dramatically from their 67-win season. Dallas won 51 games, traded Devin Harris for Jason Kidd at the trade deadline, and lost in the first round to the New Orleans Hornets.

To Howard, he had never played better. "That was my peak," Howard told *SLAM* magazine in 2014. "That's when I figured, if I'm doing this at this rate and this clip and still not getting the notoriety, it's never going to come."

Not everyone agreed. Fans complained that Howard's increase in scoring came at the expense of his defensive effort. He stopped slashing to the basket and drawing free throws, opting to shoot contested step-back jumpers instead. Howard had a strange aversion to the fourth quarter, too. He scored best in the first quarter, did alright in the second and third, and then saw his points and shots dip in the final frame. The statistics backed this up—both for his career and during his highest scoring seasons from 2005 to 2008.

At the same time, Howard became embroiled with a number of off-court events. During the 2006 NBA Finals, he infamously called a timeout the Mavericks didn't have in the final seconds. When Dallas lost, many fans unfairly blamed him. Right before the 2008 series against New Orleans, Howard talked openly about his marijuana usage during the offseason. After the team was in a 3–1 hole following its Game 4 loss, Howard distributed fliers in the locker room for the birthday party he was hosting later that night.

That offseason was more of the same, as Howard was arrested for street racing (he was reportedly going 95 mph in a 55 mph zone) and was caught on video two months later saying he didn't celebrate the national anthem because he was black. In some ways Howard was an athlete ahead of his time. Today, marijuana usage and national anthem protests are hot issues among athletes. But at the time, coupled with the other poor decisions, it was too much for Howard to ride out.

The Mavericks traded Howard at the next year's trade deadline, and it was a move they had to make. For a couple seasons, Howard had looked like the homegrown talent that Dallas was always wanting to put next to Nowitzki. Like his methodical rise,

Howard's fall from grace took a steady downward path until it was obvious he and the Mavericks had to part ways. Four games after the trade, Howard blew out his knee.

You can put the "partier" label on Howard, or the "player who never worked hard enough." Both are fair given what we know about his last few seasons with the Mavericks, including at least one reported instance of missing a game with a "stomach illness" that was really a hangover. Factor in his off-court controversies, and it's easy to see Howard one way.

Be wary before characterizing him. Never mind he was born bowlegged, spending weeks with his legs in casts as a child so that they would grow correctly. Never mind his father abandoned his family at birth. Never mind an aunt and a childhood friend being murdered while Howard was growing up as a kid. Never mind that when Howard's SAT scores weren't nearly close enough to be admitted to Wake Forest University—the school Howard was sure he would attend growing up—that he didn't give up but instead enrolled in a military academy for a year only to be admitted to Wake Forest the following fall.

Howard was on his way to a steady role as a veteran bench player with the Minnesota Timberwolves in 2012 but then tore his other ACL. Once again, he humbly worked himself back from injury to join the D League's Austin Toros for several months. In 2014 when a quiet stint with the New Orleans summer league team failed to earn him another job tryout, he retired.

Maybe Howard flew too high, too soon, like Icarus. But then again, maybe Howard accomplished more than he was ever supposed to in the first place. For that, he should be commended.

69 The Mavericks and Hip-Hop

"I'm the one living lavish /like I'm playing for the Mavericks," raps Future on his 2015 smash banger "March Madness." On the joint Nicki Minaj and Beyonce ballad, Nicki drops the line, "I do balls, Dal Mavericks." And we've got to mention Tyler the Creator, who must have set the studio ablaze when he rapped this: "Fall back like LeBron's hairline against the Mavericks, he lost."

There's a line you probably have heard before: rappers want to be ballers, and ballers want to be rappers. Hip-hop and the NBA have been linked together for decades now because of shared demographics with the league consistently appealing toward a younger audience, just like rap. It's the music of the youth and sport of the city; of course, they're linked. Sometimes, the two even collide directly. There's an artist named "Lil Durk," and Kanye West once wore a retro green Dallas snapback.

The Dallas Mavericks earned several shoutouts from mainstream musicians. Dirk Nowitzki—whose preferred musical taste involves Counting Crows, Matchbox Twenty, and The Avett Brothers, the last one whom he actually appeared onstage with in Dallas in 2012 playing the tambourine—has earned himself several references. "Sipping on Texas, Dirk Nowitzki," goes the hook of a song that's actually called "Dirk Nowitzki" and is by an Atlanta rap group called Migos. "Forty-one shots, Dirk Nowitzki," raps Quavo on that song's first verse and then, "15 Vince Carter on the wing." And Dorrough, a Dallas rapper, actually drops the line, "I rep the triple D, Dirk Nowitzki, Tony Romo" on the song "Get Big (Remix)."

By far my favorite Nowitzki reference comes from Lil B, who recorded a Kevin Durant diss track titled "Fuck KD." I've

Mavericks Players with Hip-Hop Singles

Jason Kidd
"They wanna know, they wanna know," whispers the song the moment the beat first starts playing. For a 1994 album called *B-Ball's Best Kept Secret*, which compiled a dozen NBA players onto a single mixtape, Jason Kidd raps a verse on a song called "What the Kidd Didd." Kidd is better than expected, but this still could have remained a very well-kept secret without us missing out on much.

Marquis Daniels
After going undrafted in the 2003 NBA Draft, Marquis Daniels, whose stage name was Lambo6 and then Q6, had a nice career beginning in Dallas. Unfortunately, all I can really tell you about his rap career is that it had two names involving the number six, and neither was particularly memorable.

Dirk Nowitzki, Monta Ellis, and Chandler Parsons
The Mavericks have one of the league's best digital teams over the past decade, but their best production has to be *Run DMC*, a Dirk Nowitzki, Monta Ellis, Chandler Parsons parody of the legendary 1990s Run DMC rap group. Here is Nowitzki's rap, which he delivers while wearing fake gold chains and a bucket hat: "A few years ago/some friends of mine/ wanted a ring/and we got our shine." I view my life in two stages. The first part was my unenlightened years, and then the second began immediately after hearing Nowitzki rap. It's unforgettable. It's a moment that takes your breath away and leaves you in awe. You might think Nowitzki's title or MVP is the crowning moment of his career, but that's wrong. It's this.

Maurice Ager
Ager might be the one person on this list better at music than basketball. Drafted 28th overall by the Mavericks in 2006, Ager only played 505 minutes his entire career. In 2013, though, Ager was nominated for a Grammy Award for his song "Far From Home" due to his superb production abilities.

The Matrix
Shawn Marion's debut single, the factually correct "I'm a Champion," came out on the 2014 album titled *Full Court Press Vol. 1*. In the album he raps, "like Neo, welcome to the Matrix," which is really the only reason to listen to it.

When he wasn't throwing down dunks for the Mavericks, Shawn Marion was rapping for his album, Full Court Press Vol. 1.

interviewed Lil B before and I honestly think he believes he could beat Kevin Durant in a game of one-on-one. In a hilarious music video for the profane song, he says, "3 point on a bitch like Dirk Nowitzki / Up in the club like Dirk Nowitzki /See me on the court if you wanna diss me / Let's play a game of 21, it's really fun."

The Phantom Foul

It's June 18, 2006, and the remaining seconds are ticking off in Game 5 of the NBA Finals. Dwyane Wade catches the inbounds pass in the backcourt, eludes Jason Terry near the sideline, and attempts a wild layup while splitting through Devin Harris and Dirk Nowitzki.

Let's briefly imagine that referee Bennett Salvatore, who is all the way back at half court, doesn't blow his whistle. Imagine that the ball bounces harmlessly off the backboard as the final buzzer sounded instead of Wade making yet another trip to the free throw line. Imagine the Mavericks holding on to their narrow 100–99 lead and heading back to Dallas with a 3–2 lead.

It's not hard. Whether the Mavericks won or lost the 2006 NBA Finals may have come down to that fated whistle. To this day Dallas players insist it wasn't a foul. Fans argue in every YouTube comment section and whenever someone else will give them an audience, pointing to Wade's absurd 97 free throw attempts in that six-game series and questioning the validity of the game-deciding foul in Game 5. "Hey, nobody touched him," DeSagana Diop told ESPN around the series' 10-year anniversary. "But the refs saw something different than everybody else. He had two free throws and he knocked them down. It was tough, man, it was tough."

It was an incredible play from Wade to elude four Mavericks defenders and even end up near the rim. Still, if there was contact on the play, it wasn't more than a fingertip and it wasn't a call made by the two closest officials near the play. Instead, Salvadore changed the series with that whistle, one he still defends. "I want you to do one thing," he told ESPN in 2007. "Look at Dirk. Dirk knows that he fouled him. You don't see any reaction from Dirk at all. Dirk knew."

Nowitzki himself, though, wouldn't really agree. "I'm still not sure," he said, "I fouled Wade on that last drive."

71 Al Whitley

An NBA equipment manager's job description includes maintaining the team's uniforms, according to the league's standards; taking any special requests, such as providing headbands or an extra pair of socks or new compression gear; ordering anything the team needs; doing laundry of the jerseys the team does have; and chest bumping Dirk Nowitzki after any clutch shot.

Alright, so that last one might only apply to Al Whitley.

You may not know his name, but there's a good chance you've seen Whitley on television. The Mavericks' longtime equipment manager sits right on or behind the bench and he's sometimes one of the first ones out onto the court celebrating huge moments with players like Nowitzki. His real job is an important one, no doubt. The celebrations just happen on the side. "My job is to make sure they have no distractions so they can just play basketball," Whitley told the *Fort Worth Star-Telegram* in 2006. "I'll take care of the rest."

Whitley came to the Mavericks with Steve Nash, who was one of his best friends, and he has kept the job ever since. Even though much of his job involves socks and underwear, it's hard to call it mundane—not when he's interacting constantly with star athletes and starring as an extra in dozens of television broadcasts each year.

Road games are the busiest. Whitley starts by passing around each player's practice gear and making sure all the team's equipment is loaded onto the bus headed to shootaround. While the team practices, Whitley and others set up the locker room. He's always on the early bus back to the arena and makes sure everything is packed up after the game so the team can fly home... or to another road game to do it all over again. If all goes well, there's at least one chest bump mixed into that day's agenda, too.

72 Dick Motta

Still a brand new team trying to find their way in the NBA during the early years of the franchise, the Mavericks went on the road to face the Golden State Warriors. But Mavericks head coach Dick Motta, who always embraced the unorthodox, wasn't happy with his team's energy during the first half. For Motta, the solution was asking a small favor of the halftime entertainer, a tiger tamer. Could he borrow his tiger?

Motta strolled into the locker room with the tiger on a leash, intending to jolt his young team into a better second-half performance. The players—understandably—were spooked by the sudden appearance of the large cat. According to *Sports Illustrated*, one player, Jim Spanarkel, tried sneaking back into the showers. "Don't!" Motta barked. "He'll just corner you in there."

This amusing anecdote is a perfect example of the type of eccentric coach Motta was in the NBA. He once had center Wayne Cooper goaltend a free throw, insisting to the referees that there was no rule that prevented it. (There was.) Motta was known to give younger players actual homework assignments about offensive schemes and for calling his general managers at 3:00 AM in the morning after a loss, demanding changes to the roster.

In 1978 Motta won a championship with the Washington Bullets. Two seasons later, after the Bullets finished under .500 and missed the playoffs, Motta was ready to move on. Always apt for a rebuilding project, Motta latched onto the Mavericks in their inaugural season. For the first seven seasons, Motta led Dallas from a ragtag expansion team to a legitimate playoff team. From 1984 to 1987, the Mavericks made the playoffs four straight seasons, though they were unable to get past the conference semifinals. Criticized by fans for talking with the Los Angeles Clippers and New York Knicks about potentially leaving Dallas for head coaching jobs in those cities, Motta abruptly resigned that May. He didn't join either of those teams and actually didn't rejoin the NBA as a head coach for three seasons until he took over the Sacramento Kings. Certainly, the Mavericks did nothing to drive Motta out.

The story has a coda, though. In 1994 Motta rejoined the Mavericks and coached them for two seasons during the Three J's era. It ended unsuccessfully—Dallas went 62–102 in those two years—but the players praised Motta nonetheless, describing a coach who was mellow and relaxed and nothing like the hot-headed figure many associated with him in his early days.

He coached 25 seasons, and his 1,952 games are the seventh most in NBA history—even if he lost slightly more games than he won. Besides Don Carter and Norm Sonju, Motta is perhaps the most important figure in the early Dallas history, making sure the expansion team ultimately became successful.

73 The Three-Point Streak

For 5,038 days, the Dallas Mavericks made a three-pointer in every regular-season game they played.

In February of 1999, Michael Finley and Erick Strickland combined to hit three triples in a 97–90 win against the Sacramento Kings. It started a 1,108 regular-season game streak, which remains the longest in NBA history as of the start of the 2017–18 season.

It, though, is no longer an active streak. In December of 2012, the Mavericks attempted 13 three-pointers in a game against the Toronto Raptors. With Dirk Nowitzki still absent due to preseason surgery, O.J. Mayo hoisted a team-high four. Derek Fisher jacked up three, Vince Carter added a couple of attempts, and three other players took at least one. All 13 shots missed, and, unceremoniously, a streak that seemed like it might stretch on forever died that night in Toronto. For a brief moment, it looked like it would keep going, but a fourth-quarter jumper originally ruled as a three was overturned upon review. After 14 seasons—120,912 hours, or 7,254,720 minutes, or 435,283,200 seconds—the streak died.

Two teams are poised to pass the Mavericks' record in the 2017–18 season. The Phoenix Suns and Golden State Warriors both have active streaks that will push them past the Mavericks' one halfway through the season, and with the increasing importance of the three-point line, it's highly likely that will happen.

The streak proves the Mavericks were ahead of the curve during the early 2000s, when Don Nelson let Nowitzki play the game like he wanted. While other teams pounded the ball into their seven-footers in the post, Nelson let Nowitzki start fast breaks and pull up behind the arc whenever he was open. There's no doubt that helped extend the Mavericks' streak that long.

The streak brought great memories. Fifteen times during the streak, the Mavericks hit only one three. Nowitzki once kept the streak alive by coming off the bench early in his career. On another occasion in 2005, Darrell Armstrong even subbed into garbage time to knock down the team's only triple with five minutes left in a game.

The most memorable instance came in the last regular-season game in 2006. The Mavericks rested their starters, and the team still hadn't hit a three with less than a minute left in the contest. To give the team one last chance, Avery Johnson drew up a play for backup center DeSagana Diop, who had three attempts beyond the arc in his career. He nailed it. It's the only three-pointer he made in his 12-year career.

The Mavericks begin the 2017–18 season with a 387-game streak. Assuming they make a three in every game going forward, they'll catch the old one in about a decade.

74 Roy Tarpley

Roy Tarpley should have been a star. Everyone who played with Tarpley believed that, and he was as gifted as anyone who ever played in Dallas. He moved around the court with the ease of a guard despite standing 6'11". One possession after hitting a silky smooth turnaround jump shot, he could bang away inside for an offensive putback. Yes, Tarpley would have been a star if he hadn't suffered from addiction. Instead, he ended up permanently banned from the NBA.

The Mavericks drafted Tarpley with the seventh overall selection in the 1986 NBA Draft after Tarpley had completed four stellar seasons at the University of Michigan. Once his problems came to light years later, Mavericks general manager Norm Sonju insisted the team research his history, knowing many college athletes were susceptible to drug use in that era. No, they were told, Tarpley did not have any problems.

During Tarpley's first few seasons, the future seemed bright. He made the NBA's all-rookie team during his first season and he followed it up the next year by averaging nearly 14 points and 12 rebounds off the bench. It was enough to earn him the NBA's Sixth Man of the Year award. Tarpley was incredible in the 1988 playoffs, too, averaging 18 points and 13 rebounds before the Mavericks lost in Game 7 of the Western Conference Finals.

It was the following year that Tarpley's problems began, when he was arrested for driving while intoxicated and resisting arrest. He missed most of the next two seasons, playing just 64 games combined. Poised for a comeback at the start of the 1990–91 season, Tarpley tore a ligament in his knee five games into the season and ended up missing the rest of the year. That March he was arrested again for driving under the influence and was banned from the league after a third violation several months later.

The suspension lasted three seasons before Tarpley successfully appealed the decision. Now 30 years old, Tarpley played 55 games for the Mavericks in the 1994–95 season. He was still effective on the court even if he was nowhere near his former self. But in December 1995, Tarpley violated the terms of his court-imposed personal aftercare program by drinking alcohol. This time the NBA's ban was permanent. "If Roy had stayed healthy, he could have been one of the top 50 players ever. He could do it all—shoot, score, rebound, pass, and defend," Brad Davis, one of Tarpley's Mavericks teammates, told *The Dallas Morning News* upon Tarpley's passing in 2015. Tarpley was only 50 years old, but his liver reportedly failed him.

It's important not to conflate Tarpley's addictions with who he was as a person. Many doctors and researchers believe addiction is predisposed for some people because of their genetics. Sadly and tragically, Tarpley wasn't able to successfully fight his addiction. Everyone who spent time around him attests how genuine and enjoyable to be around Tarpley was. "Roy, he was his worst enemy in a lot of ways," Derek Harper, another teammate, told the *Fort Worth Star-Telegram.* "But in spite of him having the addiction and the problem that he had, I don't think anybody has ever said he was a bad person. He was a great person."

After he was banned, Tarpley kept playing in local and professional leagues in China, Greece, and Russia. He sued the Mavericks and the NBA in 2007 for not treating his addictions as a disability, and the suit was ultimately settled out of court in 2009. Tarpley only ended up playing 280 games in the NBA—far too few for a player who was naturally gifted for the sport and for a person who had a condition he could never conquer. "But the disease of drugs basically stopped his career short," Harper said. "We just don't know how good he would have been, unfortunately."

75 1998 Nike Hoop Summit

When receiving his invitation to the 1998 Nike Hoop Summit, Dirk Nowitzki considered declining. He had never been to the United States before, and his professional team had a huge playoff game coming up that same week. Sure that they would talk him out of it, Nowitzki didn't tell his teammates until he had left. Fortunately, they won the game without him.

It was the fourth year of the annual game, featuring the USA Basketball Junior National Select Team against an invited group of international players from around the world. That March game was held in San Antonio. Nowitzki actually flew into Dallas, where the Mavericks were gracious hosts. "It was just an amazing week," Nowitzki told *USA TODAY*. "We went to some Mavs games and took the Mavs' plane to San Antonio on Saturday, where they took us to the semifinals of the Final Four. That was a blast, just being with the guys and meeting new people."

Nowitzki knew the NBA was on his radar, which is why he chose to make the trip stateside. Still, he wasn't sure if he was ready yet—and didn't realize at least 40 scouts from NBA teams would be in attendance. "I didn't know how big this game was going to be," Nowitzki said. "I had played the Euros [European championship] with my under-16 national team, and there were a couple of colleges there. This game was broadcast live on ESPN2."

It was still months before Dallas eventually drafted Nowitzki and a few years before he started growing into a household name. The announcers compared his skills to Detlef Schrempf, the fellow German shooter whose career had begun in Dallas, before the game started. The chyron on the television spelled his name as "Nowitzski," the misspelling proof that no one knew who he was yet.

By the time the game was over, they did. Nowitzki dominated in the Team World victory, scoring 33 points while feasting at the free throw line. It was his first basketball game outside of Europe, but none of the American defenders, including future NBA players Al Harrington and Rashard Lewis, could stop him.

Using his dribbling ability to break Team USA's press defense, advance the ball up the floor, and seek out contact in the lane, many of Nowitzki's free throws came in transition. Nowitzki shot 23 free throws in that game, making 19 of them. Nowitzki's 33 points was a record that stood until 2010, while his 14 rebounds is still the most ever recorded by a player in the game, though three others have equaled him. Clearly, the game was a sign of things to come.

76 Dennis Rodman

Dennis Rodman's unforgettable Hall of Fame career ended in Dallas. It was a short-lived epilogue, lasting only 12 games before a one-sided breakup. Rodman, who hadn't played since the previous season, signed with the Mavericks in February 2000 after the team had won 8 of its last 12 games. Mark Cuban saw the Mavericks as a young team making a playoff push and Rodman as the player who could help them make it despite the colorful big man's reputation of often being so difficult to work with.

Cuban put up Rodman in his own guesthouse, and the big man's debut was the second largest crowd in Reunion Arena's history and most watched game on the regional networks in seven years. It turned out the 38-year-old Rodman was still great at the things he was famous for: in those 12 games he notched 171 rebounds despite only scoring 34 points, was ejected twice, and earned a one-game suspension.

In March, Cuban and Donnie Nelson agreed they should release him. Once it became obvious the Mavericks weren't going to make the playoffs, he was a distraction the young team didn't need, so they waived him. Rodman wasn't pleased. "I think it's an injustice because I'm me, Dennis Rodman," Dennis Rodman said. "I haven't done anything wrong. I thought I was doing a good job. I thought I lived up to my expectations. I don't get it. I really don't get it. I get the short end of the stick every time. What am I doing wrong?"

But despite his complaints, the Mavericks held firm. Rodman didn't play in the NBA again. Rodman had ties to Dallas before those fateful 12 games. He had grown up in south Dallas and went to high school at South Oak Cliff before going to college 100 miles north at a small college called Southeastern Oklahoma State. From there, he was drafted in the second round by the Detroit Pistons.

It was in Detroit, and later Chicago, where the Rodman persona began in earnest. As part of the Bad Boys squads, Rodman's hard-nosed defense and rebounding fit right in. After a stint with the San Antonio Spurs, Rodman joined Michael Jordan and Scottie Pippen with the Bulls, where he won three championships during his three seasons there. With dyed hair, piercings, and colorful off-court antics, Rodman became famous across the country.

Rodman arrived in Dallas promising to be a workhorse, but he didn't rule out being a showoff. "It's not about me fighting the system," Rodman said. "It's not about me trying to be the best. It's not about me trying to get all of the glory, this and that. They just know I'm a guy who goes out there and does it, does his job. If I have the opportunity to give everyone a little entertainment here and there..."

Just a week after his season debut, Rodman was ejected on two technicals, the first for arguing with a foul call and the second for sitting down on the court. He immediately challenged the NBA commissioner to a fight. "I wish me and David Stern could put some damn gloves on and go in the ring," Rodman said afterward. "We'll see who comes out the winner. I've been a marked man for years. That's the first person they're going to look for, Dennis Rodman."

Rodman's criticism extended to his teammates and then the team's personnel. Finally, Rodman criticized Cuban himself. "He doesn't need to be hanging around the players like he's a coach or something," Rodman said. "That's like Jerry Jones, and it's dumb. That's why the Cowboys went down. He needs to be the owner, step back, and put people in who can get this team in the right direction."

The next day Rodman was released. Cuban said the comments had nothing to do with it—he was letting the man crash in his guesthouse, after all—but you can judge that for yourself.

Rodman's time with the Mavericks was emblematic of who he was as a player. It is an insignificant part of the team's history at this point but an entertaining one nevertheless.

77 Mavs Fans Can't Stand These Players

Sports are inherently emotional. It's why they can make us euphoric and then break our hearts moments later. It's why we hurl expletives at inanimate television screens and curse players who play well against our teams in the heat of the moment. Sometimes, a player will do something that legitimately pisses off a fanbase. Here are the players whom Mavericks fans still love to hate on, no matter what.

DeAndre Jordan
Going by the rulebook, DeAndre Jordan had every right to change his verbal commitment and decide to re-sign with the Los Angeles Clippers. But there's another rule in the same book that says, "If a player agrees to sign with a team and then several days later decides he isn't actually going to sign with that team, then the fans of that team are legally obligated to boo that player for as long as he lives." Okay, so that might not be an actual rule, but for Mavericks fans, it might as well be. Jordan will never have his face shown on a Dallas

Jumbotron without fans reminding him with boos how awfully he handled that situation.

Derek Fisher

Fisher's tenure with the Mavericks lasted nine games. How can three weeks of basketball build up so much ill will? Well, the briefness of Fisher's stay was exactly the problem. The then-38-year-old joined Dallas early in the 2012–13 season, but with Dirk Nowitzki missing the first quarter of the season, the Mavericks piled up losses. Fisher asked to be released by the team, citing the difficulty of being away from his family and a minor injury he suffered. As it turned out, Fisher missed his family so much he signed with the Oklahoma City Thunder—a contending team—just a couple months later and even came back the next season to play 81 games.

It's not just the fans, who thought Fisher using his family as an excuse to get out of a situation was a cheap move. In 2014 when asked about Fisher's commitment level to coaching the New York Knicks, Cuban caustically told reporters, "I'm more concerned with his health and welfare. I know how hard it is for him to fly and travel and be away." There's still no love lost between Fisher and the Mavericks.

Lamar Odom

It's much easier to understand Odom's struggles when he joined the Mavericks in 2012 now that we know about his battles with addiction. When he was traded to Dallas, coming off winning the Sixth Man of the Year, Odom was viewed as an absolute steal. Instead, he averaged six points on 35 percent shooting while playing 50 games, and the two sides mutually decided to part ways before the playoffs started. At the time nobody understood why Odom crashed and burned with the Mavericks. From an outside observer, it looked like Odom didn't care. Hopefully, Odom can successfully fight his demons. He played one more season in the NBA after his brief stint with the Mavericks before retiring from the NBA.

Erick Dampier

Dampier came to Dallas in a situation that was completely unfair to him. Earlier that summer in 2004, the Mavericks had let Steve Nash sign with the Phoenix Suns, fearing his injury history and not believing he could reach MVP levels of play. Instead, in an eight-player sign-and-trade deal, the Mavericks received the lumbering Dampier from the Golden State Warriors and handed him a seven-year, $73 million contract.

For most of the next six seasons, Dampier started at center for the Dallas Mavericks. The best way to describe him is perfectly average. His best skill was rebounding, and he was an adequate rim protector and, while he constantly disappointed offensively, he still made enough shots to stay on the floor. For the contract Dampier received, it was fair to expect more. Still, Dampier played as well as he could, and the hate he has gotten from Mavericks fans always seemed overblown. It was Dampier who allowed the Mavericks to trade for Tyson Chandler before the championship season. If nothing else, Dampier deserves credit for that.

Kiki VanDeWeghe

VanDeWeghe was the Mavericks' first ever draft pick. As a brand new franchise in 1980, Dallas selected him with the 11th overall pick, but he never played a minute for them. In fact, as a college kid coming out of UCLA, VanDeWeghe refused to join the team and demanded a trade. They ended up dealing him that December, and Mavericks fans ended up booing him the rest of his playing career.

The Mavericks, though, ended up employing VanDeWeghe as a coach in the late 1990s until he was hired as a general manager by the Denver Nuggets in 2001. VanDeWeghe has been cited as a huge early factor in Dirk Nowitzki's development and has had a great relationship with the team in the years since.

78 The Rajon Rondo Debacle

The last time Rajon Rondo wore a Dallas Mavericks jersey was in the Houston Rockets' visiting locker room. With media waiting to talk to him, Rondo dressed silently, put on a pair of headphones, and breezed past without even acknowledging our presence. In my time spent in NBA locker rooms, I've never seen a stranger scene.

Rondo joined the Mavericks in one of the most short-sighted trades in the team's history. The Mavericks started the 2014–15 season with a 19–8 record but felt compelled to make a trade to shore up a weak point guard position in a ridiculously strong Western Conference. (That year, their 19–8 start somehow only had them as the sixth seed.) But despite free-flowing offense dominating the league, Dallas traded for Rondo, a mercurial point guard who couldn't shoot and preferred slow, methodical offensive pacing.

It didn't work. The Mavericks' offense tanked, their defense didn't improve much, and the team finished with only 50 wins despite a 58-win pace before the trade. Rondo publicly screamed at Rick Carlisle during a regular-season game, resulting in a one-game suspension. The two formed an uneasy truce the rest of the year, but emotions finally came to a head in the postseason. During Game 2 against the Rockets during the playoffs, Rondo had a miserable first half that included an eight-second violation for being too slow walking the ball up the court. To begin the second half, Rondo committed two lazy fouls against James Harden and a technical that caused Carlisle to angrily yank him from the game.

Rondo never played another second for Dallas and walked out on the media after that game. The Mavericks announced the next day—covering for him perhaps at the request of his agent, even though the truth was obvious—that Rondo had a back injury and would not return during the playoffs. When asked if he expected Rondo to ever wear a Mavericks jersey again, Carlisle bluntly said no. It was later reported the team voted that Rondo would not receive the monetary playoff share that the players split among themselves, which almost never happens.

Rondo's tenure was the most disastrous that has ever happened for Dallas, and it remains a forgettable chapter in their history. Rondo left a bad taste in the mouth of everyone associated with the team, and there's no doubt Carlisle is right when he said he'll never be in Mavericks blue again.

79 Fall in Love with the Pre-Rondo Mavericks

It was the middle of November 2014 when the Dallas Mavericks obliterated the Los Angeles Lakers. In a game at the American Airlines Center, the Mavericks roasted their frequent rivals for 140 points, which is tied for the sixth most points in franchise history and a figure the team hasn't topped in a non-overtime game since 1992. Dirk Nowitzki led the way with 23 points while seven of his teammates scored in double figures. It was a shellacking so brutal there aren't enough adjectives to properly describe it.

That Mavericks team was the best since the 2011 championship...and they were never even given a chance. We know the obvious fallout from the Rajon Rondo trade—the fighting with Rick Carlisle, him quitting in the playoffs, the team taking an unprecedented vote to withhold his playoff shares. But the Rondo trade looks even more disastrous after considering how it broke up the team and how they never recaptured that magic.

What follows is the biggest "what if" for the Mavericks in the past decade. The day before the Mavericks traded for Rondo, they were 19–8 and on a 58-win pace. The team's 113.6 offensive rating—which is just points scored while adjusted for 100 possessions to put every team on equal footing—was the best in the league. In fact, it was the best offensive output the league had seen in a decade.

That Dallas offense was mesmerizing. It had the typically brilliant Dirk Nowitzki paired with Tyson Chandler yet again. Monta Ellis touched the ball the most as the team's leading scorer, Chandler Parsons filled in as a secondary ballhandler, and backup big man Brandan meant the team could toss alley-oops for days. If defenses packed the paint to stop Wright or Chandler from rolling right down the middle, every player in the rotation was capable of hitting three-pointers.

The Mavericks, obviously, were worse at defense. At the time of the trade, they ranked 20th in defense. They eviscerated bad teams during those first two months, but Dallas had only gone 0–5 against Western Conference playoff teams so far that season. That stat was thrown around frequently in the aftermath of the trade by the Mavericks and by media members alike, even though four of the five losses had been by single digits.

Jameer Nelson was the other problem. The 32-year-old starting point guard had been underwhelming that season even as the Mavericks dominated offensively. He was horrendous at defending the pick-and-roll, shot less than 40 percent from the field, and clearly was out of place as a starter on that team.

The timing of that Mavericks' team could not have been worse. In any other season, 19–8 should have put them within the top four in their conference. Yet on December 18, the day before the Rondo trade happened, Dallas was sitting in the sixth seed. The Western Conference was historically good that year. Six different teams had winning percentages better than .700. (The East only had five teams above .500.) Those six teams—of which Dallas was sixth—didn't even include the defending champion San Antonio Spurs.

That's why the Mavericks traded for Rondo. They did it despite Rick Carlisle warning the front office it might not work because Dirk Nowitzki was certain it would. They didn't know that the 2015 trade deadline would be the wildest one in recent memory, or that Goran Dragic (who in theory would have been a perfect fit) would end up being dealt.

Rondo shredded that league-leading offense. Where the Mavericks had run tempo, Rondo slowed it down. With shooters all over the floor, Rondo botched it with an ineffective jump shot that opponents basically ignored. Even worse, the Mavericks dealt Wright and Jae Crowder in the trade. They especially missed Wright's rim running in the months that followed.

It's "what if" time. What if Raymond Felton, who had arrived along with Chandler that summer, hadn't suffered a terrible high ankle sprain early that preseason? Given how well he played the following season, if he was healthy, there's a good chance he starts over Nelson, and the Mavericks don't feel pressured into the trade.

What if the Mavericks had beaten the Spurs on opening night—a one-point loss—or the Houston Rockets in November, a game they lost by just three points? The Mavericks went 31–24 after the Rondo trade, and their .563 winning percentage was almost 15 points lower than before.

What if Rondo had been traded to the Rockets, another rumored suitor for the guard? Houston was 19–5 at the time of the trade, a few games ahead of Dallas, but Rondo likely would have slowed them down as well. The Mavericks eventually lost to the Rockets in the first round that series, but keeping that original team together—with a healthy Felton, maybe, or even someone like Dragic—could have allowed them to pass the Rockets in the standings and potentially make a run to the second round.

This is all speculation. The only facts we know is that the Rondo trade turned a team that was a joy to watch into one that was a slog. He hurt Ellis, who had been the de facto point guard, and now had to play off the ball more frequently in a role that he wasn't as good at, and Parsons, who was forced into a role that made him even more of an off-the-ball player than Ellis. With the Mavericks and Boston Celtics, respectively, Al-Farouq Aminu and Crowder both broke out that season as high-quality, defensive-minded wings. Crowder played sparingly early that season, but perhaps both could have earned minutes and helped stiffen the defense.

That team probably wasn't a contender, while the Rondo trade—in some bizarre world—might have made the Mavericks one. That's what the team ultimately gambled on, and it's understandable why they felt it necessary. But while hindsight is still undefeated, it's hard not to wish that 2014 offensive juggernaut had remained intact. They were so fun, so enjoyable—and maybe, just maybe—better than we realized at the time.

80 How the Mavericks Got Their Name

Would you root for the Dallas Express? What about the Wranglers? Those were the two names that the "Mavericks" nickname beat out during the franchise's inception. Despite the team's logo and the team's equine mascot, Champ, a Maverick isn't actually a horse.

According to the *Merriam-Webster* dictionary, there are two definitions for the word *maverick*, and Dallas' team name was selected with the second one in mind.

1. An unbranded range animal; especially: a motherless calf
2. An independent individual who does not go along with a group or party

Fans sent in 4,600 postcards for the vote on the team name, and *Mavericks* was chosen to represent the new Dallas team at the 1980 All-Star Game when the franchise was approved. It also referenced *Maverick*, a 60-minute comedic Western series that aired on television from 1957 to 1962. In that show James Garner starred as Bret Maverick, a traveling poker player who constantly found himself in hijinks throughout the American Old West or even on Mississippi riverboats. The lead—first Garner but later Jack Kelly, Roger Moore, and Robert Colbert as the Maverick brothers—often had to weigh financial gain with a decision that was morally right and usually ended up on the ethical side. Despite lasting only five seasons, the show was popular especially during Garner's two seasons. (Garner ended up as a part of the ownership group that funded the Mavericks' expansion costs.)

Clearly, the fictional Maverick brothers represented the word's second definition well. You could argue it fits Mark Cuban well, too, whose entrepreneurial spirit put him in a position to own the team. Because of the first definition, the horse motif the team uses works well—even if *maverick* was more a term used for cattle than horses.

In a league where the Jazz represent Utah and the Raptors hail from Canada, this nickname is intrinsically Texas. It fits the city of Dallas, which has a long history in the cowboy and cattle industry, and meshes well with the team's other professional sports teams— the Dallas Cowboys, the Texas Rangers, and the Dallas Stars. The only controversy remaining about the Mavericks name was that it was also being used by the University of Texas at Arlington. Dallas ultimately pushed forward with it anyway, and now two types of Mavericks exist in the Dallas metroplex.

81 Brad Davis

Two Mavericks jerseys hang from the rafters in the American Airlines Center. One belongs to Rolando Blackman, the co-star of the Dallas playoff squads of the 1980s who spent 11 seasons with the franchise and scored more than 16,600 points. But as of the 2017 season, the only other player to receive that honor is Brad Davis.

That Davis did so much for this team that his jersey was retired speaks to how highly the franchise regards him. No one confused Davis for an all-time great; his career averages were only 8.2 points and 4.9 assists. Davis had loyalty, though. After playing 78 total games his first three years in the league, Davis didn't have teams lining up to sign him during the summer of 1980. Dallas picked up the journeyman point guard in their inaugural season, and Davis ended up starting virtually every game at point guard for the team the next five years, averaging 11.2 points, 6.8 assists, and shooting 53 percent from the field.

By the 1986 season, Derek Harper had surpassed him, and a 30-year-old Davis had no problem accepting his move to backup point guard. Davis played 503 more games for Dallas across seven seasons before back issues forced him into retirement. Shortly afterward, Davis joined the Mavericks as a coach and a radio broadcaster. Davis has been with the organization ever since, mostly as the team's radio broadcaster with a brief foray into television. You can find him helping Dirk Nowitzki warm up on the road or working with the franchise in community relations. Whatever he does, he's a beloved figure in the organization.

There's no doubt Harper and Michael Finley's jerseys should join him in the rafters, and, of course, Nowitzki's will be there as soon as his playing days are over. Jason Kidd, Steve Nash, and Jason Terry all could join him.

82 Three Franchise-Altering Trades

Fans love trades. Of course they do. Trades can radically change teams, and radical change brings out the passion from anyone who is heavily invested in something. These three trades, in particular, worked to perfection.

The Jason Kidd trade

The toughest part about the 2008 trade for Jason Kidd was giving up Devin Harris.

It made sense why the trade was divisive. Kidd was one of the league's best point guards, but he was 34 while the Mavericks draft pick, Harris, was 24. Kidd was a true point guard, something the Mavericks hadn't had since Steve Nash. (Jason Terry and Harris, the two players who had mostly played there since, were more shooting guards with passing skills than floor generals.)

After one false start involving including Jerry Stackhouse in the deal, the Mavericks did eventually pull the trigger in mid-February. Kidd struggled his first half season in Dallas as Avery Johnson frequently played him off the ball, while Harris' best year of his

Acquiring point guard Steve Nash is one of the best trades in Mavericks history.

career came in his first full season with the New Jersey Nets. But as Harris' injury problems caused a decline in his play, and Kidd led the Mavericks to a championship, it was clear Dallas won this swap.

The Tyson Chandler trade

Chandler came to Dallas intending to be a backup center. It's still wild to think that the catalyst for the 2011 championship run came from a player who planned to come off the bench.

The trade was Chandler and Alexis Ajinca for Erick Dampier, Eduardo Najera, and Matt Carroll. The Mavericks had been flaunting Dampier as a trade chip for a while because his expiring deal was partially guaranteed and could instantly save teams money if they cut him.

The Steve Nash trade

The Mavericks had desired a trade for Steve Nash for months before the Phoenix Suns finally relented. The push behind the deal was Donnie Nelson, the budding executive who had worked with the Suns before joining Dallas and had seen the talent of Phoenix's backup point guard firsthand. After the 1998 draft, on the same day the Mavericks chose a young German named Dirk Nowitzki, Phoenix finally relented and shipped out Nash.

Dallas, of course, watched Nash grow into a star point guard for six seasons, as he and Nowitzki helped the Mavericks become a perennial playoff team. They thought the Suns' backup point guard was good, sure, but no one could have predicted he would be *that* good.

83 Chandler Parsons

It's appropriate that Chandler Parsons' time with the Mavericks began and ended in a club. The first one was an Orlando nightclub, where Mark Cuban and Parsons initially signed the offer sheet that eventually made him a Maverick. It's always a gamble to pursue restricted free agents, but Dallas rolled the dice on a three-year deal worth $46 million for a small forward who they believed was underused with the Houston Rockets. A selfie taken that night—Cuban wore a T-shirt with the papers on the table beneath him, and Parsons was behind him, sporting a gold chain—went viral and immortalizes that night.

The second came two years later at an Oklahoma burlesque-themed spot called Dollhouse Lounge. A day before a Mavericks playoff game against the Oklahoma City Thunder and with Parsons sidelined with his second season-ending injury, the Hollywood forward and his nearly-as-flamboyant owner bantered back and forth in the dimly lit bar with a few celebrity friends. One was comedian and actor Amy Schumer, who posted a selfie that Parsons and Cuban posed for.

As Parsons left that evening, he and his entourage took the cab, which had been called for Cuban. In a scene described by an ESPN article in 2016, Parsons rolled down the window and shouted, "Max or nothing, motherfucker!" at Cuban as the car rolled away. It was playful, just like the rest of the evening. Still, it illustrated the one problem with the future of the Cuban-Parsons relationship: that Parsons wanted a maximum contract that the Mavericks were never going to offer him.

When Dallas' season ended five games later, Parsons' time there did, too. Parsons, if nothing else, was one of the most entertaining athletes the Mavericks ever employed. When Rick Carlisle called him overweight in his very first training camp with the team, Parsons responded by posting a photo of his sculpted abs on Instagram. That set an appropriate tone for his expensive fashion tastes, part-time modeling in the offseason, supermodel girlfriends, and a glamorous Instagram account, featuring vacations around the globe.

Entertainment alone wasn't enough to make up for the disappointment of his on-court performance. In Parsons' two seasons in Dallas, he showed flashes of being an elite pick-and-roll ballhandler. During the occasional moments when he could get the ball out of Monta Ellis or Rajon Rondo's hands, Parsons played best in his first season. At 6'10" his ball handling, passing, and scoring gave him a skillset unique to only a few other players his height.

In a game against Oklahoma City during his first season, Parsons took over the fourth quarter of a thrilling four-point win. He scored 13 points in the final 5:08, and almost all the points came on layups from driving to the rim off pick-and-rolls before he iced the game with a turnaround jumper. That is the player the Mavericks paid for, and in an alternate timeline somewhere, that must have been exactly who he became. Unfortunately, in this one, he never did.

Parsons didn't play in the final six games of the 2014–15 regular season because of a knee injury, but Dallas was facing the Rockets, Parsons' former team, in the first round. There was no way he was missing it, so he powered through Game 1 while visibly limited. Late in the second quarter, Parsons tweaked it and limped back to the locker room while a hostile Rockets crowd booed him. But he came out and finished the second half anyway—a moment forgotten by Mavericks fans in the years that followed.

Still, playing on that knee may have been reckless. At worst, you could speculate he injured his knee even further, though there never has been definitive proof. Regardless, it was announced

Parsons needed season-ending knee surgery shortly before Game 2. The Mavericks fell to Houston in a gentleman's sweep, winning only Game 4 at home in the five-game series.

That summer the Mavericks were vague about Parsons' injury. By the time free agency rolled around, though, it had been nearly forgotten, and Parsons spent weeks recruiting DeAndre Jordan, a move that he and Cuban were convinced would push the Mavericks back toward contender status in the Western Conference. It nearly worked, too. You can't really blame the Mavericks for the debacle that followed, when Jordan verbally committed to the team, second-guessed his decision the next day, and ultimately broke his verbal agreement to re-sign with the Clippers a week later.

It turned out Parsons' surgery was a form of microfracture surgery, one of the worst knee procedures an athlete can have. Even though the two ballhandling guards that disrupted last year's offense were gone, Parsons started the season slow, working his way back into shape on a severe minutes restriction. It was an exasperating two months before Parsons was "healthy" and it was another one before he started to look like himself again.

In January and February that season, Parsons was superb. Over his final 26 games in Dallas, Parsons averaged 19 points, six rebounds, and three assists on sparkling efficiency, even as the Mavericks themselves were struggling. But the team could only be so sympathetic when Parsons went down for the year yet again. After he missed a couple games with hamstring tightness, the Mavericks announced Parsons was undergoing arthroscopic knee surgery and would miss the playoffs for a second straight season. The two sides didn't talk much after that, and Dallas let him walk that offseason without ever officially offering him a contract.

Parsons was a smart signing that didn't work out. The small-but-vocal percentage of Mavericks fans who trashed Parsons after leaving—booing him upon his return and accusing him of "stealing" Dirk Nowitzki's money because Nowitzki's pay cut had helped facilitate his signing—never made much sense.

It's false reasoning to think that because Parsons had a lavish lifestyle off the court, he couldn't also care about basketball. After all, there are enough hours in the day for both pleasure and business. But in hindsight, it's pretty clear the decision to let Parsons walk was the right one. Though Parsons and Nowitzki had an amusing lighthearted relationship, it was clear the Big German meshed better with Parsons' replacement, Harrison Barnes—a gym rat with a subdued off-court persona.

Barnes won't be posting 1:00 AM selfies with Cuban. He has a vastly different lifestyle and famously claimed the Golden State Warriors' championship champagne in 2015 was his first alcoholic drink ever. It's hard to imagine anyone having quite the relationship Parsons did with Cuban, to be honest. The most outgoing player in the NBA paired up with the most sociable owner resulted in a bond between two unlikely parties. In retrospect, especially with other teammates frowning in private at the influence Parsons had, it might have been for the best that both parties separated when they did.

Still, the breakup won't be forever. Not if Cuban has his way. In a scene described by ESPN, the two met up for drinks shortly before training camp in 2016. That night Cuban raised his glass saying that his boy, Parsons, would be back in one role or another someday in Dallas.

84 Other Rivalries

The San Antonio Spurs will always be the Mavericks' most important rival. They've dueled too many times over the years and they've competed so closely as the winningest franchises since 2000 that they're inseparable. There are other teams, though, with whom the Mavericks have shared a heated history. These three stand out the most.

Los Angeles Lakers

Three times, the Mavericks met the Los Angeles Lakers in the playoffs in the 1980s. Three times, the Mavericks lost. It may not have been the most competitive rivalry in the postseason, but Los Angeles frustrated Dallas more than any other team. Mavericks players and fans will always remember the 1988 Western Conference Finals. In 1984 and 1986, the Lakers had twice beaten Dallas convincingly in the semifinals, but the '88 series felt different. Mavericks fans packed the stadium, and chants of "Beat L.A." resonated through Reunion Arena, but Dallas lost in seven games. Surprisingly, Dirk Nowitzki and Kobe Bryant only faced off once in the playoffs, a four-game sweep in 2011 during the championship run. But the memories of the two teams battling in the '80s will never leave those who lived it.

Houston Rockets

Even putting aside sports, Dallas and Houston are rivals. The cities share a not-always-friendly rivalry, and their sports teams are just the easiest manifestation of the locales' mutual desire to one-up each other. In the past few seasons, the Mavericks and the Rockets' rivalry has grown even more real.

The proximity helps. That Chandler Parsons left the Houston Rockets to sign in Dallas in 2014 added fuel during his two years here, too. Mavericks fans can't stand James Harden's uncanny knack for drawing fouls—or "flopping" as they call it.

Utah Jazz

This was a rather one-sided rivalry since the Mavericks consistently roasted the Utah Jazz. They only met in the playoffs once when Dallas upset the Jazz in 2001 thanks to Calvin Booth's last-minute layup. Dirk once called Utah, though he meant Salt Lake City, "a bad city." Though the quote was taken out of context, Jazz fans used it as an excuse to boo him for years afterward.

85 The 11-Win Season

Eleven wins. Seventy-one losses. Only four teams in NBA history have ever had a worse season than the Mavericks in 1993. It's a year Dallas fans wish they could douse in gasoline, light on fire, and launch into space. Through 76 games their 8–68 record is the worst of all time. If the team hadn't won three of their final six games, Dallas would have an even more infamous spot in the record books. Instead, the Philadelphia 76ers have both a nine and a 10-win season that save Dallas from utter embarrassment. Still, an 11-win season cannot be bragged about and it included the Mavericks' worst loss in team history—a 58-point decimation at the hands of the Sacramento Kings.

Instead of dwelling on the losses, though, we'll look at the silver lining and focus on the 11 games the Mavericks did win that season.

November 14, 1992
Mavericks 113, Hawks 105
Dallas' first win that season came against the Atlanta Hawks—a very average squad that finished with 43 wins—thanks to the best game of Terry Davis' life. Davis was a journeyman big man, but against the Hawks, he looked like he had stolen Dominique Wilkins' powers. Davis finished with 35 points and 17 rebounds for the only 30-point game in his career. In fact, he never scored more than 24 in any other game.

December 16, 1992
Mavericks 102, Lakers 95
After running the league (or at least the Western Conference) for the 1980s, the Los Angeles Lakers came back down to earth for a few seasons. They only won 39 games that year and they were the second team to lose to Dallas. Terry Davis had a much more ordinary performance of 16 points and eight rebounds.

January 19, 1993
Mavericks 113, Pistons 103
Dallas lost 15 games in a row before adding another game to the win column. The Detroit Pistons were on a downswing from their consecutive championships in 1989 and 1990, but they still had Mavericks star Mark Aguirre, who scored just two points off the bench.

February 5, 1993
Mavericks 105, Pacers 104
Only nine games later, the Mavericks won again. Like the other three teams, the Indiana Pacers were enduring a middle-of-the-road season, going exactly 41–41 that year. While Reggie Miller dropped 30 points, Derek Harper's 22-point, 13-assist night led the way for a Dallas victory.

March 17, 1993
Mavericks 102, Magic 96
After the win against Indiana, the team went on its longest losing streak of the year and lost 19 straight games. Amazingly, Dallas topped it the following season, losing 20 straight. That second streak still stands as a franchise record. This win was weird. Only one Mavericks starter (Jim Jackson) scored in double figures against the Orlando Magic, but four bench players did. The 51 points from the reserves carried the day.

March 19, 1993
Mavericks 89, 76ers 87
A streak! An honest-to-God winning streak! (Do two straight victories count as a winning streak?) It wasn't pretty against the Philadelphia 76ers, but a 24-point evening from Terry Davis led the way.

March 24, 1993
Mavericks 101, Bullets 98
Jim Jackson, the team's top pick, didn't play until March. Once he did, it was clear why Dallas had picked him fourth overall. His 27 points, eight rebounds, and seven assists against the Washington Bullets in the Mavericks' seventh win of the year clearly showed his potential.

April 6, 1993
Mavericks 109, SuperSonics 107
The Seattle SuperSonics were by far the best team Dallas beat in 1993. Led by Ricky Pierce, Shawn Kemp, and Gary Payton, they finished with 55 wins before reaching the Western Conference Finals and losing to the Phoenix Suns in seven games. But despite a totally healthy roster, the Sonics couldn't top the Mavericks in

this late-season game. Led by Jim Jackson's 18 points, eight Dallas players reached double figures.

April 16, 1993
Mavericks 99, Nuggets 86
The Denver Nuggets only won 36 games that season, but they earned a more infamous honor: they were the only team Dallas beat by more than 10 points all year. I hope everyone who was on that team still wakes up at night ashamed of themselves.

April 23, 1993
Mavericks 103, Timberwolves 100
Jimmy Jackson's season-high came in this game. On the second-to-last day of the regular season, he scored 32 points on 11-of-21 shooting against the Minnesota Timberwolves.

April 24, 1993
Mavericks 128, Rockets 123
The Houston Rockets were the other good team Dallas beat, albeit on the last day of the season without a couple rotation players in Vernon Maxwell and Robert Horry. Houston was a season away from back-to-back championships, but it still had 55 wins that year. Jim Jackson and Derek Harper combined for 41 points while the bench chipped in 44 points combined—enough to push Dallas to a final win that year.

As you can tell, this season could have been even worse. Jackson's late debut was a major reason why the Mavericks only had four wins halfway through March. Thankfully, Dallas won enough late in the year to avoid total embarrassment—well, as much as an 11-win season can avoid embarrassment.

86 Devin Harris

Devin Harris began his career with Dallas trapped in the middle of an internal political struggle, reprised his role years later as a backup guard, and became an NBA All-Star somewhere in the middle of those two former things. Since becoming the franchise's only top five selection since Jason Kidd, he's had a strange career.

Technically, the Washington Wizards selected Harris in the 2004 NBA Draft, but it was at the Mavericks' request. Shortly after the selection, the Mavericks dealt them Antawn Jamison in exchange for Harris, Jerry Stackhouse, and Christian Laettner in a prearranged deal. Dallas had planned to groom Harris as a point guard to back up Steve Nash, but that idea was derailed when Nash left in free agency that summer.

The relationship between Mark Cuban and head coach Don Nelson had already been deteriorating, but Cuban's decision not to match Phoenix's offer to Nash was a final blow for Nelson. Many think he subtly retaliated during that 2004 season. "[Nelson] started Devin Harris ahead of Jason Terry," said Jeff Wade, a Mavericks announcer and longtime Dallas radio host. "I think that was a middle finger up in the air. Devin Harris wasn't ready to start at point guard, but it was, 'Oh, you're going to take my guy away? Here's a rookie, have fun with this.' That's how I perceived it."

Harris started the first 19 games that season before being moved to the bench. Despite being jerked around as a front-office pawn, Harris showed flashes that season of his incredible quickness and playmaking skills.

The trajectory on Harris' career changed when Nelson resigned later that season and left Avery Johnson in charge. Johnson discouraged Harris from shooting three-pointers (he only attempted

71 total the next two years) and generally encouraged him to play conservatively over the next few seasons. "Avery kept that entire team bottled up, and it worked right up until it didn't," said Kirk Henderson, longtime editor at the Mavericks blog Mavs Moneyball. "I had no idea he had some of the scoring ability he showed in New Jersey."

Many Mavericks fans still believed Harris could continue developing, but after the 2006 NBA Finals fiasco and the embarrassing first-round upset the following year, Harris was dealt to the New Jersey Nets in the Jason Kidd trade. Dealing a 24-year-old point guard for a 34-year-old one didn't make everyone happy, though there were plenty of fans who supported the deal as well.

Initially, it looked like Dallas had been fleeced. Harris had a career year during the 2008–09 season, making the All-Star team and averaging more than 21 points per game with his newfound offensive freedom. During one Mavericks game in New Jersey, fans even chanted, "Thank you, Cuban!" By the next season, though, Harris was already declining. Injuries began popping up that would nag at him the rest of his career, and Harris has played more than 70 games in his career only two seasons since. The Nets dealt him to the Utah Jazz as part of the Deron Williams deal in 2011, and he played there for a year before moving on to the Atlanta Hawks. In the summer of 2013, Harris reunited with the Mavericks in free agency. "I also didn't think he'd play as long as he has," Henderson said. "Point guards are a challenging position to hoist the 'future of the franchise' label on because it's really hard to tell how long their prime will last."

87 The Best Dirk Quotes

Dirk Nowitzki's dry, often self-deprecating humor has helped endear himself to fans almost as much as his play on the court. He doesn't take compliments well, blames himself for losses, and nitpicks his performance even when he plays well individually. But once you get him talking, especially after a win, he's more than happy to crack jokes and poke good-natured fun at his teammates. Over the years, we've been treated to dozens of wonderful Nowitzki one-liners and more thoughtful answers about his career. Here are 10 favorites.

"You should learn Chinese because you'll be in China soon."
Nowitzki might not act arrogant off the court, but when he's hooping, his (mostly) friendly trash talk is legendary. In both practices and games, Nowitzki will roast anyone who comes at him, and one of his favorite quips is the one above. Nowitzki also enjoys calling players "burgers," which is probably meant as a slight but just ends up being hilarious.

"You are my guy, but your head weighs 500 pounds."
Don't mess with Nowitzki on Twitter. He fired off this zinger to teammate Zaza Pachulia back in 2016.

"Utah is a bad city."
Let Nowitzki explain this incredible gaffe: "We come back here for Game 2, and there was like one camera guy, and he asked me, 'So why did you guys not stay in Utah?' I said, 'Well, Utah is a bad city,' meaning it's the playoffs, and we shouldn't spend too much time there, it's hostile. I come back here, and they blew the whole

thing up. They were talking about it on the TV that night already. I mean, they were trying to call my hotel room. It was awesome. Then, like I said, I came out with 90 minutes on the clock, and they were already booing. There was a sign up there: 'Germany is a bad city.' They got me good." Nowitzki was booed in Utah—well, Salt Lake City—for years because of this quote. Fortunately, he took it in stride.

"Shut it down! Let's go home!"
Bless whoever's idea it was to give Dirk Nowitzki a microphone while he was injured in 2012. What was an in-game interview turned into Nowitzki serving as totally biased, completely hyped color commentator, shouting in glee when Brandan Wright threw down a big dunk. It's a top five moment in his career, and nobody can tell me differently.

"My Crocs game is strong."
When Zaza Pachulia posted a photo of Dirk Nowitzki wearing Crocs—the popular slip-on shoe renowned for its ugliness—it caused nearly everyone to poke good-natured fun at the Big German. Hey, Nowitzki stuck by the footwear all the same. "When my daughter wants to play, I'll take her out, and it's rained a little bit and it's a little wet, so I put on my Crocs," he told the media. "And one day I must have just not paid attention and I walked out in my Crocs and went to the arena. Everything broke loose from there. The guys were killing me, and the pictures were taken and sent out on social media. My Crocs game is strong."

"I came up with my own Dream Shake, I guess, the white version."
Nowitzki talks humbly about his signature one-footed fadeaway after passing Hakeem Olajuwon for all-time points scored.

"For a white guy, it's pretty impressive."
Nowitzki rarely ever says something raunchy, especially when he knows he's on camera. That makes this rare exception even better. A few days before, Shaun Livingston had earned a flagrant foul for bizarrely whacking Nowitzki's…well, his groin area. (I don't think my editors would let me print anything more descriptive than that.) Talking about the play at a charity event, Nowitzki uttered this flawless joke with a hilarious implication. "We talked a little bit afterward," he said, already starting to smile. "He said, 'For a white guy, it's pretty impressive.'"

Even Rick Carlisle, sitting next to Nowitzki, cracked a smile.

"That was the realest thing, probably ever in my entire life. That's when you know, 'Now this is all you. This is a responsibility for now on, for the rest of your life.'"
That's what Nowitzki said about parenthood after he and his wife Jessica took home their first newborn daughter. It's not the only time Nowitzki talked about being a parent, and this quote is an amazing insight into who he is as a person. "I'm glad I had kids later in my career, where I can enjoy it more," he said. "Sometimes I'm like, 'I don't think I could have done this in my 20s, when I was super intense, when everything was so goal-driven.' I still love to compete, but now if I don't sleep my eight hours it's, 'Okay, just deal with it.' But in my 20s, I would have been paranoid."

"Don't feel bad for me."
This is my favorite quote from Nowitzki. When he was asked about potentially not winning another championship, this response really put sports and winning in perspective.

Here's the full quote: "I see, obviously, reports on Twitter all the time, guys hitting me up, 'I feel bad for Dirk.' Don't feel bad for me. I love what I do, and we get paid a lot of money to do what we do. I love competing and I love the sport still. I've been lucky to do it for a long, long time, came here, whatever, 18 years ago not knowing what to expect, and it's been an incredible journey. I don't want anybody to feel sorry for me. I'm going to compete like I always have, and then one day it'll be all over."

"I always wanted to be a basketball player—nothing more, nothing less."
And damn, he was a great one.

88 Wesley Matthews

When DeAndre Jordan backed out of his verbal agreement with the Mavericks, Mark Cuban gave Wesley Matthews an option. Matthews had also agreed to sign with the Mavericks, and Cuban told him he would understand if Matthews wanted to back out now. "I told Wes that I would not hold him to his commitment if he wanted to go elsewhere," Cuban wrote on his Dust message application. "I can't print his exact response, but suffice it to say he is excited to play for our Mavs."

For jilted Mavericks fans, it's exactly what they needed to hear.

Matthews' career in Dallas since that moment has had some ups and downs, but the Marquette University product is set to play for the Mavericks through at least 2019, and the franchise is all the better for it. He's a fiercely loyal teammate who helps maintain the perfect temperament in a locker room and he's stubborn as hell when anyone tries to question what he believes. Even during his worst shooting stretches, Matthews will swear up and down that his next dozen shots will go in. Even when the Mavericks started 4–17 during the 2016–17 season, Matthews always believed the team would make a playoff run.

Poised to be a marquee free agent on the 2015 market, Matthews suffered the biggest setback of his career when he ruptured his Achilles tendon. Matthews was playing for Portland then, where he spent five of his first six seasons, and the Trail Blazers were 41–19 when his injury occurred. Portland, a team that had even been rumored as a dark-horse championship contender by several smart pundits, wasn't the same after that and won just one game in the playoffs.

An Achilles rupture is basketball's worst muscular injury of the ones that occur on a somewhat regular basis. We hear a lot about torn ACL muscles because they're more common and familiar, but Achilles injuries require an even more difficult recovery process. "The Achilles tendon attaches the calf muscle to the heel bone," Dr. Kevin Stone, a longtime orthopedic surgeon, told me. "It's designed to stretch, it's designed to absorb force when the athlete lands from a jump. It's designed to provide power for push-off when taking a running step."

An Achilles rupture, Stone said, is normally just bad luck if a basketball player suffers it. In Matthews' case his nickname is "Ironman," and he once played 250 consecutive games before that streak ended in 2012. Heading into the 2015 offseason was unfamiliar territory for him, but the Mavericks valued his work ethic and trusted he could recover. They signed him to a four-year max contract anyway.

Matthews said right away his plan was to start Game 1 for the Mavericks. Miraculously, he did despite the injury, playing 78 games that season while logging the fourth most minutes of his career. After a red hot December, including a game where he hit seven threes, Matthews struggled with his shot much of the rest of the season. Given he was returning from injury, it wasn't a huge surprise he posted career low percentages shooting from the field and behind the three-point line.

Any concern that Matthews would never recover was put to rest the next year. Matthews even earned himself an invitation to participate in the Three-Point Contest during 2017 All-Star weekend. As the Mavericks build for the future, Matthews is exactly the type of player you want in the locker room.

89 Deron Williams

Deron Williams' career in Dallas will always come with a "what if?" In the 2012 offseason, when people still debated whether he or Chris Paul was a better point guard, Williams chose to re-sign with the Brooklyn Nets instead of joining Dallas. The decision permanently altered both franchises.

Williams grew up in Carrollton and went to high school in The Colony, two Texas suburbs about 30 minutes down the highway from Dallas. His junior and senior seasons, Williams led his high school to consecutive seasons where they lost just twice. As Williams' career progressed, he emerged as one of the two best point guards in the league. The third overall pick in 2005, Williams averaged 17 points and nine assists during his first six seasons with the Utah Jazz. From about 2007 to 2010, the Williams vs. Paul debate could start a lively debate at virtually any bar in America.

Utah traded Williams to the New Jersey Nets at the 2010 trade deadline. He had another year left on his current contract and as he gave signs that he might leave in free agency, the Jazz wanted to strike when the point guard still had plenty of value. Williams had a mediocre season and a half with the Nets, still putting up numbers but posting career low percentages, thanks to a lack of talent around him. It brought him to free agency and a choice that would shape the rest of his career.

The Mavericks had shed much of their players from their 2011 title team because they expected to have several great chances at landing a superstar. Williams was first in line, and with Dallas being his hometown, the team expected to have a pitch that could sway him. After Williams met with both teams, it was reported to be a 50-50 decision. The Nets pushed a bright future on Williams: they had a new owner, Russian billionaire Mikhail Prokhorov, who promised to spend; they had Jay Z as a part owner, who helped push a monochromatic rebrand to the Brooklyn Nets; they had traded for Gerald Wallace, who was coming off a down year with the Portland Trail Blazers but was still considered in his prime. The Nets could also offer Williams more money since they retained his Larry Bird rights.

In Dallas the pitch was simpler: we just won a championship, we have Dirk Nowitzki, and we're your hometown. On July 2, as Williams was still mulling over his two options, the Nets swung a terrible trade for Joe Johnson. They dealt nearly six players and a first-round draft pick for Johnson, a former All-Star who was a good player but owed an outrageous $90 million over the next four seasons. The move crippled their future, but it was thought to be the move that swayed Williams to choose Brooklyn.

The story ends poorly: the Nets won 49 games the next season with their massive payroll, fell to 44 the following year, tumbled below .500 the year after, and now have a muddier path back to relevancy than any team in the league. In 2015 Williams requested and was granted a buyout from the Nets, telling Yahoo! Sports he questioned if he even wanted to keep playing basketball during his final months in Brooklyn.

After his buyout Williams' choice in free agency was clear. The point guard, who was clearly on the decline, chose to return home to Dallas that summer, joining the team in the wake of the DeAndre Jordan fiasco and helping lead a surprising recovery effort by the Mavericks' front office. One thing was very clear: it was good to be home. "It's home," Williams told *The Dallas Morning News* in 2015. "I am a homebody. We have been on the road, so I haven't really got a chance to get out much. But it's a great city, great people, great food. I love Mexican food. I definitely missed Tex-Mex when I was gone. That's probably missed the most— Tex-Mex and barbecue. So I get my fair share of that now. I've got to stay away from it more than anything. Those are two great things about being back, for sure."

Williams never regained his old form in Dallas, but no one expected him to. His steady presence was welcome. He meshed well with Rick Carlisle and mentored the young roster Dallas fielded in the 2016–17 season before Dallas waived him so he could join the reigning champions, the Cleveland Cavaliers. He missed games both years but gutted through a hernia injury in the first-round series against Oklahoma City in 2016, playing through a visibly painful injury to score 13 points in the team's only win that series. He ended up being sidelined for all but one minute the rest of the series, but his play in that game helped vindicate previous notions that Williams was "soft."

Williams almost certainly would have been more successful in Dallas if he had chosen them in 2012, though part of his failures in Brooklyn came from his body slowly breaking down. Even the Mavericks' lauded training staff couldn't have reversed that completely.

90 Watch the Dirk Nowitzki Documentary

There's a Dirk Nowitzki documentary you must watch called *Nowitzki: The Perfect Shot*. It was released by the Mark Cuban-owned Magnolia Pictures in 2014 and is widely available for purchase online.

There are several Nowitzki documentaries, but this one was directed and produced by two German filmmakers, features interviews with legends like Kobe Bryant and Yao Ming, and offers the most real look at Nowitzki's career you'll ever see. It starts with Nowitzki growing up in Wurzburg, Germany, and progresses throughout his career, showing every high and low he experienced.

The documentary even addresses one awkward moment in Nowitzki's life: a bizarre relationship with Cristal Taylor, who he was briefly engaged to before she turned out to be a con artist and was arrested on charges of fraud. For months she maintained that she was carrying Nowitzki's child before it was revealed she wasn't even pregnant. The documentary also shows Nowitzki's happy marriage to his current wife, Jessica, just a couple years later.

Here are a few other highlights from the documentary:

- Nowitzki still asks for gas money from his mom when he visits Germany.
- His MVP trophy is also at his parents' house in Germany, sitting right next to his dad's Player of the Year handball award.
- Holger Geschwindner calls his basketball training academy the "Institute of Applied Nonsense" and even has business cards with that exact phrase printed on there.

91 Best Places to Take In Mavericks Fandom

Dallas will forever be a football city first. Football culture begins in high school and is carried on by Cowboys, Longhorns, and Aggies, whose fandom is a bond treated as strong as family. But Dallas is a basketball town, too. Dirk Nowitzki making the Mavericks good—for damn near two decades—was the best way to push the fanatics who filled Reunion Arena into die-hard fans that permeated the entire Metroplex. At the start of the 2017–18 season, the American Airlines Center has sold out a league-best 637 straight Mavericks games. Google "2011 Mavericks championship parade," and I guarantee you've never seen downtown look quite like that.

You can find signs of Mavericks loyalty all throughout the Dallas area, but here are the best spots.

The Deep Ellum Murals

You have to visit the Mavericks murals painted onto the team's corporate office in Deep Ellum, the city's leading entertainment district just northeast of downtown. Both of them feature an even larger-than-life Dirk, one celebrating 2011, and another with arms fully outstretched and his name prominently on the back of his jersey. They're sure to improve your Instagram feed—that much is for certain.

The Hangar

The Mavericks reopened a fan shop in Victory Park right by the American Airlines Center. It's the best place for gear and other team items.

City Tavern and Taco Joint

Look carefully and you'll see jerseys and memorabilia in bars and restaurants all over Dallas. City Tavern, the best bar downtown in my humble opinion, has a signed Dirk Nowitzki jersey. Taco Joint, a local chain that sells…well, tacos…has murals with Mavericks scenes woven in.

Bullzerk

Two married graphic designers opened this Dallas-centric T-shirt shop that sells other various city-related memorabilia, too. You can usually find something related to the Mavericks here, and if not, visit anyway since it's a cool place.

92 The Best Dirk Nicknames

Dirk Nowitzki is already an incredible name, but the Big German hasn't gone two decades in the NBA without picking up some great ones. See, I just used one and I swear I wasn't even meaning to. Note that these rankings have been arbitrarily decided by me alone and thus are flawless and without critique. Thank you.

12. The German Wunderkind

The joke here is that *wunderkind* (definition: a person who achieves great success when relatively young) is a word with German origins, like Nowitzki, and it describes him. It's an alright nickname! But it hasn't aged well, now that Nowitzki is no longer relatively young.

The Bavarian Bomber (aka the German Wunderkind) employs his patented one-legged jumper to score his 30,000th career point.

11. Der Dunkinschnitzel, Der Dribblemeister, Der DunkinmeisterBaron von Slamminstein, Admiral von Slamminhausen, and Kaiser von Dunkinslammin

When Conan O'Brien hosted his show in Dallas for a week, he had Nowitzki rattle off his many nicknames.

10. Dirk Diggler

Diggler is a character in the cult movie *Boogie Nights*. He's an actor in adult movies, though, so no real tie-in to Nowitzki besides the first name.

9. The Seven-Foot Schnitzel

Schnitzel—specifically, wiener schnitzel—is the national dish of Austria. Unfortunately that's not Germany, though it's common in Germany.

8. ReDirkulous

It's not really a nickname, more of an adjective with a clever turn of phrase. Either way, it is pretty good and quite common.

7. The Berlin Tall

The play on words of the Berlin Wall is clever. This is good stuff.

6. Dunking Deutschman

Deutschman is such a great word all by itself that it carries this nickname. But you say, does Dirk really dunk much? Only 352 times in his regular-season career, thank you very much. He was a lot more spry than people remember in his first five seasons. It's also a play on words of the "Dunking Dutchman," the nickname of former Indiana Pacers center Rik Smits, who was born in the Netherlands.

5. The Bavarian Bomber

Wurzburg is located in the German region of Bavaria, so this nickname gets extra credit for being very geographically accurate.

4. Blonde Bomber

This nickname worked best when Nowitzki had his shaggy locks rather than the more mature closer cut. It's still solid.

3. Ghostface Drillah

Created in honor of rap emcee Ghostface Killah, this nickname is too good. When Nowitzki drilled a clutch shot over your favorite team, you could only shake your head.

2. Dirty

Just Dirty. That's what he is. That's who he has been. It's unbelievably simple and so perfect that only one can truly top it.

1. Tall Baller From the G

And it's this one. It has rhythm. It has soul. They're all great, but this has to be my favorite.

93 Rodrigue Beaubois

The obsession started with a video. It was a grainy five minutes and 32 seconds, uploaded to YouTube in April 2009, set to Michael Jackson's "Thriller," and titled simply, "highlights BEAUBOIS." Who knows how it even got there; the account that posted it has never uploaded anything else.

For people whose Mavericks fandom was cultish—at the time that included me—that was all we could find out about Dallas' first-round pick in the 2009 NBA Draft. No one really knew anything about Rodrigue Beaubois when he went No. 25 overall, but the mystery just made him more fascinating.

Oh, that video. In those glorious five-and-a-half minutes, Beaubois did everything. The 6'0" guard rained down three-pointers, blocked jump shots, confidently ran fast breaks, and even threw down alley-oops. The competition was unknown French leagues, but his potential—along with a 39" vertical leap and 6'10" wingspan—stood out even then.

The Mavericks started 12–3 in the 2009–10 season, and Beaubois started 12 of those games. Because Dallas preferred Jason Terry as the sixth man, there always was room for a provisional starting two-guard, something Roddy B was perfect for. Three weeks into the season, he played 19 minutes in a game against the Detroit Pistons, scoring 14 points on 6-of-6 shooting with four assists and no turnovers. Mavericks fans' slow-growing fondness for the rookie began turning into a craze.

Beaubois fell in and out of the rotation that year, but he dazzled offensively in most of his minutes on the floor. He had a seven-game stretch early in March where he scored double digits every time, including a brilliant performance against the Chicago Bulls while filling in for Jason Kidd, and not a single Chicago defender could stay in front of him. Then on March 27, against the lowly 2010 Golden State Warriors, Beaubois painted his Mona Lisa—40 points, nine three-pointers, and eight rebounds to go along with 68 percent shooting.

The hype had never been higher. "Rodrigue Beaubois, the 22-year-old future of the franchise," wrote *D Magazine* before the 2011 season. "The Mavs' season depends on Beaubois bursting out and coach Rick Carlisle using him properly. Beaubois is the only hope," wrote Tom Ziller for AOL NBA FanHouse. "Championship? If It Happens, It's Because Of That French Dude," wrote another dude, clearly out of his mind. Okay, yes, it was me. It definitely wasn't because of that French Dude, but at least the championship part came true. The point is that Beaubois hysteria had reached impossible levels. "I'm not going to trade Roddy," Cuban told reporters a few days before the 2010 trade deadline. "There are maybe one or two guys in the league I'll trade him for. Other than that, he's pretty much untouchable."

The Mavericks had totally bought into the young Frenchman, but unfortunately, Beaubois' anointment as the Mavericks' next great star came to a screeching halt before the 2011 season. While practicing for the French national team, Beaubois broke the fifth metatarsal in his foot. He wouldn't return until February, when he started 26 games with mediocre results. He didn't play a minute in the championship run.

Carlisle continued to treat him as a rotation player the next season, but Beaubois simply couldn't produce consistently enough. After hitting 41 percent of his three-pointers as a rookie, Beaubois could never crack 30 percent in his following three years with the Mavericks. Between those shooting struggles, his fragile injury history, and an inability to put it all together, Beaubois faded out of the league after his contract expired in 2013 and hasn't re-signed with an NBA team since. He still plays basketball professionally and lives in Dallas during his offseason, but even if Beaubois does attempt an NBA comeback, he'll unfortunately never live up to what we all thought he could be.

Mavericks fans had gone years without a truly impressive young prospect when Beaubois arrived, so there's no surprise he captured everyone's attention as easily as he did. Perhaps in an alternate universe somewhere, Beaubois never got injured and turned into a top 10 guard in the NBA for an entire decade. Instead, we're left with the one video. It's still on YouTube, still scored by Michael Jackson, still featuring Beaubois at his best, still taunting us.

94 Mother's Day Massacre

The Mavericks were never better during the 2011 championship run than in Game 4 of the Western Conference Semifinals against the Los Angeles Lakers. On the verge of sweeping the two-time defending champions and sending Phil Jackson into an unceremonious retirement, Dallas left no doubts. The Mavericks led by 25 points in the first half, tied a then playoff record with 20 three-pointers, and finished with a 122–86 eviscerating win.

Here are the 20 three-pointers.

1. Just 34 seconds into the game, DeShawn Stevenson buried the game's first three-pointer. It was wide open. You'll find that's a trend.
2. Jason Kidd nailed the second three of the game after curling up from the baseline to the right wing. He and Stevenson were starters, but the bench was responsible for 17 of the next 18 makes.
3. Jason Terry didn't enter the game until 2:53 remained in the first quarter. When the Lakers overplayed Dirk Nowitzki, Terry drained his first three off Nowitzki's pass to the opposite corner.
4. On the next play, Peja Stojakovic hit for the first time.
5. In the second quarter, Steve Blake gambled for a steal and came up short, giving Terry enough space for his second three.

6. Terry was open again in the opposite corner, and this time it was off an offensive rebound.

7. "The JET flaps are down, and Jason Terry is 4-for-4 behind the long line," television announcer Mike Breen said after Terry found himself wide open. "How you doing, JT?"

8. Mavericks fans had brought brooms to "sweep" the Lakers away and signs screaming, "BEAT L.A." That was the old chant Dallas fans used in the 1980s, when Los Angeles emerged as the bitter rival that knocked the Mavericks out of the post-season. When Terry hit his fifth three on five attempts off a gorgeous pass from Nowitzki, those chants started back up in earnest.

9. On the very next possession, Stojakovic buried a corner three that barely moved the net. "Another one," Breen yelled. The Lakers called a timeout.

10. Stojakovic was several feet behind the line when he fired up his next attempt. It was money.

11. Terry hit one more three with 30 seconds left. The Lakers retreated to the locker room, shellshocked.

12. Seconds after Terry checked into the second half, he was open for a three. It was his seventh in eight attempts.

13. Terry struck again. This time he passed the ball out, dribbled baseline, kept running to the corner, and got the ball back once he arrived. It's like the Lakers forgot about him the second the ball left his hands.

14. Terry hit his ninth and final three. He probably could have hit five more if he tried, but Terry wasn't forcing any shot. Every single attempt was a catch-and-shoot jumper.

15. Stojakovic got back in on the action with a transition triple, his fourth. Though it's on a smaller scale, this must've felt satisfying for him. A decade before, Stojakovic's Sacramento Kings had lost to Los Angeles in the 2002 Western Conference Finals. Thanks to questionable refereeing that gave the Lakers 73 free

throws in the final two games, it was still one of the most controversial playoff series in the league's history.

16. Dirk Nowitzki was left alone at the top of the arc. It's like Los Angeles forgot he could shoot back there, too.

17. It was Stojakovic again.

18. And Stojakovic struck one more time. He finished 6-of-6 on threes, while Terry was 9-of-10.

19. The final two threes both came from the same right corner. J.J. Barea hit the first one while the shot clock was running down and with Sasha Vujacic in his face.

20. Finally, Brian Cardinal launched a shot that tied what was then the NBA playoff record. The TV broadcast cut to a shot of Mark Cuban, and even he looked like he couldn't believe his eyes. And with that, the Mavericks ended the Lakers' chance at a three-peat and moved on to the Western Conference Finals.

95 Blog About the Mavericks

Mark Cuban became a billionaire because of the Internet and often wrote directly to Mavericks fans on his own personal blog. We'll ignore that he once banned "bloggers" from the locker room after a dispute with one media member. All in all, Dallas has an incredibly gracious credentialing process for blogs that are serious about covering the team.

That's how I started, joining SB Nation's Mavs Moneyball as a writer in 2010 before I began attending games in 2012. If you're a Mavericks fan and don't read the site, I'd say you're missing out on a great companion that can guide you through every game and offseason move the team makes.

Blogs used to be a novelty, but they're an essential part of any sports writing career now. Every journalist writes for the Internet, and every one has a Twitter presence, which is still called a "micro-blogging service" even if that term seems wholly outdated. It allows fans to connect to players and even us writers more than ever before. For example, I'll always respond to tweets if you mention me @tim_cato.

Dallas has had a rich blogosphere, though some have fallen to the wayside. The Two Man Game was a classic, and its successor Mavs Outsider Report ended up losing steam as well. We'll never forget the soft rock video breakdowns from TMG. In addition to Mavs Moneyball, other valued blogs in the Dallas blogosphere are dallasbasketball.com, mavsfanatic.com, and The Smoking Cuban, which is part of the FanSided network. All three have produced great work and quality reporting.

96 Binge-Watch Mavericks Videos

It's late Tuesday afternoon, and your boss has already left the office. It's 9:00 PM on a Friday, and your plans fell through, but it's too early to go to bed. I'm not here to judge your YouTube binges, when just one video somehow leads you down a rabbit hole, and suddenly you're watching a video teaching you how to make creme brulee, even though you burned the only batch of cookies you ever tried to bake. I'm just here to guide you along the journey.

Let's start nice and simple—just search "Dirk Nowitzki." If you want to see him light up some random team, add a number between 30 and 45 to the end. "Dirk Nowitzki 38" would work, for example, since Nowitzki has scored 38 points in a game nine times in his career, and at least a couple of those have dedicated videos for him. "Dirk Nowitzki game winner" is another good search if you want a shorter video.

Nowitzki's highest scoring game was a 53-point shootout with Tracy McGrady, who scored 48 points himself. For years we were stuck with grainy highlights of the game, but in 2016 the NBA uploaded a high-definition video of the two players facing off. The title starts with "Dirk Nowitzki VS Tracy McGrady HD," and if you put that into the search, it should come up. It's absolutely worth watching.

I ran Mavs Moneyball for years, but I can't take credit for our YouTube channel. One of our editors, Austin Ngaruiya, has loaded the page full of obscure, old highlights like Michael Jordan as a Washington Wizard and Nowitzki combining for 59 points in a game from 2003. Either search Mavs Moneyball on YouTube or type in youtube.com/user/sbnmavsmoneyball to dive into some old school, mid-2000s goodness.

The Dallas Mavericks' official account constantly uploads content. I'd advise sorting by "most popular" on their video page since a lot of it is filler you won't be interested in. Two more accounts that have great Mavericks videos are "kietassss" (that's four S') and "D-Mavs."

There's another Nowitzki documentary called "How Dirk became DIRK (full movie)." It's a great 50-minute documentary on the Dallas sports hero.

Finally, one more thing I cannot recommend highly enough: search "2011 mini movie." One of the best things the NBA does with its official media is creating mini documentaries (about 10 minutes long) for all the NBA Finals, including 2011. These are great watches, no matter what mood you're in. That's how you YouTube binge the Mavericks. Don't be ashamed, since we all do it. Now you can do it better.

97 The Best All-Time Guards

The franchise has existed for almost 40 years, meaning there are strong candidates for every position on a list of the Mavericks' all-time team. You're bound to disagree with me on a spot or two as well. Let's start with the two guard positions, which will earn the strongest arguments. Here's who I would choose.

Point Guard

The floor general for this Mavericks super lineup we're creating comes down to personal preference since the top three candidates are all more than qualified. Choosing between Jason Kidd, Steve Nash, and Derek Harper almost requires a coin flip.

Despite six seasons in Dallas, Nash only played 408 games, the lowest of the three. He was a great player but not quite the two-time MVP he became with the Phoenix Suns, averaging about 15 points during his time in Dallas along with seven assists. He was named to the All-Star team twice and he made the All-NBA third team a couple times as well. He and Nowitzki would still have flawless chemistry in this hypothetical experiment, so there's another point in his favor.

Kidd played exactly 500 games in a Dallas uniform. His stats are by far the lowest—10.5 points, 8.4 assists, and 5.5 rebounds—but he's the only one who was on the 2011 championship squad. If he had played another season or two with the Mavericks to begin his career, instead of asking for a trade after just two seasons, this would be a no-brainer. Although Harper was never better than Kidd or Nash at their peaks, he does have longevity. He played 872 games here in Dallas or about 28,000 minutes. That's more than 19 straight days of basketball if you were to put his minutes back-to-back. (Don't actually play basketball that long. It's not healthy.) He's the team's all-time leader in steals and assists, and even Michael Jordan acknowledged he was a fine defender.

Though my heart wants to pick Nash, my brain says Harper. He was a stellar all-around player with the third most games played on franchise history, while the other two candidates weren't on the Mavericks during their prime.

Selection: Derek Harper

Shooting Guard

It's pretty clear that the best shooting guard in the Mavericks' history comes down to Jason Terry, Rolando Blackman, or Jim Jackson.

We all know Terry, a man so confident he inked a tattoo of the championship trophy onto his bicep in the preseason before the Mavericks won that very trophy. JET played eight seasons in Dallas, recorded nearly 10,000 points in a Mavericks jersey, and finished sixth all time in games played. His confident play paired perfectly with Dirk Nowitzki, and the two-man game between that duo may be unmatched among teammates throughout Nowitzki's career.

Blackman played more than 200 more games in Dallas than Terry and he's the fourth all-time leader in games played in the franchise's history. Drafted in the franchise's second year, Blackman spent 11 of his 13 seasons with the Mavericks. He was a foundational building block to the franchise and an unforgettable part of the team's proudest moments from the 1980s. After his rookie season, Blackman never averaged fewer than 17 points per game, ending up as the team's second all-time leading scorer.

Jackson's resume doesn't stack up to those two, but he deserves a mention. Although the Three J's crashed and burned during the 1996–97 season, and Dallas shipped all three out of town, but Jackson still ended up playing five seasons with the team because he was the first one drafted. For various reasons Jackson's career never had stability after that as he played for 11 other teams after leaving Dallas. While in a Mavericks uniform, though, Jackson played nearly 300 games and scored 5,660 points.

Both Terry and Blackman are great choices for this hypothetical team, but Blackman might have been slightly better at his peak and played several more seasons with the team when compared to Terry. Plus, picking him makes Terry the sixth man on this team, which is just fitting.

Selection: Rolando Blackman

98 The Best All-Time Forwards

It's easier to figure out the two greatest forwards than it is to determine which guards stand out most. One spot, obviously, is already locked down. Here's my best attempt at choosing the best player for each spot.

Small Forward

Let's give apologies in advance to Josh Howard, whose one All-Star appearance was his only great season, and Shawn Marion, who was perennially underrated with the Mavericks but not quite good enough for this discussion. When it comes to the best Mavericks small forward, this is a two-man race.

Mark Aguirre was the first overall pick in the 1981 NBA Draft—and for good reason. The 6'6" forward could do it all on the basketball court, but most importantly he could score.

By his third season in Dallas, Aguirre averaged 29.5 points per game, meaning he's one of just 39 players to this day who has averaged at least 29 points for an entire season. He was named an All-Star three times—the most by any Maverick not from Germany—and he was an ironman, too. He played at least 74 games per season throughout his eight years in Dallas, excluding his rookie year and the final one when he was traded halfway through.

Coming along a decade later, Michael Finley arrived by trade. The expectations for Finley weren't nearly as high, but he quickly exceeded them anyway. Finley arrived a couple seasons before Dirk Nowitzki was drafted, and they ended up being teammates for six seasons. It was Finley's team for the first couple years, but the forward from the University of Wisconsin had no problem handing the reins to Nowitzki when it became clear how special he was becoming.

Finley and Aguirre both used their strength and deft touch from the midrange during their seasons in Dallas. Aguirre averaged more than 20 points, and Finley nearly averaged that many. If there was a difference, it was where they operated: Aguirre had an unbelievable post game, while most of Finley's scoring started on the perimeter first. It's Aguirre who's the third all-time leading Mavericks scorer with 13,930 points, but Finley's 12,389 rounds out the top five.

With his three-point shooting, Finley fits on this team better. (Aguirre developed the shot later in his career and was never particularly proficient with it.) Both players served crucial roles with the Mavericks, especially Finley sacrificing his own alpha role on the team so that Nowitzki could grow into the top 20 all-time player that he did.

Selection: Michael Finley

Power Forward

The thing about Dirk Nowitzki, who is obviously the choice here, is that he has been a Maverick for so long that there aren't even any other good choices. Dallas briefly employed Antawn Jamison, who

One of the best forwards to ever play for the Mavericks, Michael Finley slashes to the hole during a 1997 game.

won Sixth Man of the Year, but the Mavericks let him walk after just one season because of obvious position overlaps with Nowitzki. Harrison Barnes could soon become the next best Mavericks power forward, but only time will tell. Dennis Rodman is in the Hall of Fame, but his 12 games in Dallas were disastrous.

The two best Mavericks power forwards outside of Nowitzki are two players from the 1980s—Sam Perkins and Jay Vincent. Perkins is No. 8 all time on the Mavericks' scoring list, while Vincent is 10th overall with 6,766 and 6,464 points, respectively. Both had important roles pushing the franchise forward early on, but Nowitzki has been so good for so long that most of the team's power forwards are nothing more than backups.

Nowitzki is the star of this hypothetical five-man lineup, regardless of the talent around him. We didn't reunite him with his buddy Steve Nash or his championship partner Jason Kidd in the starting five, but he would adjust to this hypothetical all-time squad just fine. If there is one skill of Nowitzki's this book hasn't mentioned enough, it's his adaptability. Put him with virtually any lineup and any player, and Nowitzki's pure offensive genius and the gravity of his shooting made his teammates better. He's the best power forward and by far the best player in the Mavericks' history and he'll start at power forward here.

Selection: Dirk Nowitzki

99 The Best All-Time Center

Four players are worth mentioning at center. The first two, Erick Dampier and Shawn Bradley, earn appearances solely based on longevity. Dampier started most of his six seasons in Dallas, doing a wholly adequate if unspectacular job as a lumbering defender who dropped a few too many passes. Bradley is actually the team's all-time leading blocks leader, recording exactly 1,250 blocks during his nine seasons in Dallas. Neither, however, are serious contenders for the title of best center in Mavericks history. That is either Tyson Chandler or James Donaldson.

It would easily be Chandler's if he re-signed after the title season. After the Mavericks declined to re-sign him, Chandler had a couple of the best statistical seasons of his career, including winning Defensive Player of the Year in 2012. His return for the 2014–15 season reinforced his status as an all-time Mavericks great even if that season didn't end up going anywhere after the disastrous Rajon Rondo trade. Still, Chandler only playing two seasons in Dallas hurts his candidacy.

The other candidate is James Donaldson, who can boast about his longevity in Dallas. Donaldson came to the Mavericks via a trade in 1985, the first of seven seasons he spent in Dallas. He was a fundamental center who knew his role on the court, playing solely around the basket and averaging 8.8 points and 9.8 rebounds throughout his Dallas career. Donaldson is also the only Mavericks center to be selected to an All-Star Game, representing the team during the 1988 game as an injury replacement. (A fun fact: despite 26,000 minutes played, Donaldson never attempted a single three-pointer. No player has ever logged more minutes without attempting at least one than Donaldson.)

Still, this choice is Chandler all the way. Nowitzki never had a center fit better next to him than Chandler, both in playing style and in personality. The two together won a championship, and you can never discount that.

Selection: Tyson Chandler

100 An Oral History of the 24 Hours After the 2011 Finals

When writing about the championship, this book mostly deals with what happened on the court and what it meant for everyone involved. Here is a different look at the night the Mavericks won the title. With interviews from more than a dozen people who were there that night, this is an oral history of the 24 hours immediately following Game 6 of the 2011 NBA Finals.

* * *

The scoreboard reads "MAVERICKS 105 HEAT 95" when the final buzzer sounds on June 12, 2011.

DIRK NOWITZKI: All the work you put in, all the people that have stuck with you and you've worked with, all the disappointments from year to year, from the MVP season to losing in the playoffs all the time, a little bit of everything—it just overcame me with emotions. I felt it already before the buzzer because it wasn't really a close game.

SCOTT "SCOOTER" TOMLIN, Mavericks media relations: Dirk is going to do an interview with Doris Burke on the stage, so he doesn't have to do a walk-off interview.

SARAH MELTON, Mavericks media relations: You didn't think he was going to go anywhere!

SCOTT TOMLIN: I see Dirk walk back to the tunnel because the tunnel's basically toward the center of the court. And I'm thinking, *That's strange. Where's he going?* Then I see Tim Frank, (vice president) of communications with the NBA, kind of walking behind him like trying to also figure it out, so I thought *I don't know what's going on, but Dirk's about to accept the MVP award.*

TYSON CHANDLER: I didn't recognize Dirk (had left) until he had come back, but it makes complete sense. It made all the sense in the world…He felt the same way I felt.

DONNIE NELSON: I totally, totally understood. When you go through something like that, it's hard to put into words, you know? Let's just say the other time we went to the Finals was probably…there's not a lot of people that could have recovered in the way that he did.

SCOTT TOMLIN: Tim and I see him in the shower, I walk over to him, and I said, "You need to get back out there. They're going to present the trophy, and you're about to get the MVP of the Finals trophy." He said, "Okay, give me 30 minutes," and I said, "We don't have 30 seconds. We've got to go."

DIRK NOWITZKI: I remember Scooter and Tim Frank from the NBA following me and I was laying there. They have a bench in the shower and I laid down, and they're like, "You've got to go back out there. They're about to present the trophy." And I said, "Give it to somebody else."

SCOTT TOMLIN: I said, "Look man, when they hand that trophy to your team, you're going to want to be there. You're going to want that picture. You're going to want to be on the stage with your teammates. You don't want to miss out on that."

DIRK NOWITZKI: I actually went back out, and it actually wasn't bad anymore. After that first emotional wave, I got over it. I needed five minutes and then I was fine.

Nowitzki returns to the court, where his team is crowding onto a podium to accept the Larry O'Brien trophy.

EDDIE SEFKO, Mavericks beat writer since 2004: After the game, everything's a zoo. Everyone's racing around trying to get stories in the paper, stories online, and everything else. And I just remember, there was always something else to do, you couldn't give people enough, they wanted to know everything.

DONNIE NELSON: I was initially looking for Pat Riley just to shake his hand as you do, couldn't find him, ended up finding (Heat vice president of operations) Andy (Elisburg), who's his right-hand man, and he said Pat was kind of in a meeting or something like that, couldn't come out.

JEFF "SKIN" WADE, Mavericks announcer and Dallas radio host: I'm (shown) on the ABC broadcast as the camera's floating around, interviewing JET (for ESPN Radio). I'm wearing a goofy green T-shirt with a robot on it. So my memory of the trophy presentation was the chaos of being on the floor, making sure I took care of my radio gig and also just trying to be professional as I was losing my shit.

BEN ROGERS, Wade's longtime radio co-host: All season long, I'd be calling them the "one-and-done boys." Even when they get to the playoffs, I have no confidence they're going anywhere. So meanwhile, we're traveling on the team plane. Every single person on that team plane either works for the Mavericks or is on the broadcast. They're wearing a Mavericks logo on their shirt, except me. I've been a die-hard Mavs fan my whole life, but in that case, I was on the radio every day, saying I don't believe in this team. The minute they won, they handed Mark Cuban the trophy, and he said, "They called us the 'one-and-done boys.'" So I'm on the court in Miami listening to Mark Cuban saying, "They called us the 'one-and-done boys,'" and I'm like, 'Holy shit, this is surreal, did that really just happen?'"

MARK CUBAN: At the dais, I was screaming for (the Mavericks' first owner) Mr. Carter…(I remember) my wife screaming: "Wait for me," looking for Don Carter, having it cross my mind that I should get naked just to fuck with David Stern. And just thinking, *Oh my God. Oh my God. Oh my God.*

TYSON CHANDLER: I used to hate watching celebrations. Up to that moment, every single time, I would watch the end of the Finals and then I would leave because everybody would be watching it at my house…I just couldn't stomach it because I wasn't sure if it would ever happen for me.

SCOTT TOMLIN: Before I left (for vacation that summer), I framed the picture (of Nowitzki) holding the trophy and went over to his house and gave it to him because I know that he wanted that.

JEFF WADE: (The trophy is) a heavy bad boy.

The celebration moved back to the Mavericks' locker room, where the champagne was set up.

RICK CARLISLE: All that (champagne) went fast. It was being squirted all over the place.

MARK CUBAN: Tyson did the nicest thing ever. When everyone was getting ready to blow out the champagne, I was in the hall, and he went out and got me. So that picture over there (in the Mavericks training room) with the champagne, that doesn't happen with me in it unless Tyson goes and gets me. That was really cool.

TYSON CHANDLER: I remember going into the shower area, pausing, taking a break from the celebration and I remember DK (Mavericks director of sports psychology Don Kalkstein) coming up to me and I remember being able to tell him, "I don't get it. I can't shake it" because it was hard for me to imagine that it was actually over, that we had won the championship, and I was in such a zone, a competitive edge, that it was hard for me to actually celebrate.

RICK CARLISLE: I had to go do the media. That was probably 30 minutes. After that I was in my office in the locker room with my friends. I had four very close friends at the game, and we got together and had a beer.

The Mavericks then moved to Club LIV to continuing celebrating.

JEFF WADE: Sunday night was Lil Wayne night. He was the host of that night, every Sunday there in Miami.

MARK CUBAN: I don't know if I'd rather spend $140,000 on the championship rings or the bar tab that night.

BEN ROGERS: It almost felt like a convention center. It was so big, but the area the Mavs had roped off wasn't like a club in a club. It was right in the middle of everything. There was just velvet ropes and couches squaring off a little private area, and so the Mavericks were in that roped-off area, and the rest of the club was raging, and people were trying to get as close to the Mavs as they could.

IAN MAHINMI: There's still some parts of the night that are still blurry, but we had a hell of a time.

BEN ROGERS: It was so crowded you could barely move. I just remember all drinks were on Cuban. It was so loud you couldn't really talk. It was just smiling and laughing.

MARK CUBAN: My AMEX got declined. It was a new card. It hadn't gotten authorized yet.

COREY BREWER: (Cuban) partied hard that night. I think everyone partied really hard. But to win a championship, that's worth it.

TIM MACMAHON, Mavericks beat writer since 2008: Cuban (was) a sweaty, hugging mess.

JEFF WADE: Lil Wayne night was a $100 cover charge, and so I did one of the douchiest things I've ever done, went to the very front of this long line. I went up to the guy at the door, I said, "I'm on the Mavericks TV broadcast. I'm supposed to be in there at that party." I don't have a Mav credential or anything, and he looks at me like I'm an idiot. I googled myself, and showed him a picture, and he said, "Come on in."

BEN ROGERS: I went to my room and fell asleep…I finally wake up, my phone's ringing, and I missed it. (Wade) had left me a message, and it's like, this loud music, "DUDE WAKE UP, WAKE UP, WE GOT A CALL TO GO CELEBRATE, WE'RE AT THIS CLUB. YOU'RE NOT GOING TO BELIEVE THIS." I felt like I woke up late for a test or something and I'm panicking.

JEFF WADE: Nowitzki looks over at me and yells, "Where's Ben?" I go, "He's at the hotel, I think he's sleeping."…An hour later I look down, and Ben is in the middle of the party.

TYSON CHANDLER: I remember walking in, saw my teammates, walked to the top level, and I walked down…And I left. Because I didn't want to celebrate with the rest of the people in Miami.

RICK CARLISLE: Mark had a group of people who went out somewhere. They hooped it up a little bit. I didn't go with them, but there were pictures tweeted and stuff like that. That night, the next day, that stuff got out there. But from my standpoint, it was pretty low-key.

EDDIE SEFKO: I got back to the hotel and I sent a text to Rick that just said, "Congratulations, you guys did a great job, happy for all you guys." He sent me a text right back that said, "Where are you?" And I said, "I just got back to the hotel." He said, "Come up to my room." So he tells me where he was, and I went in there and I took a couple of cold beers I'd stolen from somewhere, and we sat there and drink a couple beers and just kind of reminisced and relived the whole thing. He had a big grin on his face, naturally.

TYSON CHANDLER: I went back to my hotel, and my mom was there, and my brothers and sisters, and my wife and some friends. We ordered room service and we just sat and kinda reminisced, and that was it. I had a quiet night.

Club LIV was still going strong, though.

DIRK NOWITZKI: The craziest thing is we had no food. We had no food in the locker room, they had no food in the club, so I just remember being completely exhausted. I even ordered food at like five or six in the morning, ordered a hamburger or something. This was back at the hotel.

JEFF WADE: (Nowitzki's trainer) Holger, who is sitting underneath the landing, (is) having champagne poured all over him. He doesn't look up. He is sending messages, obviously, to Germany, I'm assuming. He's sitting there on this landing. It's like a cave. It's like a mystic cave, (and he's) sending messages to Germany. I'm five feet away from Dirk. And at this point, it's 1 in the morning, and I'm like, "I am not fucking moving from this spot until the night is over." I'm standing on a platform five feet away from Dirk and I stand there all fucking night. Ben and Skin have a radio show that morning. The flight left midday, but the bus to the airport took off in the morning. Almost no one had gone to bed that night for any significant portion of time.

BEN ROGERS: We did not sleep the entire night and went and did a show on ESPN sleepless and just did three hours (of radio) celebrating. You know what, I would be willing to bet if you went back and were somehow able to listen to the show, it would have been just terrible. I mean, if you were a Mavs fan and you had stayed up all night, maybe it would have been the best show ever, but anyone else, we were probably delirious and overly excited fanboys. But I don't even remember the show.

EDDIE SEFKO: Of course, the next morning almost all the players had not slept. Getting on the plane, Cuban and they were all still drunk. I was on the flight home. The police escort was great, and then the door had not shut, and the champagne corks were already popping on the plane.

STEVE CHAVERA, Mavericks web producer: I missed the bus. I blame (play-by-play announcer Mark) Followill. He gave me the wrong bus time. I wasn't the only one. I'm not going to throw him under the bus, though. None of us had slept that night. I went back to the hotel, took a swim, went to my room, got dressed, and when I got down, they were gone.

EDDIE SEFKO: Everybody was in different stages of drunk, hungover, recovering, and drunk again.

RICK CARLISLE: It's an unforgettable experience.

DIRK NOWITZKI: That was just an awesome night. You just have that feeling that you're on top of the world. You're with your teammates. You just won it all, something you'd worked toward for so long. I just remember it being such a fun night. Cuban getting the bottle, that was this big. It was an incredible night.

Acknowledgments

Let me start by thanking Josh Williams, my editor Jeff Fedotin, and everyone else at Triumph Books who helped with this project.

Thanks to Austin Ngaruiya, my roommate throughout the writing process and lifelong friend. He was an invaluable help when I demanded he recall everything he could about a random team or player from the early 2000s.

Thanks to Tim MacMahon, who vouched for me on this project and from whom I've learned so much in the Mavericks locker room. I still owe you a beer in any city but Houston.

Thanks to Bobby Karalla, Jonny Auping, and Jonathan Tjarks, who helped me brainstorm this book at our Pluckers summits. We all write about sports for a living now, which is wild. Also, thanks to everyone I've met in the Mavericks press box over the years. You're all good people.

Thanks to Lisa Rotter, who hired me at Mavs Moneyball and then trusted me to run the site upon her retirement. Thanks for putting up with a kid who was still trying to figure everything out.

Thanks to Sarah Melton, Scott Tomlin, and Alan Rakowski, the unflappable Mavericks PR team who has always put up with me over the years. Sarah granted me my first credential when I was a clueless college freshman, and that was one of the first steps along my path to becoming a published author.

Thanks to the Mavs Moneyball crew: Rebecca, Kirk, Kate, Josh, Ian, Doyle, and everyone else who has helped us build the best damn Mavericks blog on the planet over the years. Specifically, without Rebecca running the site in my absence, I never would have had the time to write this book. She's a rock star. I know I can trust you all to keep up the amazing work the site does.

Thanks to Mike Prada and Paul Flannery, my SB Nation editors who encouraged me to take on this project and make me a better writer constantly. Shout-out to the SB Nation youths, too. As we say, yeet!

Thanks to the many players and people associated with the Mavericks who gave me time for interviews: Dirk Nowitzki, Rick Carlisle, Casey Smith, Tyson Chandler, Jeff "Skin" Wade, Ben Rogers, Derek Harper, Eddie Sefko, Scott Tomlin, and everyone else.

Thanks to Mark Cuban, who didn't hesitate for a moment when I asked him if he'd write a foreword.

Finally, thanks to Bruce, Sue, and Andy. You're all very good family, and I appreciate your unfailing support, even if you thought majoring in journalism was a bad idea. (I think it turned out alright.) I won't use "I'm writing a book" as an excuse not to visit anymore! Well, at least until the next one.

Sources

I'm lucky to have entered sports journalism right when we all decided it was alright to have fun. For as long as I've written professionally, my work has been a mix of blogging and reporting, and this book was written the exact same way.

I conducted about 20 interviews with various players, coaches, and people connected to the Mavericks, while also drawing on my five seasons covering the team with a season credential. I've attended a few hundred Mavericks games in my life and several playoff series. As often as I could, I drew from those experiences and used it to inform and enhance my writing.

The rest came from months of research online and from my own memory watching this team. Some chapters were written in a more traditional newspaper style, while others could only exist on an online blog. This was an intentional choice.

A massive amount of my research came from stories penned by the current Mavericks beat writers over the past decade: ESPN's Tim MacMahon, *The Dallas Morning News*' Eddie Sefko, and the *Fort Worth Star-Telegram*'s Dwain Price. Jeff Caplan, who also worked at ESPN throughout the NBA Finals season, had many excellent stories that helped me remember amazing details from that championship run. I also drew information from Earl K. Sneed and Bobby Karalla at Mavs.com.

This book could not have been written without basketball-reference.com. It is the most valuable, comprehensive, and thorough database of NBA statistics and information and it constantly helped me remember records, coaches, players, and nearly any statistic that I needed to properly write this book.

A book called *Tales from the Dallas Mavericks Locker Room: A Collection of the Greatest Mavs Stories Ever Told* written by Jaime

Aron was a crucial source of information for the first two decades of the franchise. I must also thank Jim Karalla, whose excellent memories of the early Mavericks squads helped me make sure I was on the right track.

Other sources of information included: Mavs Moneyball, SB Nation, *D Magazine*, *The Oklahoman*, Fox Sports, Grantland, Yahoo's Ball Don't Lie blog, the great *San Antonio Express-News*, Mark Cuban's blog, the Dallas-Mavs.com message board, the *New York Daily News*, NBA.com, *USA TODAY*, *Dallas Observer*, Rap Genius, and *The Wall Street Journal*. *Sports Illustrated* and the *Los Angeles Times* both had easily accessible archives of stories from the 1980s and 1990s that were extremely helpful. One quote was taken from a sister publication: *100 Things Raptors Fans Should Know & Do Before They Die*. Two Nowitzki documentaries, *How Dirk Became Dirk* and *The Perfect Shot*, were both useful information sources as well.

While sports journalism is a changing profession, it is not a dying one. It will always be necessary to celebrate, amplify, and hold accountable professional sports, those billion-dollar industries that we enjoy so much. This book could not have been possible without the difficult, dedicated, and tireless work of sports journalists who came before it and hopefully it will push sports journalism forward in a small but similar way.